THE ATLANTA PARADOX

THE ATLANTA PARADOX

David L. Sjoquist, Editor

A VOLUME IN THE MULTI-CITY STUDY OF
URBAN INEQUALITY

RUSSELL SAGE FOUNDATION | NEW YORK

Library of Congress Cataloging-in-Publication Data

The Atlanta paradox / David L. Sjoquist, editor.
    p.   cm.
  "A volume in the Multi-City Study of Urban Inequality."
  Includes bibliographical references and index.
  ISBN 0-87154-808-9
  1. Atlanta (Ga.)—Social conditions.   2. Atlanta (Ga.)—Economic
  conditions.   3. Atlanta (Ga.)—race relations.   4. Equality—
  Georgia—Atlanta.   I. Sjoquist, David L.   II. Series. Title
  HN80.A8 A86   2000
  305.8'09758'231—dc21   00-020793

RUSSELL SAGE FOUNDATION
112 East 64th Street, New York, New York 10021
10 9 8 7 6 5 4 3 2 1

The Multi-City Study of Urban Inequality

The Multi-City Study of Urban Inequality is a major social science research project designed to deepen the nation's understanding of the social and economic divisions that now beset America's cities. It is based on a uniquely linked set of surveys of employers and households in four major cities: Atlanta, Boston, Detroit, and Los Angeles. The Multi-City Study focuses on the effects of massive economic restructuring on racial and ethnic groups in the inner city, who must compete for increasingly limited opportunities in a shifting labor market while facing persistent discrimination in housing and hiring. Involving more than forty researchers at fifteen U.S. colleges and universities, the Multi-City Study has been jointly funded by the Ford Foundation and the Russell Sage Foundation. This volume is the third in a series of books reporting the results of the Multi-City Study to be published by the Russell Sage Foundation.

Contents

Contributors

DAVID L. SJOQUIST is professor of economics in the Andrew Young School of Policy Studies at Georgia State University.

RONALD H. BAYOR is professor of history at Georgia Tech and editor of the *Journal of American Ethnic History*.

IRENE BROWNE is associate professor of sociology and women's studies at Emory University.

OBIE CLAYTON JR. is professor of sociology and director of the Morehouse Research Institute of Morehouse College.

NIKKI MCINTYRE FINLAY received her doctorate from Georgia State University and works for TrueShopping Inc.

CHRISTOPHER R. GELLER is lecturer in the School of Economics at Deakin University, Victoria, Australia.

GARY PAUL GREEN is professor of rural sociology at the University of Wisconsin, Madison.

ROGER B. HAMMER is research associate in the Applied Population Laboratory and a graduate student in sociology at the University of Wisconsin, Madison.

TRUMAN A. HARTSHORN is professor of geography in the Department of Anthropology and Geography at Georgia State University.

CYNTHIA LUCAS HEWITT is assistant professor of sociology at the University of Georgia.

KEITH R. IHLANFELDT is professor of economics in the Andrew Young School of Policy Studies at Georgia State University.

SAHADEO PATRAM is senior research associate of the Morehouse Research Institute and director of the affiliated State Data Center program at Morehouse College.

TRAVIS PATTON is adjunct professor of sociology and associate director of the Morehouse Research Institute of Morehouse College.

MARK A. THOMPSON is associate dean of the School of Business and associate professor of economics at Quinnipiac University.

LEANN M. TIGGES is associate professor of rural sociology at the University of Wisconsin, Madison.

1

THE ATLANTA PARADOX: INTRODUCTION

David L. Sjoquist

ATLANTA offers a sharply contrasting mosaic: the poverty of its public housing projects versus the sprawling riches of its suburbs; the mansions in Buckhead versus the weathered wooden row houses in Cabbagetown; the glistening office towers and glitzy shopping in Midtown and Lenox Square versus the abandoned stores on the Southside; the grocery carts filled with aluminum cans versus the BMWs filled with gray-suited executives; suburban jobs that go wanting versus a city black poverty rate of 35 percent.

These contrasts reflect what we call the Atlanta paradox. It is a paradox of substantial racial segregation in a community with a reputation for good race relations and of high inner-city poverty in the face of substantial economic growth.

Consider that in 1987, *The Christian Science Monitor* declared Atlanta the "mecca of the black middle class" (Ingwerson 1987), and *Ebony* listed it among the top five cities for black businesses. Indeed, Atlanta has been a magnet for blacks. Between 1970 and 1996, the black population in the Atlanta region increased by 158 percent, while the white population increased by just 78 percent.[1] Yet, despite surviving racial integration with relatively little violence and undergoing recent improvement, Atlanta remains a very racially segregated city (Farley and Frey 1994, chap. 5).

Or how does one explain the contrast between economic growth and persistent poverty? The Atlanta region's economy has been one of the highest growth areas in the country; between 1980 and 1996, the number of jobs in the Atlanta region increased by 804,843, or 4.1 percent per year. Employment in the city proper increased by only 62,157, however, or 1.0 percent per year (Atlanta Regional Commission 1997). Mean real family income in the Atlanta metropolitan area grew 20.6

percent between 1969 and 1989, compared with 10.7 percent for the country as a whole. Yet despite the phenomenal regional growth, mean real family income in the city between 1969 and 1989 declined, both absolutely and relative to the suburbs (Walker 1997).

Despite the economic growth, the poverty rate of blacks in the city in 1990 was 35 percent, an increase from 29 percent in 1970. The poverty rate in the city of Atlanta is the fifth highest among central cities, exceeded only by Detroit, Cleveland, Miami, and New Orleans. While employment growth in the city of Atlanta has not been dramatic, it has exceeded that of these four other cities, for which employment either declined or increased only marginally. In addition, employment in the metropolitan areas of these four other cities increased at rates of less than 1 percent per year, substantially below that for the Atlanta region.

The economic growth experienced in the Atlanta metropolitan area might have been expected to "lift all boats." Timothy Bartik (1991), for example, conducted an extensive study of the effects of metropolitan growth on various labor market outcomes and found that economic growth within a metropolitan area tends to lead to higher real earnings and to individuals being promoted into higher-paying occupations. In other words, the economic growth is not immediately offset by increased migration, but rather benefits local residents. Furthermore, and of real interest here, he finds that the effects of growth on real earnings are significantly higher for blacks and for less-educated workers. His results suggest that the effects of economic growth on earnings are extremely progressive.

Likewise, Paul A. Jargowsky (1997) finds that ghetto poverty is determined largely by dynamic metropolitanwide processes, the most important factor being the overall economic conditions in the area. He finds that neighborhood poverty is linked with the level and distribution of income in the metropolitan area.

This "Atlanta paradox" is the motivation for this book.[2] It is a paradox of extreme racial and economic inequality—of abject poverty in a region of tremendous wealth, of a poor and economically declining city population in the face of dramatic economic growth, and of a black mecca in a "city too busy to hate" (a slogan adopted in 1955 by Mayor William Hartsfield) confronting a highly racially segregated population and the substantial problems associated with racism and poverty that pervade the city.

In many ways, Atlanta personifies the problem of urban inequality. There is a wide disparity in income between those living in the city and those in the suburbs. Atlanta not only has one of the smallest middle classes of any major city, but the ratio of white household income to black household income is an astounding 2.76 (Walker 1997). Furthermore, poverty is highly concentrated, with 84.1 percent of the city's poor living in the city's poorest neighborhoods (Ihlanfeldt 1998).[3]

Atlanta has also experienced substantial urban sprawl. Robert D. Bullard (1998) argues that this has had a detrimental effect on blacks, pushing people farther apart geographically, politically, economically, and socially, and fueling disinvestment in the central city.

This book is an exploration of urban inequality in Atlanta, part of a larger study sponsored and funded by the Russell Sage Foundation and the Ford Foundation. The project, known as the Multi-City Survey of Urban Inequality, was designed to examine the role of racial attitudes, residential segregation, and the functioning of the labor market in explaining urban inequality. A household survey and two employer surveys were conducted in each of the four cities studied (Atlanta, Boston, Detroit, and Los Angeles). Much of the research reported here is based on the Atlanta household survey, known as the Greater Atlanta Neighborhood Study (GANS). Details of the GANS survey are presented in the appendix to this chapter.

To place the story of urban inequality in Atlanta in context, one must understand the recent socioeconomic changes that the region has undergone. Thus, we begin with a description of the economic and demographic dynamics that help explain the continued inequality in Atlanta's labor market and housing market.

Urban inequality in Atlanta is synonymous with racial inequality, so one must first grasp the city's racial history. The roots of inequality lie in the legal segregation long practiced in Atlanta. But the end of legal segregation and the dynamic growth in Atlanta in recent decades have not eliminated or even substantially reduced inequality. This is an attempt to find out why, with explanations that explore the following arguments and themes:

- In the work of William J. Wilson (1987) and others, much is made of the growth in the spatial mismatch between residential location and job growth. Atlanta suburbs that are inaccessible by public transit have experienced significant job growth. Thus, spatial mismatch may be a contributing factor to the Atlanta paradox.

- Douglas S. Massey and Nancy A. Denton (1993) argue that the rise of the black underclass is due in part to a set of mutually reinforcing spirals of decline that develop through residential segregation of the poor. If true, it is important to determine the forces that maintain racially segregated housing, including the possibly deliberate choices by blacks to live in racially segregated neighborhoods and discrimination in the housing market.

- Human capital arguments suggest that labor market outcomes are the result of differences in education and job skills. Do racial differences in human capital explain racial differences in labor market outcomes?

- Labor market outcomes are also affected by discrimination. Is there evidence that labor market outcomes are worse for minorities because of discrimination?

- Information regarding job opportunities and job search strategies have been shown to influence labor market outcomes. If minorities have worse job information or use ineffective search methods, then they may experience worse labor market outcomes.

- Social capital provides advantages, both socially and economically, in much the same way that human capital does. The lack of social capital among less skilled workers, perhaps resulting from the concentration of poverty, could thus result in inferior labor market performance.

There are, of course, other possible explanations. For example, the persistence of concentrated poverty in the city could be the result of "population churning"—a process whereby the poor move out of the city when they reach middle-class status, to be replaced by poor in-migrants—or of a self-perpetuating culture of poverty. Panel data that would follow individual households over time would be required to investigate these possibilities, but are, unfortunately, not available. What the chapters in this book provide are analyses of a rich assortment of potential explanations by both economists and sociologists.

The analysis in this volume is largely restricted to comparisons between blacks and whites. Other racial and ethnic groups, such as Hispanics and Asians, account for such a small fraction of Atlanta's population (2 percent each) that the issue of urban inequality is clearly one of black and white.

Atlanta is an interesting case for investigating the causes of urban inequality. It is a city that presents a paradox of phenomenal growth in contrast to the unexpected high level of inner-city poverty and economic stagnation, and of a black mecca in contrast to the unexpected high level of segregation. The Atlanta paradox and attempts to find explanations for it are the impetus for and the focus of the research reported on in this book.

Overview of the Book

The Atlanta paradox is developed in detail by Truman A. Hartshorn and Keith R. Ihlanfeldt (chapter 2 herein), who also provide a historic and spatial profile of the economic and demographic changes in the city of Atlanta and the Atlanta region. As late as 1960, the metropolitan area had a population of only 1 million, compared with today's size of over 3.5 million. The growth rate in the Atlanta area during the past thirty years has been nothing short of phenomenal. Job growth has paralleled the population growth.

The city of Atlanta has not fared nearly as well. Between 1960 and 1990, it lost about a fifth of its population. Jobs increased marginally.

Ronald H. Bayor (chapter 3) notes that blacks had historically been confined to a small geographic area. With the end of legal housing segregation, the black population began to decentralize. While blacks increased throughout the MSA, the growth was concentrated largely in areas adjacent to existing concentrations of blacks, namely, south DeKalb County and south Fulton County, just beyond the city of Atlanta (see map 1.1). As blacks moved into these areas, whites fled. The result of these dynamics is that better than 65 percent of the jobs are located in the northern half of the region, while more than 71 percent of the blacks are located in the southern half of the region. Furthermore, the poor are housed in the city (71 percent of the area's poor are there).

Evidence suggests a spatial mismatch between the residential locations of poor blacks and the locations of available jobs, and the large number of female-headed households residing within the city suggests a significant welfare-dependent population that may be untouched by the economic growth in the region. The picture is one of dramatic growth, but growth that has missed parts of the region, in particular, the city of Atlanta. It is also a picture of inequality by race and geography in the face of rising incomes.

The Atlanta paradox has deep historic roots. Current racial differences have their origins in the deliberate antiblack policies and actions adopted by whites since the Civil War. Bayor's history of race in Atlanta (see chapter 3) details how the white community restricted blacks' choice of residence and employment opportunities, and neglected them when it came to schooling, transportation, and city services. For example, through zoning restrictions, highway construction, and other policies, blacks, who represented 65 percent of the city's population in 1965, were restricted to just 22 percent of the land area. It is no wonder that the population continues to be segregated twenty to thirty years after the end of legal segregation.

Race has always played an important role in Atlanta, and much of the character of the city is a result of policies driven by racial concerns. Since racial attitudes and economic inequality are associated, it is important to understand the current racial attitudes and perceptions of Atlantans. Using the extensive set of questions in the GANS that explore

MAP 1.1   *The Atlanta MCSUI Area*

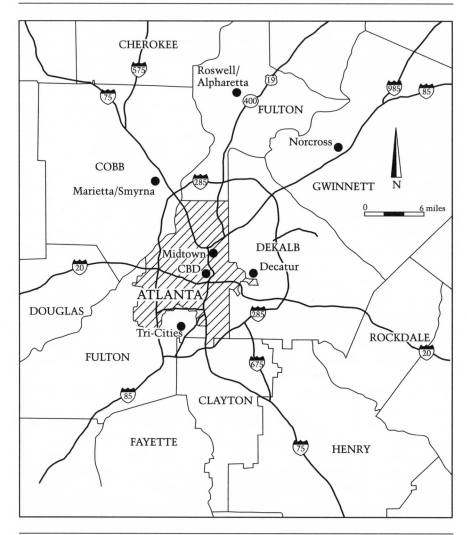

Source: Cartographic Research Laboratory Department of Geography, Georgia State University 1999.

racial attitudes and perceptions, Obie Clayton Jr., Christopher R. Geller, Sahadeo Patram, Travis Patton, and I (chapter 4) provide an overview of racial differences in attitudes and opinions regarding residential segregation, racial stereotyping, and racial competition.

They find that race certainly matters, and in some ways it matters a great deal. For example, a small percentage of either blacks or whites is willing to live in a neighborhood comprised largely of the other race, and many whites still hold unfavorable stereotypes of blacks. There is room for optimism, however, as the results suggest that whites and particularly blacks are willing to live in communities that are much more integrated than what exists presently, and the more severe forms of racial stereotyping have largely disappeared.

In Chapter 5, Mark Thompson uses the GANS to explore reasons for the continued existence of residential segregation in Atlanta. He first considers whether racial differences in economic conditions mean that blacks are unable to afford housing in white suburban neighborhoods. While it is true that on average black residents of the city of Atlanta have lower incomes, Thompson finds that it is economically feasible for many central city blacks to obtain suburban housing. Thus, he concludes that economic factors are not a prime contributor to residential segregation. A second hypothesis is that blacks perceive that suburban housing is more expensive than it actually is. Thompson finds some support for this hypothesis.

Third, building on the analysis in chapter 4, Thompson provides strong evidence that residential segregation is not the result of a desire by blacks to live in segregated housing. In addition, racial differences in the perceptions of respondents as to the desirability of specific neighborhoods are small. However, Thompson does find that given the stated preferences of whites, integration of neighborhoods does not appear to represent a stable equilibrium.

One of the explanations for the poor labor market performance of inner-city minorities is the spatial mismatch hypothesis, an explanation originally framed by John F. Kain (1968). Essentially the argument is that low-skilled, inner-city minorities are unable to find housing in the suburbs, where the relevant jobs have shifted. Lack of job access leads to higher unemployment, lower wages, or longer commutes. Spatial mismatch has become a popular explanation of poor labor market performance of inner-city blacks (Wilson 1987). Ihlanfeldt and I (chapter 6) provide a critical look at recent evidence on the existence of spatial mismatch and conclude that there is increasing evidence that supports the spatial mismatch hypothesis as an explanation for at least part of the poor labor market performance of low-skilled, inner-city minorities.

As noted, despite phenomenal economic growth, substantial income inequality continues to exist in Atlanta. In chapter 7, Ihlanfeldt and I explore the level and change in earnings inequality in the Atlanta metropolitan area between 1980 and the mid-1990s. In many ways Atlanta parallels what has been observed across the United States: an increase in earnings inequality both across and within groups. We document that the earnings inequality increased regardless of race, that the earnings of blacks fell relative to whites, and that earnings of city blacks fell relative to suburban blacks. It is not that blacks in the Atlanta area did badly during the 1980s—in fact, in comparison with other cities, they did well. But relative to whites in Atlanta, black earnings fell, and the level of racial inequality remained higher in Atlanta than in other cities. What is puzzling is that the change in the distribution of earnings in Atlanta closely paralleled the change in the United States, even though Atlanta experienced such dramatic economic growth.

There are many possible explanations for racial and gender differences in earnings. Three chapters of the book are devoted to exploring these differences. Ihlanfeldt and Sjoquist begin that analysis in chapter 7, exploring human capital factors associated with the level of earnings. It is further explored by Irene Browne and Leann M. Tigges in chapter 8, who focus on the earnings of black females within the context of the "multiple jeopardy" hypothesis, which states that the disadvantages in the labor market associated with race and gender interact in a multiplicative way for black females. They use the richness of the GANS to explore the process that results in the observed labor market inequality for black females, and find that the disadvantages faced by black females appear to be driven by institutional processes.

Cynthia Lucas Hewitt (chapter 9) expands on the analysis of racial and gender earnings inequality by exploring earnings difference between blacks who are employed in a job with majority white co-workers and those in an equivalent job with majority black co-workers. Using the GANS, Hewitt finds that in the Atlanta region the former earn more than the latter. But this leads to the question of why the difference exists and why blacks have not been more fully assimilated into majority-white jobs.

Chapters 10 and 11 use the GANS data to consider job search and social networks. In chapter 10, Nikki McIntyre Finlay explores the effect of the job search process on labor market outcomes, and addresses whether the poor use less effective search strategies. The existing literature points to the importance of using family and friends for job referrals. Using a two-stage estimation procedure that controls for the effect of the expected outcome and individual's characteristics on the choice of search strategy, she finds that search strategy has only a small effect on the outcome of a search.

One of the concerns about families in poverty is that they become socially isolated, and that the social contacts they do have do not provide them with the support they may need to secure a job, such as money, child care, and transportation. If this is true, then poor households become trapped in the sense that being poor reduces or eliminates the social resources that might assist them in coping with or escaping from poverty. Gary Paul Green, Roger B. Hammer, and Leann M. Tigges (chapter 11) find evidence that social isolation is higher for individuals in poverty households, but that their smaller social networks do not prevent them from receiving help, although the ties tend to be with family members, whose level of support is frequently small.

As a whole, the chapters in this volume provide evidence that there are many and complex causes of the Atlanta paradox, which argues for the importance of addressing the problem of persistent poverty on multiple fronts. The concluding chapter presents a discussion of policy options.

Some might say that the situation in Atlanta is no different than that in other cities. In some ways that is true. What makes Atlanta unique is its contrasts between the perception of racial harmony and the past and present residential and employment segregation, and between the dynamic economy and the growing economic inequality. The research reported on in this volume provides us with a better understanding of the Atlanta paradox and the nature and causes of the urban inequality that exists in Atlanta.

Appendix
The Survey Data

This volume is based largely on research that employs a unique household survey, the Greater Atlanta Neighborhood Study (GANS). The survey is part of a larger project, the Multi-City Study of Urban Inequality, examining the causes and consequences of urban inequality in four metropolitan areas: Atlanta, Boston, Detroit, and Los Angeles. As part of the larger project, each city conducted similar surveys, all funded by the Ford Foundation and the Russell Sage Foundation. In addition to the household surveys, two related surveys of employers in all four cities were conducted.

The Greater Atlanta
Neighborhood Survey

Mathematica Policy Research, Inc., conducted the sampling and data collection for the GANS under the direction of a consortium of four schools: Emory University, the University of Georgia, Georgia State University, and Morehouse College.

The sample was a four-stage area probability sample that involved:

first, selecting a sample of census block groups; second, selecting blocks within the sampled block groups; third, listing and selecting households from sampled blocks; fourth, randomly selecting one adult from each selected household. Household weights are provided. The frame represented the nine most central countries in the Atlanta area (see map 1.1).

Half the sample selected was in predominantly black neighborhoods and half was in mostly white neighborhoods. The face-to-face interviews lasting well over an hour were conducted between June and November 1993. A total of 1,529 interviews were completed. Among the respondents, 651 were white, 829 were black, and 49 were of other races. The overall completion rate was 73.2 percent; 87 percent of all interviews were completed by interviewers of the same race as the respondent.

Each interviewee was asked extensive questions covering several topics, including: demographic and household composition; socioeconomic characteristics; the current and previous residential location of the respondent; the respondent's perceptions of his or her current neighborhood; attitudes and perceptions regarding inequality, discrimination, and various racial groups; activities, attitudes, and experiences related to the labor market; attitudes regarding residential segregation; and social networks.

The Multi-City Study of Urban Inequality Employer Surveys

A companion survey of businesses was also conducted in the four cities by Harry J. Holzer. (See Holzer 1996 for a more complete discussion of the employer survey.) The employer survey, conducted between June 1992 and May 1994, was administered to 800 employers in the metropolitan areas of each of the four cities. The interviews, which lasted an average of thirty-five minutes, were conducted by phone with the individual responsible for hiring. Questions focused on overall employer and employee characteristics, such as number and demographic composition of employees and recent hiring; numbers and characteristics of vacant positions; and characteristics of the most recently filled job in the establishment and of the person who filled that job.

The sample of firms was drawn from two sources. The first was a random sample of firms, stratified by establishment size. The second was the employers of respondents in the household surveys. Approximately 1,000 firms came from the second source. The overall response rate was approximately 67 percent among firms that were successfully screened.

A second employer survey was conducted by Joleen Kirschenman, Philip Moss, and Chris Tilly. Their data consist of a unique, large set of in-depth interviews with employers at firms in the Atlanta, Boston, Detroit, and Los Angeles metropolitan areas conducted as part of the Multi-City In-depth Employer Survey. This survey consisted of telephone interviews of several hundred employers per city and a face-to-face, in-depth survey of forty-five employers each in Atlanta and Los Angeles, forty-six in Boston, and thirty-eight in Detroit, for a total of 174. Firms were surveyed between the summer of 1994 and the summer of 1996.

The sample for the in-depth employer survey was drawn from the list of firms that had been identified by household respondents holding jobs requiring no more than a high school education, and had successfully completed a telephone survey. The response rate for screened firms in this subset of the telephone survey was 69 percent; the response rate for the in-depth survey was also about two-thirds. Interviewers spoke face-to-face with up to three (and, in a few cases, more) respondents per firm: the chief executive officer at the site or another top manager; a personnel official involved in hiring for the sample job; and a line manager or supervisor who managed employees in the sample job category. This strategy gathers the differing knowledge and perceptions of these various categories of managers. In smaller firms, these functions were often performed by just one or two people, so fewer interviews were conducted. In total, 354 interviews were conducted with 364 respondents (with some interviews gathering multiple respondents).

The in-depth interview involved a series of structured questions and follow-up probes. Questions gathered the details of the recruiting, screening, and hiring procedures used in filling the sample job, and what each procedure is designed to do. They also assessed employer attitudes toward different groups in the workforce and different neighborhoods in the metropolitan area in question, and probed any recent business location decisions. All questions were open-ended, and interviewers were trained to encourage respondents to elaborate, telling the story of their business's relationship to the labor market.

All the surveys are available from the Inter-university Consortium for Political and Social Research at the University of Michigan.

Identified Geographic Areas

Several questions in the GANS refer to certain geographic areas. These areas are identified in map 1.1. The demographic characteristics of these areas are described here.

Decatur

Decatur is a suburb located to the east of the city of Atlanta. The area is recognized as one of the most integrated in the metropolitan area. Through the 1980s, as the Atlanta metropolitan area experienced rapid population growth, Decatur's population fell from 18,404 to 17,336, a decline almost exclusively in its black population. Blacks accounted for 39 percent of Decatur's population in 1990 and 26 percent of the Atlanta-area population. The mean housing value in 1990 was $107,600, slightly in excess of the average for the Atlanta metropolitan area of $106,800 (1990 census).

Tri-Cities

The area known as Tri-Cities consists of three small suburban cities (College Park, East Point, and Hapeville) located adjacent to and south of the city of Atlanta, near Hartsfield International Airport. The area is older than most of the region and is characterized by aging industrial complexes. The Tri-Cities have not shared in the metropolitan area's rapid population growth; population there fell by 11.6 percent between 1980 and 1990. In 1990, blacks accounted for 64 percent of the population. Mean home value in 1990 was $68,450, far below that for the metropolitan area.

Midtown

The Midtown area is within the city limits of Atlanta, stretching north from the central business district. Population in Midtown fell during the 1980s. The area has a significant representation of blacks (26.5 percent in 1990). Housing prices in Midtown are higher than average for the metro area; mean home value in 1990 was $162,400.

Marietta-Smyrna

Marietta-Smyrna consists of two small cities located to the northwest in Cobb County. The area's population expanded by nearly 47 percent between 1980 and 1990. In 1990, 18.5 percent of the area's population was black. The location has experienced significant growth in jobs, new housing, and retail outlets. Average home value was $99,300 in 1990.

Roswell-Alpharetta

Rosewell-Alpharetta consists of two cities located to the north of Atlanta, still in Fulton County. The area is predominantly white (93 percent in 1990). Like Marietta-Smyrna, this area has experienced rapid growth in population (nearly tripling between 1980 and 1990), employment, retail trade, and housing. Home prices (average value in 1990 was $167,000) and household incomes are well in excess of the metro-area average.

Norcross

The population of Norcross, located northeast of the city in Gwinnett County, also nearly tripled between 1980 and 1990. Like the other two northern suburbs, this area is predominantly white (86.9 percent) and has experienced rapid economic growth. The average home price in 1990 was $140,000.

Notes

1. The Atlanta region refers to the ten-county planning area of the Atlanta Regional Commission.
2. For a discussion of some of the social and economic problems facing Atlanta, see Walker (1997).
3. High-poverty neighborhoods are defined as census tracts with a poverty rate of 20 percent or more.

References

Atlanta Regional Commission. 1997. *Employment 1996*. Atlanta: Atlanta Regional Commission.

Bartik, Timothy J. 1991. *Who Benefits from State and Local Economic Development Policies?* Kalamazoo, Mich.: W. E. Upjohn Institute.

Bullard, Robert D. 1998. "Introduction: Anatomy of Sprawl." In *Sprawl Atlanta: Social Equity Dimensions of Uneven Growth and Development*, edited by Robert D. Bullard, Glenn S. Johnson, and Angel O. Torres. Atlanta: Environmental Justice Resource Center, Clark Atlanta University.

Farley, Renolds, and William H. Frey. 1994. "Changes in the Segregation of Whites from Blacks During the 1980s: Small Steps Toward a More Integrated Society." *American Sociological Review* 59: 23–45.

Holzer, Harry J. 1996. *What Employers Want: Job Prospects for Less-Educated Workers*. New York: Russell Sage Foundation.

Ihlanfeldt, Keith R. 1998. *Breaking the Concentration of Poverty*. Atlanta: Research Atlanta.

Ingwerson, Marshall. 1987. "Atlanta Has Become a Mecca of the Black Middle Class in America." *Christian Science Monitor*, May 29, p. 1.

Jargowsky, Paul A. 1997. *Poverty and Place: Ghettos, Barrios, and the American City*. New York: Russell Sage Foundation.

Kain, John F. 1968. "Housing Segregation, Negro Employment, and Metropolitan Decentralization." *Quarterly Journal of Economics* 82: 175–97.

Massey, Douglas S., and Nancy A. Denton. 1993. *American Apartheid: Segregation and the Making of the Underclass*. Cambridge, Mass.: Harvard University Press.

Walker, Mary Beth. 1997. *A Population Profile of the City of Atlanta: Trends, Causes, and Options*. Atlanta: Research Atlanta.

Wilson, William J. 1987. *The Truly Disadvantaged*. Chicago: University of Chicago Press.

2

GROWTH AND CHANGE IN METROPOLITAN ATLANTA

*Truman A. Hartshorn and
Keith R. Ihlanfeldt*

ATLANTA remained a small town until the post–Civil War era. At the beginning of the war, the city numbered about 11,000 residents, but by war's end, despite being burned by Sherman's troops, it had grown to a city of 15,000.

The leading city in Georgia in the late nineteenth century was the coastal port of Savannah. The second-ranking cities in the state at the time were the inland fall-line manufacturing cities of Augusta, Macon, and Columbus (see map 2.1). They maintained close ties to Savannah with both rail and water connections. Savannah, in turn, had close European ties for the import and export of goods. Not until the Reconstruction era did the focus of growth in the state shift toward Atlanta, with its superior railroad connections to northern cities.

Atlanta grew to a population of 75,000 by 1895, and overtook Savannah as the leading city in the state in the early twentieth century, as its population topped 100,000. By the 1920s it had become the center of the country's cotton and textile industry. The Forward Atlanta campaign, an aggressive advertising blitz launched in national magazines in 1925, aimed to lure northern investment to the city. It proved very successful. The city's growth was also helped by its designation as a stopover on the U.S. Postal Service's airmail route between New York and Miami in 1930. Expansion stopped in its tracks during the Great Depression, but resumed with the coming of World War II.

Post–World War II Atlanta benefited from the demand for housing among returning soldiers and the reinstatements of job production in the private sector. Many ills that had befallen the city needed to be addressed, including slum housing conditions in older neighborhoods and

MAP 2.1   *Population Change in Georgia, 1980 to 1990*

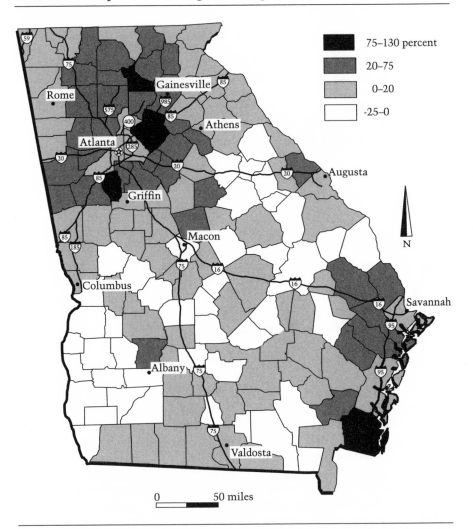

75–130 percent

20–75

0–20

-25–0

N

Rome

Gainesville

Athens

Atlanta

Augusta

Griffin

Macon

Columbus

Savannah

Albany

Valdosta

0   50 miles

Sources: Cartographic Research Laboratory, Department of Geography, Georgia State University, 1999; U.S. Department of Commerce 1982, 1992.

making room for the rapidly growing African American population. The Plan for Improvement adopted in 1952 expanded the northern boundary of the city, more than tripling its size and increasing its population by 100,000. The urban renewal and expressway building program that began in the 1950s targeted many run-down neighborhoods. The Atlanta

Housing Authority provided new housing units in massive housing projects that began ringing the Downtown Area at this time. (See chapter 3 for a discussion of the historical treatment of blacks in Atlanta.)

Suburbanization

The post–World War II era launched a suburban building boom that was to carry the region over the next fifty years into its greatest growth period ever. The city of Atlanta, and Fulton and DeKalb counties joined in 1947 to form the first publicly supported multicounty planning agency in the country, the Metropolitan Planning Commission. This agency would be the predecessor to the present ten-county Atlanta Regional Commission (ARC; see map 2.2).[1] But the big story concerning suburbanization in Atlanta, then as now, has been the prevailing laissez-faire market economy–driven approach to growth, which has created a very pro-growth and highly competitive atmosphere that itself has stimulated development in the region. Unlike the situation in many other parts of the country, in Atlanta comprehensive county-level service providers, known as urban county units, emerged. To this day, most of the suburban population in Atlanta resides in these urban county settings in unincorporated neighborhoods.

By 1960, the Atlanta region reached the one million population threshold, and was composed of five counties: Fulton, DeKalb, Cobb, Gwinnett, and Clayton. Atlanta was described at the time as "a city too busy to hate," a wooded city with lovely homes and a desirable climate. The populations of these five counties have mushroomed in the past forty years, and it is now justified to think of them as urban, not suburban, counties. Another ring of four counties can be thought of as the "new" suburban counties of the region: Rockdale, Henry, Fayette, and Douglas. These nine counties comprise what we refer to as the Atlanta Regional Commission region. The nine-county ARC region grew by 31 percent in the 1980s and by 18 percent between 1990 and 1996 (table 2.1).

The current twenty-county census-defined Atlanta Metropolitan Statistical Area (MSA) includes the nine-county ARC area and another band of eleven largely urban fringe counties (see map 2.2). This MSA designation was made following the tabulation of the 1990 census findings. The fact that the Atlanta MSA contains more counties than any other metropolitan area in the U.S. largely reflects suburban sprawl, which has resulted from high population growth and an ability to continue to develop outward without encountering legal or geographical barriers. This sprawl is dramatically illustrated in the growth of the ur-

TABLE 2.1   *Atlanta Region Population, 1980 to 1996*

County	1980	1990	Rate of Change 1980 to 1990 (Percentage)	1996	Rate of Change 1990 to 1996 (Percentage)
Clayton	150,357	182,052	21.1	202.427	11.6
Cobb	287,718	447,745	50.4	538,832	20.3
DeKalb	483,024	545,837	13.0	589,796	8.0
Douglas	54,573	71,130	30.3	84,463	18.8
Fayette	29,043	62,415	114.9	81,891	31.2
Fulton	589,904	648,951	10.0	718,336	10.7
Gwinnett	166,903	352,900	114.4	478,001	35.4
Henry	36,309	58,741	61.8	90,969	54.9
Rockdale	36,747	54,091	47.2	65,219	20.6
Regional total	1,844,578	2,423,863	31.4	2,849,934	17.6
City of Atlanta	425,022	394,017	−7.1	401,907	2.0

Source: U.S. Department of Commerce 1982, 1992; Atlanta Regional Commission 1981, 1991, 1997.

banized (map 2.3), which is an area defined by the U.S. Census Bureau as the central city and the surrounding area with population density exceeding 1,000 people per acre.

Power Sharing

The 1970s witnessed the breakdown of the traditional white elite business/political leadership group, with the election in 1974 of the first African American mayor, Maynard Jackson. Not only did the political leadership in the city shift to African American control at that time, but also a new group of developers, bankers, and community leaders emerged in the white community, thus making decision-making more broad-based, if also more complicated and contentious. In short, economic control remained in white hands and political power resided in African American hands.

National Population Ranking

The Atlanta MSA increased in population ranking in comparison with other metropolitan areas in each recent census decade. In 1970, the Atlanta region ranked 20th nationally; in 1980, it was 15th; and it reached 13th in 1990 (see table 2.2). As of 1996, it was ranked 11th, having outpaced all other metropolitan areas in population growth during the 1990s, except Phoenix.

MAP 2.2   *Atlanta Geographical Areas*

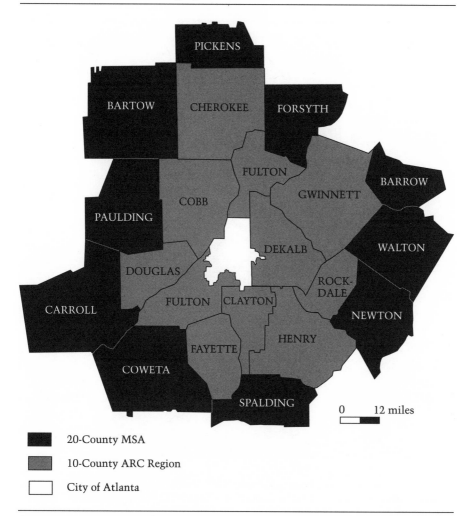

Source: U.S. Department of Commerce 1992; the Cartographic Research Laboratory, Department of Geography, Georgia State University, 1999.

During the 1970s, the Sunbelt received top billing in national population growth, as 10 major metropolitan areas in the South and West, including Atlanta, grew faster than the United States as a whole. Strong metropolitan growth rates continued in the United States in the 1980s. The foundation of this city-building process rested on a rapidly expanding entrepreneurial job base, associated with the maturing of the service

MAP 2.3   *The Atlanta Urbanized Area, 1950, 1970, and 1990*

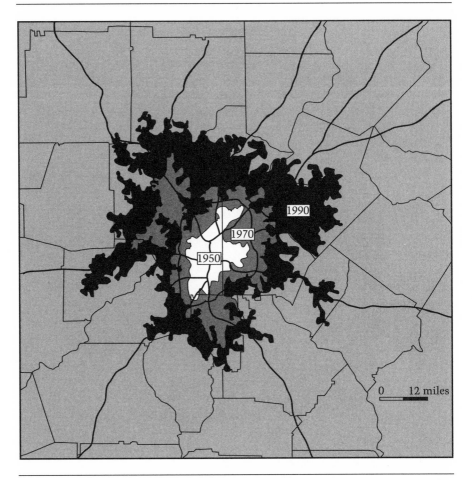

Sources: U.S. Department of Commerce 1952, 1972, 1992; Chris Carver; the Cartographic Research Laboratory, Department of Geography, Georgia State University, 1999.

economy and information age. Expansion of high-technology industry and growing affluence fueled this growth, as did an explosion of white-collar office employment and the growth of producer services associated with the information age, especially top management office functions. Not only did Sunbelt cities such as Atlanta boom, but many northern cities threw off the shackles of decline associated with their heavy industrial past.

TABLE 2.2   Metropolitan Area Population Rankings, 1980 to 1996

1990 Rank	Metropolitan Area	Population (in 1,000s) 1980	1990[a]	Percentage Change 1980 to 1990	Population (in 1,000s) 1996	Percentage Change 1990 to 1996
1.	New York–Northern N.J.–Long Island CMSA[b]	18,713	19,342	3.4	19,846	2.1
2.	Los Angeles–Riverside–Orange County CMSA	11,498	14,532	26.3	15,495	6.6
3.	Chicago–Gary–Kenosha CMSA	8,115	8,240	1.5	8,600	4.4
4.	Washington–Baltimore CMSA	5,791	6,727	16.1	7,165	6.5
5.	San Francisco–Oakland–San Jose CMSA	5,368	6,253	16.4	6,605	5.7
6.	Philadelphia–Wilmington–Atlantic City CMSA	5,649	5,893	4.3	5,973	1.4
7.	Boston–Worcester–Lawrence–Lowell–Brockton MA/NH CMSA	5,336	5,686	6.5	5,796	1.9
8.	Detroit–Ann Arbor–Flint, MI CMSA	5,293	5,187	−2.0	5,284	1.9
9.	Dallas–Fort Worth CMSA	3,046	4,037	32.5	4,575	13.3
10.	Houston–Galveston–Brazoria CMSA	3,118	3,731	19.6	4,253	14.0
11.	Miami–Fort Lauderdale CMSA	2,644	3,193	20.7	3,514	10.1
12.	Seattle–Tacoma–Bremerton MSA	2,409	2,970	23.2	3,321	11.8
13.	Atlanta MSA	2,233	2,960	33.0	3,541	19.7
14.	Cleveland–Akron CMSA	2,938	2,860	−2.6	2,913	1.9
15.	Minneapolis–St. Paul MSA	2,198	2,539	15.5	2,765	8.9
16.	San Diego MSA	1,862	2,498	34.1	2,655	6.3
17.	St. Louis MSA	2,414	2,493	3.2	2,548	2.2
18.	Pittsburgh MSA	2,571	2,395	−6.8	2,379	−0.6
19.	Phoenix–Mesa MSA	1,600	2,238	40.0	2,747	22.7
20.	Tampa–St. Petersburg–Clearwater MSA	1,614	2,068	28.1	2,199	6.3

Source: U.S. Department of Commerce 1982, 1992.
[a] 1990 population totals based on revised census metropolitan area definitions, effective December 31, 1992.
[b] A CMSA is a consolidated metropolitan statistical area that includes two or more primary metropolitan statistical areas, or cities. An MSA is a metropolitan statistical area that is centered on a single large city.

Central-City Decline and the Return to Growth

The city of Atlanta has long been hemmed in by suburban neighborhoods that receive urban services from the county government. The list of the Top 20 central-city population rankings in the U.S. shown in table 2.3 looks considerably different than the metropolitan rankings and reflects the bounded nature of the Atlanta central city. Especially notable is the absence of the city of Atlanta in the Top 20 central-city listings for 1980, 1990, or 1996. Atlanta's central city is smaller in population size in relation not only to Houston's (#4 in 1996) or Dallas's (#9 in 1996), but to those in less populated metropolitan areas such as Memphis (#18 in 1996).

The Atlanta central city population shrank by 70,000 people during the 1970s and by another 31,000 during the 1980s. Population has increased somewhat in recent years, however, rising from 394,000 in 1980 to 402,000 in 1996. Nevertheless, the city's national size rank has continued to decline, falling from 36th place in 1990 to 38th place in 1996.

Sluggish overall central-city growth rates and restrictive annexation policies, in the face of rapid metropolitan expansion, severely eroded central-city shares of the total metropolitan population at the national level in the past thirty years, with Atlanta faring worse than average. In some cases, the central-city share of the metropolitan population dwindled to about 20 percent of the total by 1980, as in the case of Pittsburgh, St. Louis, Washington, D.C., Atlanta, and Miami. By 1996 the city/suburban dichotomy was even more dramatic for Atlanta, as the city accounted for only 11 percent of the metropolitan population. This share placed Atlanta among the smallest central cities in the nation in relation to the overall metropolitan population. In fact, three suburban counties in the region (DeKalb, Cobb, and Gwinnett) now have populations greater than the city of Atlanta.

In-Migration Characteristics

A considerable portion of the growth of the Atlanta region in recent decades has come from the in-migration of residents from other parts of the country and abroad (table 2.4). Nearly half a million people moved into the Atlanta region from other areas between 1985 and 1990, mostly from other metropolitan areas.

Residential movement rates within the metropolitan area, such as shifting residence from city to suburb or from suburb to suburb, are also high. DeKalb County, for example, received a significant share of movers into the county (30 percent) from the city of Atlanta from 1985

TABLE 2.3   Central-City Population 1980 to 1996

1980 Rank	1980 City	1980 Pop. (000s)	1980 Rank Change	% Change 1970 to 1980	1990 City	1990 Pop. (000s)	1990 Rank Change	% Change 1980 to 1990	1990 Rank	1996 City	1996 Pop. (000s)	1996 Rank Change	% Change 1990 to 1996
1.	New York	7,072	NC[a]	−10.4	New York	7,323	NC	3.5	1.	New York	7,381	NC	0.8
2.	Chicago	3,005	NC	−10.8	Los Angeles	3,485	(+1)	17.4	2.	Los Angeles	3,554	NC	2.0
3.	Los Angeles	2,969	NC	5.5	Chicago	2,784	(−1)	−7.4	3.	Chicago	2,722	NC	−2.2
4.	Philadelphia	1,688	NC	−13.4	Houston	1,631	(+1)	2.2	4.	Houston	1,744	NC	6.5
5.	Houston	1,595	(+1)	29.2	Philadelphia	1,586	(−1)	−6.1	5.	Philadelphia	1,478	NC	−6.8
6.	Detroit	1,203	(−1)	−20.5	San Diego	1,111	(+2)	26.8	6.	San Diego	1,171	NC	5.4
7.	Dallas	905	(+1)	7.2	Detroit	1,028	(−1)	−14.6	7.	Phoenix	1,159	(+2)	17.7
8.	San Diego	876	(+6)	25.6	Dallas	1,007	(−1)	11.3	8.	San Antonio	1,068	(+2)	11.3
9.	Phoenix	790	(+11)	35.2	Phoenix	983	NC	24.5	9.	Dallas	1,053	(−1)	4.5
10.	San Antonio	786	(+5)	20.2	San Antonio	936	NC	19.1	10.	Detroit	1,000	(−3)	−2.7
11.	Baltimore	787	(−4)	−13.0	San Jose	782	(+6)	24.3	11.	San Jose	839	NC	7.2
12.	Indianapolis	701	(−1)	−4.9	Baltimore	736	(−1)	−6.4	12.	Indianapolis	757	(+1)	2.1
13.	San Francisco	679	NC	−5.1	Indianapolis	731	(−1)	4.3	13.	San Francisco	735	(+1)	1.6
14.	Memphis	646	(+3)	3.5	San Francisco	724	(−1)	6.6	14.	Jacksonville	721	(+1)	7.2
15.	Washington, D.C.	638	(−6)	−15.7	Jacksonville	635	(+3)	17.9	15.	Baltimore	675	(−3)	−8.2
16.	Milwaukee	636	(−6)	−11.2	Columbus	633	(+3)	12.0	16.	Columbus	657	NC	3.8
17.	San Jose	629	(new)	36.7	Milwaukee	628	(−1)	−1.3	17.	El Paso	600	(new)	16.4
18.	Columbus	565	(new)	4.6	Memphis	610	(−4)	−5.5	18.	Memphis	597	NC	−3.5
19.	Jacksonville	541	(new)	7.3	Washington, D.C.	607	(−4)	−4.9	19.	Milwaukee	590	(−2)	−6.0
20.	Boston	563	(−3)	−12.1	Boston	574	NC	2.0	20.	Boston	558	NC	−2.8
.									.				
.									.				
29	Atlanta	425	(−2)	−14.1	Atlanta	394	(−7)	−7.2	38	Atlanta	402	(−2)	2.0

Source: U.S. Department of Commerce 1998.
[a]NC = no change in the rank.

TABLE 2.4   *Origins of In-Migrants in Atlanta Region, 1985 to 1990*

County	Total In-Migrants	City of Atlanta	MSA Remainder	Different MSA	Not MSA	Abroad
		Place of Origin[a]				
Clayton	59,834	7,904 (13)	17,145 (30)	23,412 (39)	7,207 (12)	3,566 (6)
Cobb	157,217	32,680 (21)	4,738 (3)	91,023 (58)	21,740 (14)	7,036 (4)
DeKalb	173,756	51,593 (30)	10,006 (6)	81,753 (47)	17,959 (10)	12,445 (7)
Douglas	19,781	1,454 (7)	7,729 (39)	7,211 (37)	3,047 (15)	340 (2)
Fayette	27,089	977 (4)	11,310 (42)	11,362 (42)	2,318 (9)	1,122 (4)
Fulton	171,688	—	42,124 (27)	94,847 (54)	19,795 (12)	9,922 (6)
Gwinnett	136,393	6,236 (5)	40,385 (30)	67,871 (51)	15,650 (11)	6,251 (5)
Henry	21,384	1,068 (5)	14,214 (66)	3,974 (18)	1,771 (8)	357 (2)
Rockdale	16,959	475 (3)	9,207 (54)	5,109 (30)	1,673 (10)	495 (3)
City of Atlanta	81,903	—	25,320 (31)	41,772 (52)	10,153 (12)	4,947 (6)

Source: U.S. Department of Commerce 1982, 1992.
[a]Numbers in parentheses are the percentage of total in-migrants from the place of origin.

to 1990, while metropolitan counties farther away received progressively fewer immigrants from the city.

Most of the suburban counties in the region received their in-migrants from other suburban counties, typically from neighboring counties closer to the center of the region. This decentralization pattern from the central city outward provides an example of a distance-decline process (fewer long-distance than short-distance movers). This is consistent with the generalization that most intrametropolitan moves are outward, short in distance, and involve moves to locations on the same side of the city in relation to the downtown area. These data also suggest a cascade effect involving the successive shifting of population in waves from the central city to inner suburban and then outer suburban counties, a process that fueled tremendous population decentralization in Atlanta in the 1980s.

Those counties receiving the largest share of population growth from other metropolitan areas (approximating one-half of the total number of newcomers) included the more mature close-in urban counties inside of or adjacent to the I-285 perimeter highway, such as Cobb (58 percent), Fulton (54 percent), Gwinnett (51 percent), and DeKalb (47 percent). While direct data are hard to acquire, anecdotal evidence suggests, based on home sales and related data, that this population transfer is predominantly a white-collar, middle-class phenomenon. In many cases it involves an influx of a more affluent residential base into a particular county than the mix already living there. In turn, some budget-minded residents already living in the county often move over time to more peripheral counties, lending further credence to the cascade effect.

Metropolitan Atlanta counties generally do not attract significant numbers of immigrants from nonmetropolitan (rural) areas. In no instance in the nine-county ARC region did more than 20 percent of a county's growth in the latter half of the 1980s occur from nonmetropolitan areas. Nevertheless, the more densely populated counties did assimilate thousands of nonmetropolitan immigrants during the last half of the 1980s, even though their percentage of the total remained small. Cobb received nearly 22,000 rural migrants; Fulton, 20,000; and DeKalb, 18,000. These numbers translate into a 10 to 14 percent rural share of the population in-migration into each of those counties.

Ethnic Composition

An African American–white dichotomy has traditionally characterized the ethnic composition of the Atlanta region. The African American population share of the nine-county region increased from 22 percent in 1970, to 26 percent in 1980, to 28 percent in 1990 (see table 2.5). The Asian share of the population registered a 0.2 percent share in 1970, 0.6 percent in 1980, and 2.0 percent in 1990. The Hispanic population share experienced a similar increase in the past twenty years.

The African American population as a percentage of the total population in the city of Atlanta in 1970 stood at 52 percent, increasing to 67 percent in 1980, and remained essentially the same in 1990. At the same time, the Asian population share rose to just under 1 percent in 1990 and the Hispanic share to about 2 percent of the total.

These global figures belie significant subregional trends, such as ethnic suburbanization and the creation of identifiable Asian and Hispanic communities in the suburbs in the 1980s. Traditionally, residential segregation has created two housing markets in Atlanta, one white and one African American, as most census tracts in the region have either been all white or all African American. In contrast, the Asian and Hispanic populations are less segregated and created more cultural diversity within many neighborhoods by 1990. The level of African American–white residential segregation declined in the 1980s and the 1990s as African American suburbanization expanded, but distinctive residential patterns remained. We will examine these patterns in greater detail in a later section using special ARC tabulations that allow a very recent look (1996) at residential segregation within the Atlanta region.

TABLE 2.5 Population by Ethnic Group in ARC Region, 1970 to 1990

County	White Population			African American Population			Asian Population			Hispanic Population[a]	
	1970	1980 (Percentage Change)[b]	1990 (Percentage Change)	1970	1980 (Percentage Change)	1990 (Percentage Change)	1970	1980 (Percentage Change)	1990 (Percentage Change)	1980	1990 (Percentage Change)
Clayton	93,381	137,950 (48)	132,036 (−4)	4,447	10,494 (136)	43,373 (313)	247	1,097 (344)	4,729 (331)	1,242	3,624 (192)
Cobb	188,198	281,625 (50)	392,411 (39)	8,216	13,055 (59)	44,042 (237)	328	1,617 (392)	7,425 (359)	2,522	8,995 (257)
DeKalb	357,536	344,254 (−4)	292,421 (−15)	56,877	130,980 (130)	230,532 (91)	696	4,296 (517)	15,895 (270)	7,755	14,491 (87)
Douglas	26,030	51,444 (98)	64,795 (26)	2,609	2,818 (8)	5,423 (92)	21	108 (414)	381 (253)	353	816 (131)
Fayette	9,382	27,746 (196)	57,621 (108)	1,954	1,114 (−43)	3,201 (187)	27	84 (211)	1,143 (1,261)	238	903 (279)
Fulton	369,815	280,334 (−24)	310,167 (11)	236,497	303,508 (28)	323,984 (7)	1,166	2,659 (128)	8,017 (202)	7,574	13,420 (77)
Fulton outside Atlanta	NA	NA	199,411 (32)	NA	NA	84,384 (76)	NA	NA	4,899 (420)	2,251	6,080 (170)
Gwinnett	68,611	161,263 (135)	321,400 (99)	3,641	4,094 (12)	18,049 (341)	84	1,020 (1,114)	9,822 (863)	1,727	8,076 (368)
Henry	16,116	29,673 (84)	52,073 (75)	7,580	6,363 (−16)	6,017 (−5)	20	97 (385)	385 (297)	156	443 (184)
Rockdale	14,999	33,220 (14)	48,913 (47)	3,129	3,186 (2)	4,344 (36)	16	212 (1,225)	450 (112)	358	499 (39)
ARC region	1,144,068	1,347,509 (18)	1,671,837 (24)	324,950	475,615 (46)	678,965 (43)	2,605	11,190 (330)	48,247 (331)	21,925	51,267 (134)
City of Atlanta	239,268	137,878 (−42)	122,363 (−11)	255,771	282,911 (11)	264,213 (−7)	—	1,775	3,276 (85)	5,750	7,640 (33)

Source: U.S. Department of Commerce 1972, 1982, 1992.

[a] The Hispanic population was not separately tabulated by the Census Bureau in 1970. Hispanics can be of any race.

[b] The numbers in parentheses are the percentage change in population over the decade.

NA = not available.

Employment Growth

Atlanta has been among the national leaders in employment growth over the past two decades. Table 2.6 reports average annual employment growth rates broken down by industry group for the periods 1980 to 1989 and 1990 to 1997 for Atlanta and nine other metropolitan areas. Figure 2.1 shows the distribution of jobs by industry for Atlanta in 1997. The set of comparison MSAs represents major metropolitan areas located throughout the United States in each of the country's four major census regions that, like Atlanta, have large minority populations.

In both periods, Atlanta achieved the highest average annual growth rate in total employment among the MSAs listed (4.4 percent for 1980 through 1989 and 3.5 percent for 1990 through 1997), with the exception of Seattle in the earlier period.

Employment growth rates by industry show that Atlanta's growth has been broadly based, with Atlanta ranking no lower than third in any industry group, regardless of time period. Of particular interest to the Atlanta paradox is that employment growth in both periods has been the greatest in services—the industry group containing the highest proportion of jobs for lower-skilled workers. During the 1990 to 1997 period, Atlanta's services employment growth dominated by a considerable margin that occurring in any of the other comparison MSAs. Also relevant is that Atlanta has experienced positive average annual growth in manufacturing, while most of the other MSAs have lost jobs in these industries. Traditionally, manufacturing has been an important source of higher-wage jobs for lower-skilled black workers both in Atlanta and nationally.

Racial Disparities in Socioeconomic Indicators

In analyzing racial disparities across geographical areas within the Atlanta region, it is important to draw a distinction between the northern and southern suburbs. Historically, these areas have developed quite differently, with the southern suburbs lagging far behind the northern suburbs. Hence, in lieu of the standard central-city versus suburbs dichotomy, the following analysis will be based on a division of the Atlanta region into three parts: the city of Atlanta, the northern suburbs, and the southern suburbs (see map 2.4).[2]

Poverty and Income

Table 2.7 reports the number and incidence of poor people broken down by race and subregional area for 1980 and 1990. For the entire region in

TABLE 2.6   Average Annual Employment Growth Rates for Selected Metropolitan Areas (Percentage)

1980 to 1989	Total	Construction	Manufacturing	Transportation, Communication, and Utilities	Wholesale/ Retail	Finance, Insurance, and Real Estate	Services
Atlanta	4.4	5.0	2.2	3.8	4.5	5.0	6.7
Chicago	1.4	2.9	-2.2	1.2	1.9	2.9	4.2
Dallas	3.6	-1.0	1.5	2.4	3.0	4.8	7.7
Denver	0.7	-4.0	-2.2	2.4	0.8	2.0	3.5
Detroit	0.5	0.6	-2.3	-0.1	1.9	1.9	4.8
Los Angeles	1.4	1.6	-0.7	0.6	1.6	2.0	3.5
Miami	2.4	1.6	-0.7	0.2	2.8	3.9	4.3
New York	1.1	7.0	-3.3	-1.4	0.4	2.3	3.1
Philadelphia	1.5	3.3	-2.0	0.3	2.1	2.8	4.4
Seattle	4.9	8.0	4.5	3.3	4.3	3.4	7.4

1990 to 1997	Total	Construction	Manufacturing	Transportation, Communication, and Utilities	Wholesale/ Retail	Finance, Insurance, and Real Estate	Services
Atlanta	3.5	3.9	1.4	3.7	3.0	2.2	6.0
Chicago	1.2	0.5	-0.3	1.3	0.2	0.8	3.3
Dallas	3.1	7.1	0.6	5.3	2.5	0.8	5.2
Denver	3.2	8.9	-0.3	2.8	3.0	3.5	4.8
Detroit	1.1	3.0	-0.2	1.0	0.8	0.6	3.1
Los Angeles	-0.7	-2.2	-3.2	0.0	-1.3	-2.7	1.3
Miami	1.2	-1.6	-2.4	2.6	0.9	-0.6	3.0
New York	-0.7	NA	-3.9	-0.5	-1.0	-0.6	1.4
Philadelphia	0.2	-7.6	-2.3	0.4	-0.5	-1.4	2.4
Seattle	2.5	1.8	0.1	2.1	2.3	1.0	4.8

Source: Chang and Tanyi 1998.

FIGURE 2.1   *Percentage of Total Metropolitan Employment, 1997*

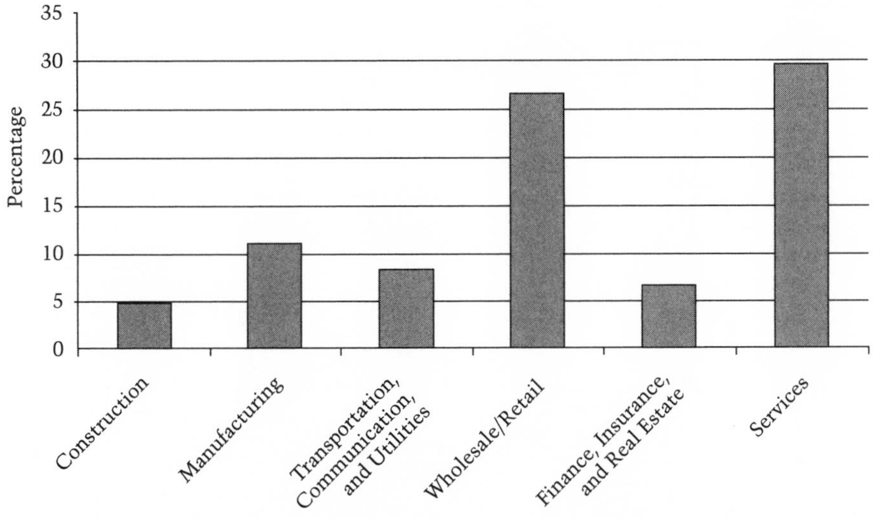

Source: Atlanta Regional Commission 1998.

1980 there were 115,201 blacks living below the poverty line, which resulted in a black poverty rate of 27.2 percent—over four times greater than the white poverty rate of 6.4 percent.

The vast majority of the region's impoverished blacks (71 percent) live within the city of Atlanta, where the black poverty rate equaled 33.2 percent in 1980. In comparison, the white poverty rate in the city was only 12.6 percent. Black poverty rates were lower in the suburbs but still high, especially in comparison to those for whites.

During the 1980s, both the black and white poverty rates declined at the regional level. Within the city of Atlanta, however, both the number and incidence of the poor increased for blacks over the decade, while both of these measures declined for whites. The remarkably high and increasing black poverty within the city during a time when Atlanta enjoyed unprecedented employment growth in both high- and low-skill jobs lies at the heart of the Atlanta paradox.

Striking a more optimistic note was the decline in both black and white poverty outside the city on both the north and south sides of the region. Particularly dramatic was the decline in the black poverty rate in the northern suburbs, where it fell from 25.6 percent in 1980 to only 13.4 in 1990. As will be explored more fully, during the 1980s the northern suburbs attracted a growing number of successful blacks and experi-

29

MAP 2.4   *Geographic Divisions of Atlanta Region (Based on Superdistrict Groupings)*

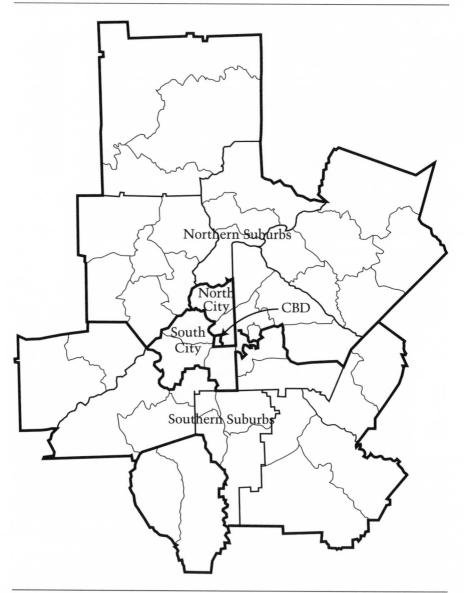

Source: Cartographic Research Laboratory, Department of Geography, Georgia State University, 1999.

TABLE 2.7   *Population Below Poverty Level*

	Region	City	Northern Suburbs	Southern Suburbs
Blacks				
1980	115,201	82,080	8,644	24,477
	(27.2)[a]	(33.2)	(25.6)	(17.1)
1990	143,655	89,124	20,511	34,020
	(21.7)	(35.0)	(13.4)	(13.5)
Whites				
1980	81,228	15,072	38,979	27,177
	(6.4)	(12.6)	(5.1)	(6.9)
1990	81,709	11,179	46,671	23,859
	(4.9)	(9.7)	(4.2)	(5.7)

Source: U.S. Department of Commerce 1982, 1992.
[a]Number in parentheses is the poverty rate.

enced the lion's share of the region's employment growth. Both of these factors led to the decline in black poverty north of the city.

The magnitude of the economic disparity within the city of Atlanta between blacks and whites can be further illustrated by focusing on racial differences in household incomes. In 1989, white household incomes registered $61,691 on average in the city, compared with only $22,322 for black households. This disparity suggests a tremendous gulf between the buying power of African American and white households in the city.[3]

The tendency for high-income whites and low-income blacks to occupy the central city is not unique to Atlanta. Research by urban economists indicates that the former group prefers a city location because they place a high value on commuting time and can afford to send their children to private schools. Low-income African Americans, on the other hand, are concentrated within central cities because of racial discrimination in the suburban housing market and the need to live in the older, less expensive housing that cities tend to offer in abundance. For those who cannot afford cars, the central city also typically offers better access to public transportation.

Income disparities by race were not as great in the suburbs as within the city, but significant differences existed. In the northern suburbs, average white household income ($54,947) was $23,495 higher than average African American household income ($31,452). A considerably smaller differential of $8,059 separated African American and white average household income on the south side: $43,072 for whites and $35,013 for African Americans. Overall, in 1989 average household income for whites was the lowest on the south side, while the average for African Americans was the lowest in the city. Somewhat surprisingly, the highest average for African Americans existed in the southern suburbs. These findings suggest the following income profile of the Atlanta region: the highest-income whites tend to live in the city; the highest-income African Americans tend to live in the southern suburbs; and highest overall household incomes in the region occur in the northern suburbs.

Poverty Concentration

The growing concern over the increasing concentration of poverty within inner cities stems from the belief that the geographical concentration of the poor is detrimental to their own as well as society's welfare. The validity of this belief has been supported by recent empirical findings.[4]

Table 2.8 shows that there are large racial disparities in not only the incidence of poverty but also its concentration within the city of Atlanta. Moreover, concentrated poverty for blacks increased between 1980 and 1990 both absolutely and relative to whites. In 1980, 41.6 percent of the city's black poor lived in a high-poverty neighborhood. The corresponding figure for the white poor was 12.5 percent. During the 1980s concentrated poverty rose to 48.7 percent for city blacks, but declined to 8.2 percent for city whites. John Kasarda (1993) has shown that for the central cities of the same set of ten metro areas listed in table 2.5, the concentration of Atlanta's black poor is fourth highest. The high and increasing poverty concentration among blacks in Atlanta is paradoxical, since research has shown that both the level and growth of concentrated poverty are lower in metropolitan areas with strong economies (Jargowsky 1997).

Employment

The disparities in income between blacks and whites can be caused by racial differences in employment, wages, and/or wealth. The numbers in table 2.9 suggest that the first factor plays a salient role. In 1980, 65 percent of black males in the region held jobs during the census reference week. The figure for white males was 15 percentage points higher. Within the city of Atlanta, the black male employment rate was lower (59 percent), but the racial gap in employment was smaller (10 percentage points). For the 1990 reference week, the black male employment rate was higher at the regional level (68 percent) but lower within the city (56 percent) in comparison to 1980. In contrast, rates for white males were higher for both the region and the city. In 1990, there was a difference of 18 percentage points in the rate of employment between white and black males living in the city. In the two suburban areas,

TABLE 2.8   *Number of Poor People Living in High-Poverty Neighborhoods[a]*

	Region	City	Northern Suburbs	Southern Suburbs
Blacks				
1980	35,475	34,124	1,351	0
	(30.8)[b]	(41.6)	(15.6)	
1990	43,391	43,391	0	0
	(30.2)	(48.7)		
Whites				
1980	1,891	1,891	0	0
	(2.3)	(12.5)		
1990	922	922	0	0
	(1.1)	(8.2)		

Source: U.S. Department of Commerce 1982, 1992.
[a]A high-poverty neighborhood is defined as containing 40 percent or more poor people.
[b]Number in parentheses is the percentage of the poor living in high-poverty neighborhoods.

employment rates were also higher for white than black males, but the differences (2 to 3 percentage points) between the races were much smaller in comparison to the city.

Differences in unemployment rates between white and black males parallel the large disparities observed in employment rates. In 1980, the white male unemployment rate during the reference week was 3.2 percent and 4.2 percent for the region and city, respectively. For blacks, these rates were over twice as high. In comparison to those for 1980, the 1990 unemployment rates for black males were higher and the black-white differences were larger. In 1990, the black male unemployment rate in the city of Atlanta was 3.7 times greater than the rate for white males. For both reference weeks, large differences, although less than those within the city, also existed in the unemployment rates of white and black males living in the suburbs. This contrasts with the similarity in suburban employment rates between the races and indicates that unemployment (rather than being out of the labor force) plays a relatively more important role in explaining the joblessness of suburban black men.

Racial comparisons in employment rates between females are much different than those for males. For both time periods and all subregional areas, black females tended to have jobs about as frequently and in many cases more frequently than their white counterparts. Unemployment rates, however, tell a story that mirrors the one told for males: rates are two to three times higher for black than white females, and within the city the racial gap was larger in 1990 than in 1980.

In contrast to black males, the relatively high unemployment rates

TABLE 2.9   *Employment and Unemployment Rates*

	Region	City	Northern Suburbs	Southern Suburbs
Employment rate[a]				
Black males				
1980	65.0	59.0	66.4	75.5
1990	68.3	55.8	80.0	74.0
Black females				
1980	55.5	49.7	56.9	66.0
1990	63.4	49.5	76.5	70.0
White males				
1980	79.9	69.0	82.4	79.0
1990	80.3	73.3	82.3	77.3
White females				
1980	54.9	48.7	57.6	51.9
1990	62.9	55.4	65.4	58.6
Unemployment rate[b]				
Black males				
1980	9.5	10.8	7.7	8.0
1990	9.9	13.4	6.9	9.0
Black females				
1980	9.2	10.0	7.8	8.0
1990	9.1	12.0	6.5	8.5
White males				
1980	3.2	4.2	2.6	4.0
1990	3.3	3.6	3.2	3.6
White females				
1980	3.8	3.9	2.1	4.7
1990	3.7	3.8	3.4	4.9

Source: U.S. Department of Commerce 1982, 1992.
[a]Employment rate equals the number of people over the age of fifteen with jobs divided by persons over fifteen years.
[b]Unemployment rate equals the number of unemployed people divided by the number of people in the labor force (employed + unemployed).

for black females do not translate into relatively low employment rates. The reason for this is that white females are less interested in working than black females: the labor force participation rate of white females in the region was 65 percent in 1990, whereas for black females it was 70 percent. This difference in labor force participation between white and black females largely reflects racial differences in family structure—another possible indicator of disparities in socioeconomic welfare to which we now turn.

Female-Headed Families

The number of female-headed families has increased rapidly at the national level in the last few decades for all racial groups. This growth means that fewer children are raised in two-parent families, which is unfortunate because child poverty is three times higher in homes without two parents.

In the Atlanta region, once again there is a large and growing racial disparity in this indicator of socioeconomic welfare (table 2.10). Among the region's black families, the share that are female-headed increased from 39.3 percent in 1980 to 41.7 percent in 1990. For white families, female-headedness declined from 11.1 percent to 10.8 percent over the decade. In the city of Atlanta, of course, the growth in the share of families headed by a female was much greater, rising from 45.1 percent in 1980 to 52.7 percent in 1990. For white females in the city, female-headedness declined. Outside the city, the incidence of black families headed by a female stayed about the same in the northern suburbs, but increased in the southern suburbs. For suburban white families, the share headed by a female remained stable at about 11.0 percent on both sides of the region. Within the three areas (city, northern suburbs, and southern suburbs), female-headed families comprise 76 percent, 56 percent, and 44 percent of the families living in poverty, respectively.

Intraregional Shifts in Employment and Population

In addition to Atlanta's remarkable employment and population growth, another factor that has dramatically altered the "spatial face" of the region in recent decades is changing locations of people and jobs. These shifts may be both a cause and a consequence of racial disparities in socioeconomic welfare.

The ARC publishes annual employment estimates for major industry groups, going back to 1980, for small planning areas called superdistricts.[5] There are forty-five superdistricts in the nine-county ARC region. They are aggregated into the same three subregional areas, except that the city of Atlanta is divided into north and south and the southern suburbs are divided into black and white areas (see map 2.4). These additional geographical breakdowns are useful in showing the juxtaposition between the spatial arrangement of jobs and racial residential segregation. The northern section of the central city consists of two superdistricts that are majority white. The southern section of the city includes the five remaining superdistricts in the city, all of which are majority black; one of these superdistricts is the Central Business District. The black southern suburbs represent the six suburban superdistricts that have a majority black population. This area borders the central city and contains Hartsfield International Airport. The white southern suburbs lie beyond the black southern suburbs and include thirteen superdistricts that are majority white. The northern suburbs consist of nineteen superdistricts, all of which are predominantly white.[6]

TABLE 2.10   *Number of Female-Headed Families*

	Region	City	Northern Suburbs	Southern Suburbs
Blacks				
1980	40,216	27,602	2,781	9,833
	(39.3)[a]	(45.1)	(34.9)	(29.6)
1990	68,584	33,143	13,189	22,252
	(41.7)	(52.7)	(34.7)	(35.0)
Whites				
1980	38,367	4,928	22,283	11,136
	(11.1)	(16.6)	(10.8)	(10.2)
1990	48,859	3,335	32,215	13,309
	(10.8)	(13.8)	(10.5)	(11.0)

Source: U.S. Department of Commerce 1982, 1992.
[a]Number in parentheses is the percentage of all families that are female-headed.

Employment totals for each of the five areas, broken down into single-digit industry groups, are given in table 2.11 for 1980, 1990, and 1996. In 1980, the city and the northern suburbs each contained 40 percent of the region's total jobs, leaving the southern suburbs with a 20 percent share. Since 1980, the city's share of jobs has plummeted to less than 25 percent; the northern suburbs' share has grown to 54 percent; and the southern suburbs' share has remained at about 20 percent. The north-side shift in the spatial distribution of jobs cuts across all industry groups, with the share increases ranging between a maximum of 18 percent for retailing and minimum of 8 percent for government.

Within the city of Atlanta, the white north side has lost less share of the region's jobs than the black south side. Between 1980 and 1996, the north side's share fell only 4 percentage points, while the south side's declined 12 percentage points. The largest share declines occurred in manufacturing and TCU (transportation, communication, and utilities), industries that have traditionally provided good-paying blue-collar jobs to black workers. Similarly, the black southern suburbs have experienced a 3 percentage point loss of share in total jobs, while the white southern suburb's share has grown by 4 percentage points.

The movement of jobs to the northern suburbs and the relative decline of the south side of the city and the black suburbs as employment locations has significantly reduced the percentage of the region's jobs located in black neighborhoods. Moreover, the many new jobs on the north side of the region may not be accessible to poor blacks living on the south side because the bus and rail system, a radial system focused on the downtown area, serves only Fulton and DeKalb counties. Hence, the reverse work trip from the city (or southern suburbs) to the northern suburbs is not well served by public transit.

TABLE 2.11 *Atlanta Region Employment*

		Central City		Suburbs		
		North	South	North	South	
					Black	White
Total employment						
1980	881,432	132,536	222,990	352,542	113,474	59,890
		(15.0)[a]	(25.3)	(40.0)	(12.9)	(6.8)
1990	1,410,000	171,561	225,586	716,167	163,421	133,265
		(12.2)	(16.0)	(50.8)	(11.6)	(9.5)
1996	1,682,200	192,125	225,558	911,173	172,980	180,364
		(11.4)	(13.4)	(54.2)	(10.3)	(10.7)
Construction						
1980	47,593	5,188	7,643	23,872	7,669	3,221
		(10.9)	(16.1)	(50.2)	(16.1)	(6.8)
1990	62,700	4,107	8,015	34,106	7,049	9,423
		(6.5)	(17.8)	(54.4)	(11.2)	(15.3)
1996	77,350	3,884	6,762	46,028	8,969	11,707
		(5.0)	(8.7)	(59.5)	(11.6)	(15.1)
Manufacturing						
1980	129,898	9,509	39,477	56,631	14,510	9,771
		(7.3)	(30.4)	(43.6)	(11.2)	(7.5)
1990	151,200	5,961	30,921	77,747	17,765	18,806
		(3.9)	(20.4)	(51.4)	(11.7)	(12.4)
1996	164,150	5,437	29,620	88,021	19,139	21,933
		(3.3)	(18.0)	(53.6)	(11.7)	(13.4)
Retail						
1980	142,454	22,421	23,599	60,760	20,910	14,764
		(15.7)	(16.6)	(42.6)	(14.7)	(10.4)
1990	257,900	26,729	22,265	143,093	31,210	34,603
		(10.4)	(8.6)	(55.5)	(12.1)	(13.4)
1996	306,100	30,887	18,084	185,124	26,745	45,260
		(10.1)	(5.9)	(60.5)	(8.7)	(14.8)
Wholesale						
1980	81,725	11,099	19,056	39,117	7,961	4,492
		(13.6)	(23.3)	(47.9)	(9.7)	(5.5)
1990	138,200	10,773	21,910	85,484	11,253	8,780
		(7.8)	(15.8)	(61.8)	(8.1)	(6.4)
1996	151,600	8,467	18,097	97,441	14,378	13,217
		(5.6)	(11.9)	(64.3)	(9.5)	(8.7)
Services						
1980	179,549	44,409	40,285	73,311	14,403	7,141
		(24.7)	(22.4)	(40.8)	(8.0)	(4.0)
1990	347,300	67,938	53,264	180,486	24,125	21,487
		(19.6)	(15.3)	(52.0)	(6.9)	(6.2)
1996	484,200	83,900	62,033	270,719	30,010	37,538
		(17.3)	(12.8)	(55.9)	(6.2)	(7.8)

(*Table continues on p. 38.*)

TABLE 2.11   *Continued*

		Central City		Suburbs		
		North	South	North	South	
					Black	White
Transportation, communication, and utilities						
1980	82,154	5,005	27,425	16,930	28,035	4,759
		(6.1)	(33.4)	(20.6)	(34.1)	(5.8)
1990	126,100	13,309	16,705	42,992	43,413	9,681
		(10.5)	(13.2)	(34.1)	(34.4)	(7.7)
1996	147,800	15,041	18,701	53,577	44,537	15,944
		(10.2)	(12.6)	(36.2)	(30.1)	(10.8)
Finance, insurance, and real estate						
1980	71,087	16,029	15,152	32,868	4,745	2,293
		(22.5)	(21.3)	(46.2)	(6.7)	(3.2)
1990	113,100	20,094	14,896	66,667	6,841	4,602
		(17.8)	(13.2)	(58.9)	(6.0)	(4.1)
1996	119,900	21,003	14,245	71,972	6,910	5,770
		(17.5)	(11.9)	(60.0)	(5.8)	(4.8)
Government						
1980	144,113	18,577	50,050	47,601	14,688	13,197
		(12.9)	(34.7)	(33.0)	(10.2)	(9.2)
1990	205,800	22,210	57,228	80,757	20,894	24,711
		(10.8)	(27.8)	(39.2)	(10.2)	(12.0)
1996	220,700	23,015	57,798	90,771	21,541	27,575
		(10.4)	(26.2)	(41.1)	(9.8)	(12.5)

Source: Atlanta Regional Commission 1981a, 1991, 1997a.
ªThe number in parentheses is the percentage of the region's jobs located in that area.

ARC also publishes annual population estimates broken down by race (white versus black and other races) for the superdistricts.[7] These estimates are updates of decennial census numbers obtained from monitoring changes in housing inventory (via building and demolition permits) and conducting field surveys.

The shift in employment in favor of the north side of the region has been accompanied by shifts in population (see table 2.12). The percentage of the region's whites living in the northern suburbs increased from 57.3 percent in 1980 to 65.4 percent in 1996. More dramatic has been the movement north of the black population. In 1990, 9.4 percent of the region's blacks lived in the northern suburbs, but by 1996 this percentage had climbed to 25.2 percent. As in the case of employment, the shift in population northward came at the expense of the city of Atlanta,

TABLE 2.12   *Atlanta Region Population*

	Central City		Suburbs		
	North	South	North	South	
				Black	White
Black and other races					
1980	497,829	20,393 (4.1)ª	267,772 (53.8)	47,020 (9.4)	137,921 (27.7)	24,723 (5.0)
1990	781,818	25,194 (3.2)	265,250 (33.9)	176,050 (22.5)	251,056 (32.1)	64,268 (8.2)
1996	870,634	29,842 (3.4)	266,561 (30.6)	219,864 (25.2)	272,787 (31.3)	81,580 (9.4)
Whites					
1980	1,346,654	85,776 (6.4)	52,284 (3.9)	771,399 (57.3)	165,188 (12.3)	272,007 (20.2)
1990	1,684,982	88,668 (5.3)	37,285 (2.2)	1,093,931 (64.9)	111,140 (6.6)	353,958 (21.0)
1996	1,966,666	92,866 (4.7)	39,060 (2.0)	1,286,851 (65.4)	119,681 (6.1)	428,208 (21.8)

Source: Atlanta Regional Commission 1981b, 1991, 1997b.
ªThe number in parentheses is the percentage of the region's population of the designated group located in that area.

where the shares of the region's blacks and whites declined by 24 and 4 percentage points, respectively. In the southern suburbs, the share of the region's blacks increased (although not nearly as much as in the northern suburbs), while the share of whites registered a modest decline.

Despite the northward suburbanization of blacks, over 60 percent of the region's blacks resided on the south side of the city and in the black southern suburbs in 1996—areas we identified as having suffered relative job losses over time. In contrast, only 8 percent of the region's whites lived in these areas.

The suburbanization of blacks within the Atlanta region suggests that housing segregation between whites and blacks may be declining. To investigate this, indices of dissimilarity were computed for each of the three years. These indices are the most popular measure of housing segregation and show what percentage of either racial group would have to relocate to achieve complete integration at the neighborhood level. A value of 0 indicates that each neighborhood has the same racial composition as the entire region, implying complete integration; a value of 100 indicates that all neighborhoods are either all black or all white, implying complete segregation.

The index of dissimilarity equaled 75.9 in 1980, 64.7 in 1990, and 61.4 in 1996.[8] These values imply that while the Atlanta region's neighborhoods remain highly segregated, they are much less so than in 1980.

However, the computation of a separate dissimilarity index value for each subregional area reveals that the reduction in segregation has occurred entirely outside the city of Atlanta. In both 1980 and 1996, the dissimilarity index equaled 78.0 within the city, while over this time span the index declined from 63.8 to 52.4 in the suburbs.

Conclusion

This chapter has documented the two simultaneous events that define the Atlanta paradox: rapid employment growth among all major industry groups and high and rising black poverty within the city of Atlanta. The plight of the city's black population is also registered by its high level of poverty concentration, low employment and high unemployment, and large number of female-headed families. In addition, city blacks live in highly segregated neighborhoods that have suffered significant job losses relative to other parts of the region.

Notes

1. The ARC region added its tenth county, Cherokee, in 1993. Cherokee's population accounts for less than 4 percent of the region's population. Because the GANS household sample is drawn from the nine-county ARC region and employment data for Cherokee are not available for earlier years, all of the regional data presented in this chapter refer to the nine-county region.

2. The nine-county ARC region is employed rather than the MSA because more recent employment and population data are available for the region. The region accounted for 78 percent and 87 percent of the MSA's population and employment in 1990, respectively.

3. Unfortunately, it could not be determined how much racial disparities in household income have changed over time, since census data for 1980 do not provide a breakdown of household income by race.

4. Ihlanfeldt (1999) describes the various mechanisms whereby the neighborhood milieu may affect individual behaviors and reviews the empirical literature on neighborhood effects.

5. ARC's employment estimates were initially based on a complete census of employers conducted in 1970. Since then, employment figures have been updated by surveying a sample of firms and relying on secondary resources, such as commercially available business lists and ES-202 data from the Georgia Department of Labor.

6. Of the nineteen superdistricts defining the northern suburbs, twelve have populations that are 10 percent black or less, and six are between 11 and 20 percent black. The remaining superdistrict is the city of Decatur, an outlier that is 39 percent black.

7. While blacks are not separately tabulated, the "black and other races" category is almost all black, because Asians represented only 2 percent of the region's population in 1990. This category will therefore henceforth be referred to as black.

8. The index was computed using ARC's population by race estimates at the census tract level.

References

Atlanta Regional Commission. 1981a. *Employment 1980*. Atlanta, Ga.: Atlanta Regional Commission.

———. 1981b. *Population 1980*. Atlanta, Ga.: Atlanta Regional Commission.

———. 1991. *Population 1990*. Atlanta, Ga.: Atlanta Regional Commission.

———. 1997a. *Employment 1996*. Atlanta, Ga.: Atlanta Regional Commission.

———. 1997b. *Population 1996*. Atlanta, Ga: Atlanta Regional Commission.

———. 1998. *Employment 1997*. Atlanta, Ga.: Atlanta Regional Commission.

Chang, Li-Ti, and Enoubi Tanyi. 1998. *Series Report*. Bureau of Labor Statistics Data. http://stats.sls.gov/database.htm (May 28, 1998).

Goquin, Deirdre A., and Mark S. Littman, eds. 1998. *1998 County and City Extra: Annual Metro City and County Data Book*. Lantham, Md.: Bernan Press.

Ihlanfeldt, Keith R. 1999. "The Geography of Economic and Social Opportunities Within Metropolitan Areas." In *Governance and Opportunity in Metropolitan America*, edited by Alan Altshuler, William Morrill, Harold Wolman, and Faith Mitchell. Washington, D.C.: National Academy Press.

Jargowsky, Paul A. 1997. *Poverty and Place: Ghettos, Barrios, and the American City*. New York: Russell Sage Foundation.

Kasarda, John. 1993. "Inner-City Poverty and Economic Access." In *Rediscovering Urban America: Perspectives on the 1980s*, edited by Jack Summer and Donald Hicks. Washington, D.C.: U.S. Department of Housing and Urban Development, Office of Policy Development and Research.

Mills, Edwin S., and Luan Sende Lubuele. 1995. "Projecting Metropolitan Area Growth Rates." *Journal of Urban Economics* 37: 344–60.

O'Sullivan, Arthur. 1996. *Urban Economics*, 3rd ed. Chicago: Richard D. Irwin.

U.S. Department of Commerce, Bureau of the Census. 1952. *1950 Census of Population and Housing*. Washington: U.S. Government Printing Office.

———. 1972. *1970 Census of Population and Housing*. Washington: U.S. Government Printing Office.

———. 1982. *1980 Census of Population and Housing*. Washington: U.S. Government Printing Office.

———. 1992. *1990 Census of Population and Housing*. Washington: U.S. Government Printing Office.

———. 1998. *Statistical Abstract of the United States: 1998*. Washington: U.S. Government Printing Office.

3

ATLANTA: THE HISTORICAL PARADOX

Ronald H. Bayor

ATLANTA mayor William Hartsfield proclaimed in 1955, in relation to the desegregation of the city's public golf courses, that Atlanta was "a city too busy to hate." That slogan, subsequently used in his political campaigns and during the 1960s civil rights efforts, grew popular, although it never came close to the truth.

Atlanta's image of racial harmony was protected and perpetuated because of concern about the city's economy. Little Rock and Birmingham lost investment and saw business stagnate during times of racial conflict, and Atlanta's political and business leaders were afraid that the city's economic growth and progress would end if it lost its positive race-relations image. Mayor Hartsfield worked hard to perpetuate the myth, as did his successor, Ivan Allen, who stated, "I could promise all I wanted to about Atlanta's bright, booming economic future, but none of it would come about if Atlanta failed to cope with the racial issue. . . . Was Atlanta gong to be another Little Rock, or was Atlanta going to set the pace for the New South?" (Allen 1971, 53–54; Bayor 1996, 37).

City leaders worked to avoid public displays of racial unrest, rather than seriously addressing the black community's legitimate grievances. Real changes in Atlanta's racial picture came slowly and reluctantly. Although Atlanta experienced much less violence than some other cities in relation to desegregation in the 1960s, its history indicates a city that certainly was not too busy to hate.

Understanding the current Atlanta paradox requires understanding the history of race in Atlanta. It is a history of continuous discrimination, to which the present inequities that exist within a booming economy can be traced. This chapter shows how the history of race relations in Atlanta laid the foundation for the Atlanta paradox.

In the period of rebirth and growth after the Civil War, Atlanta liked to think of itself as progressive, yet experienced one of the nation's most devastating race riots. A four-day riot in 1906 resulted in mob assaults on black businesses and neighborhoods, leaving a number of Atlantans dead or wounded. This racial tension so vividly revealed in the riot would continue through the twentieth century. It was also a city of rapid economic growth where white business leaders often controlled politics and set policies that enhanced the city's economy. Yet, by the early twentieth century, over one-third of its population, its black citizens, was purposely left out of the resurgence.

The desire for economic growth, the false sense of racial progressivism, and the intentional neglect and denial of a large segment of its people to contribute fully to and benefit from that growth created a city that was bustling with business activity and had a good national reputation for racial issues, but had significant problems with poverty and racism. By the time black political control rose in the 1970s, the city's race and class problems had been many decades in the making and were difficult to resolve.

Although the first black mayor, Maynard Jackson, did try to forge some equity between the races, he found it a very difficult task due to white fears. He stressed to white leaders that "black people do not want to take over Atlanta. Black people want to participate and to have our influence felt in fair proportions" (*Atlanta Constitution*, October 10, 1974; Bayor 1996, 50–51). Attacked by white business leaders as being antiwhite and realizing that he needed the white economic elite to help run the city, Jackson eventually pulled back from his early aggressive stand. He and his successor, Andrew Young, came to accept the priorities of the white business leaders, and the need to protect the city's image took on an exaggerated importance in their administrations also.

The rest of this chapter considers the making of the Atlanta paradox in relation to residential segregation, employment, schools, transportation, city services and neighborhoods, and city priorities. Racial discrimination has played a role in creating the continuing poverty that is part of contemporary Atlanta, and understanding that discrimination is key to understanding Atlanta.

Residential Patterns

Atlanta's residential racial polarization began to take shape by the 1890s, followed by official city efforts to maintain it. Between 1913 and 1931, officials passed segregation ordinances designed to prevent black movement into white areas. City blocks were designated by race in some cases; in others, African Americans could not secure housing near white public schools. The most important of the segregation acts of this era was a 1922 racial zoning law that divided most of the city's residential areas into white and black single and two-family dwelling and apartment house sections (Flint 1977, 309, 313, 320, 325–26, 341–43, 357; Bayor 1996, 54–55). Although the courts ruled against such acts, city officials continued to act and plan for Atlanta in terms of sections selected as acceptable for white or black use (Bayor 1996, 55).

What followed in the 1930s to 1960s were blacks' efforts to expand their land area and consistent white maneuvering to block that expansion. Using elaborate land agreements, zoning, highways, a stadium and a civic center, commercial and industrial designations, road paving, and public housing site selection, white officials had confined Atlanta blacks—43.5 percent of the city's population—to a mere 22 percent of the land by 1965 (Bayor 1996, 83). Indexes of dissimilarity, which measure segregation levels, increased significantly over the course of the twentieth century. While segregation increased, the low income level of blacks relative to whites that would have partly produced it had lessened. By 1960, most of the housing segregation in Atlanta could not be understood by looking at the income levels of the two racial groups. Race, not economic status, was the salient factor in explaining housing segregation (Toward Equal Opportunity 1967, 26; Bayor 1996, 77).

Some examples will illustrate the extravagant efforts made to maintain and enhance the city's racial polarization. In the 1950s the west side white communities of Center Hill and Grove Park (see map 3.1) were concerned about black movement into the area. Mayor Hartsfield emphasized to his construction chief the need to build an access road extension that would function as a racial dividing line in these neighborhoods. The biracial West Side Mutual Development Committee, which the mayor had established in 1952 to secure peaceful racial land agreements and residential transitions (he told his construction chief) "is trying to assure residents of Center Hill and Grove Park that the proposed access road will be a boundary which will protect them as Negro citizens move farther out" (Atlanta Bureau of Planning 1954; Bayor 1996, 63).

In another case, the city and Fulton County in the late 1950s agreed to cut Willis Mill Road on the southwest, to prevent black Atlantans from driving south along it to Cascade Heights, an affluent white neighborhood. Willis Mill had served as one of the main north-south roads into that community. Not only was part of the road cut, but over 100 acres of land were left empty along the abandoned parts of the road (Thompson 1986; Bayor 1996, 66). In the early 1950s, the city determined that blacks would be allowed to secure houses north of Westview Drive, in the west side's Mozley Park area, but not within 100 yards of

MAP 3.1   *Selected Atlanta Neighborhoods and Streets*

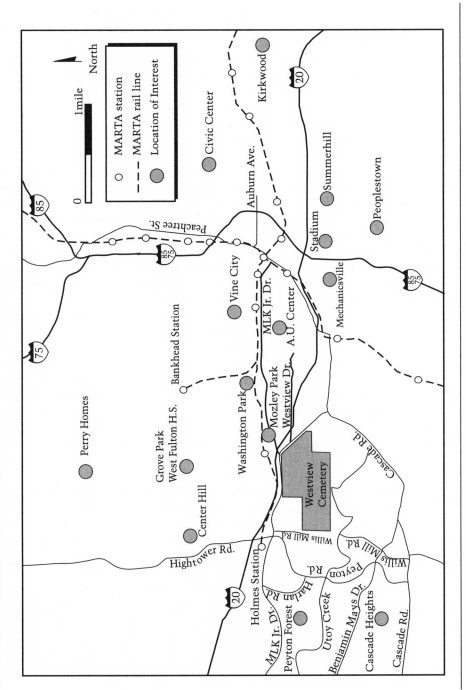

Source: Cartographic Research Laboratory, Department of Geography, Georgia State University, 1999.

that dividing line. Streets within that 100 yards were left unpaved, creating a no-man's land (Thompson, Lewis, and McEntire 1960, 21, 27–32; Bayor 1996, 65).

The most notable of these attempts was the infamous Peyton Road Wall, a concrete and steel barricade cutting Peyton and Harlan roads on the west side in 1962, in order to protect the white Peyton Forest neighborhood from black incursion. While this barricade came down shortly due to court intervention, it indicated the extremes that city officials (in this case the Board of Aldermen and the mayor) took to maintain racial division (Allen 1971, 71–72; Bayor 1996, 66–67).

The 1960s urban renewal continued the process of racial separation. By 1968, 95 percent of the individuals displaced by renewal were black (Toward Equal Opportunity 1968, 7; Bayor 1996, 70). The public housing built or planned at that time isolated its black inhabitants or severely overcrowded black neighborhoods. A 1967 Atlanta housing report noted that "many Negroes have found it necessary to live in areas which are inconvenient to their place of employment" and asked that a better match be made between public housing sites and job locations (Toward Equal Opportunity 1968, 10; Bayor 1996, 84).

The goals of renewal were both economic and racial. Redevelopment had a revitalizing impact on downtown, but the relocation process fit in with a long history of segregative policies. Where the black displacees were to be housed became a source of much concern to Atlanta's white leadership in the late 1950s and 1960s. In a number of cases (such as the abandoned Egleston Hospital site east of the central business district in 1959 to 1960, the stadium and civic center sites, and the land in the northeast part of the city), blacks either were not allowed to use the land for housing or saw their housing destroyed in an effort to move the black population away from downtown and, in the northeast area, away from affluent whites (Stone 1976, 67–71; Bayor 1996, 72–75). When these renewal policies were combined with suburban counties' refusal to build public housing and the federal government's and banks' discriminatory mortgage insurance and loan policies, it should not be surprising to see the results today: a city still residentially divided by race. So much land was being designated as racial buffers or determined as not available for black use that parts of the city were overcrowded due only to segregation policies. Before Atlanta split into a largely white suburbia and a predominantly black city, it had been intentionally divided along racial lines within the city, a precursor of what lay ahead in the racial divisions of the present. Atlanta actually saw further segregation during a period when the civil rights movement was strongest in the city; lunch counters were integrated, while neighborhoods became more segregated.

The impact of prolonged racial segregation policies has created an odd situation. The increase in black income amid the development of a substantial black middle class has not brought the housing integration that was found earlier in America's history when the income of white ethnic minorities rose. Segregated areas of affluent blacks exist in the city, and the push into suburbia has not altered the racial divisions. Housing discrimination remains even for the middle and upper classes (see chapter 5). One aspect of this is the continued discrimination in mortgage lending (*Atlanta Constitution*, March 15, 1992). Furthermore, the black poor have been isolated. This racial split in Atlanta and the metro area has a strong historical foundation and shows few signs of disappearing. This aspect of the paradox has not altered as the city's economy has improved.

Race and Employment

The racial residential split was just one aspect of the city's larger racial divisions. Employment represents another area where public policy and private decisions tried to confine the black community, in this case, to the least skilled and most poorly paid jobs. While there has always been a strong black middle class in the city, most African Americans have worked at unskilled or semiskilled manual labor jobs or in domestic and personal services (Bayor 1996, 96–97, 101, 106). The persistence during the twentieth century of a lack of opportunity, of a racial ceiling for many jobs, has been an important factor in the creation of a booming city with significant poverty tied to race. The discrimination has been severe and unrelenting. It did not slacken even when many blacks began leaving Atlanta in the World War I era, heading north for a better life, and some whites began to see the problems created by the loss of these workers. It did not abate during the Chamber of Commerce's Forward Atlanta campaign of the 1920s, which tied to promote the city's economic growth—an effort that reveals quite well the formative years of the Atlanta paradox.

During this campaign, the Chamber of Commerce worked to increase the number of companies moving to Atlanta and to make other Americans aware of the city's economic success. Atlanta's business and political leaders worked closely together to enhance the city and to provide for a profitable future. The city's attributes were emphasized, including that of a "great labor force." The venture was successful, judging by the number of companies that opened offices and factories in Atlanta by the end of the decade. But this was a campaign carried out by and for the white elite and designed to benefit them. "Campaign coordinators did not include any black citizens in the effort, did not solicit a single black company, and made no effort to gain jobs for black residents" (Kuhn, Joye, and West 1990, 90, 95). At no time were black Atlantans considered an essential part of the city's future economic development.

Economic downturns only made conditions worse for this population. For example, during the Great Depression there was a quickening pace of whites replacing black workers in jobs earlier deemed unsuitable for whites (Atlanta School of Social Work 1933; Bayor 1996, 96–99). With positions scarce, white workers pushed blacks out. Race, as was often the case in Atlanta, took precedence over economics. In a number of cases, experienced black workers were replaced with higher-paid, inexperienced whites. Job displacement, combined with race-based wage differentials and discrimination within the federal relief structure, led to a black citizenry in a more precarious economic situation than before. For example, the National Recovery Administration's minimum wages led to whites replacing blacks: white employers refused to pay what was considered a good wage to blacks and hired white workers instead (Mason 1939; Bayor 1996, 99).

Periods of plentiful jobs and rising economic opportunities did not enhance the black economic profile. Many jobs, even in the best of times for the city, continued to be closed to blacks. During World War II, when severe labor shortages and defense needs meant that employers were desperate for workers, African Americans were still not considered until pressure was applied. In regard to the Bell Aircraft factory just north of the city, blacks were initially not allowed into the training courses. Atlanta Urban League complaints to the President's Committee on Fair Employment Practices finally changed this policy (Mullis 1976, 150–53; Bayor 1996, 107). Many employers claimed that their white workers would not accept black co-workers or that black workers would make it necessary to have separate locker rooms and other facilities.

After the war, as the Atlanta economy grew, black workers still often found themselves locked out of jobs. For example, Western Electric turned down black veterans who had received training in the signal corps for positions as linemen or in any other skilled capacity. AT&T had a serious shortage of experienced linemen in the mid- to late 1940s but did not consider black applicants (Report of Conferences 1946; Bayor 1996, 108). There was no public or private efforts to make use of the talents of the large black population, integrate them into the city's economic life, or understand the problems the city would face if this growing segment was ignored.

Little changed through the 1950s. Except for some federal positions, such as post office jobs, most of the employment structure remained closed to Atlanta's blacks. City jobs could be secured, but usually in service positions (although not as firefighters or building inspectors). Many unions remained restricted and thereby kept blacks out of such jobs as plumbing and sheet metal and electrical work. In one case, the employer and union made a deal to demote blacks from permanent to nonpermanent workers so that they would not be covered by the contract and could be easily fired (Atlanta Committee for Cooperative Action, "Role of Unions"; Bayor 1996, 111). By the end of the decade, blacks still would not be hired as truck drivers in various businesses, as clerks in department stores, as office workers, or as auto mechanics, to name just a few (Atlanta Urban League 1959; Bayor 1996, 110).

A special mention must be made of Auburn Avenue, the center of the black business community. Here, black merchants and professionals served their African American clientele, and the street came to represent black economic success. Here, black workers could find jobs that were denied them in white-owned stores. And here, black customers would be treated with the respect that most white merchants would not provide (Kuhn, Joye, and West 1990, 98–99). Auburn Avenue had black-owned banks and insurance companies, including the Atlanta Life Insurance Company, started by Alonzo Herndon, a former slave who became a millionaire. Herndon's success was part of the myth created prior to integration about Atlanta being a black mecca for business. And Sweet Auburn took on mythic qualities as a street of unparalleled black prosperity.

It did not, however, continue as the center of black life and business into the present period, and this too relates to the Atlanta paradox. With the end of official segregation and the ability of black Atlantans to shop and work elsewhere, the Auburn Avenue businesses lost some of their clientele—although certainly no one would claim that segregation was preferable (Kuhn, Joye, and West 1990, 107–8). Urban renewal wiped out some nearby black neighborhoods, and dispersed these former customers of Auburn Avenue businesses. The highway system also had a pernicious effect on the street and indicates white maneuvering to dismantle the black business center.

Part of the Metropolitan Planning Commission's 1952 Up Ahead report suggested the elimination of the Auburn Avenue business area. Although it was spared due to black protests and help from white allies such as Mayor Hartsfield, it did not escape unscathed. The north-south expressway (I-75/I-85) cut through Auburn Avenue in the 1960s and split the business area as well as cut it off from many of its customers. The efforts to destroy or weaken the main black business area say a lot about the lack of white concerns of black economic success. Auburn Avenue has never recovered.

School Segregation and Desegregation

Atlanta's business and employment history is filled with persistent attempts to diminish black economic strength and significant job discrimination. The lack of adequate school and training facilities for blacks further compounded the problems of an underemployed population. Until the 1960s, the Atlanta schools operated under a dual segregated system that consistently underfunded black schools. Double sessions were common in schools in black neighborhoods, as were high pupil-teacher ratios, lack of books, run-down school buildings, and inadequate equipment. In the 1947 to 1948 school year, for example, there were 36.2 black students per teacher compared to the white student ratio of 22.6. Average per-pupil expenditure by race was $75.13 for blacks and $178.69 for whites (Atlanta Urban League 1948; Bayor 1996, 200, 215–17). The black child received less time in a more crowded classroom with fewer facilities than the white child. Putting obstacles in the way of the education of a large segment of the city's population was not a way to enhance economic growth.

Twenty years later, conditions for blacks were still dismal. Compared to whites, they had fewer textbooks, less equipment in their school buildings, and higher teacher-pupil ratios (Better Schools Atlanta 1968; Bayor 1996, 240–41). Years of underfunding majority-black schools surely had an impact in creating an undertrained and undereducated workforce. These problems would plague the city for many years and were part of the Atlanta paradox that developed. Few whites grasped the implications of this neglect for the city's future.

The civil rights efforts of the 1960s were able finally to pry open the job market, but it was a slow process that met considerable opposition within the public and private sectors. The schools, however, faced an even more difficult time. Desegregation began in 1961 but it was met with so much stalling and opposition from white school officials that the system never really desegregated. Mayor Hartsfield secured a significant public relations triumph with the initial desegregation, but it was just part of the Atlanta facade. Organized down to the smallest detail, the staged opening day of school was carefully orchestrated to emphasize racial unity and to show the country and the reporters in town that Atlanta was "a city too busy to hate."

Meanwhile, the number of black children put in majority-white schools was kept small (out of 133 black students who requested transfer to white schools in 1961, only 9 actually went). The movement was instead toward resegregation, as whites fled to suburbia or transferred to predominantly white schools, consistently urged on by the system's white leadership.

Through the 1960s, the white school leaders made numerous efforts to oppose desegregation. At Kirkwood Elementary School on Atlanta's east side, desegregation was to take place at the end of January 1965. The school was in an area of overcrowded black schools, while classrooms in white Kirkwood had empty seats. Before the black children arrived, the school superintendent sent letters to all white students at Kirkwood offering them easy transfer. By the end of January, the black students found only seven white students and the white principal remaining in this "desegregated school" (Racial Isolation 1967, 66; Bayor 1996, 233). At West Fulton High School, 150 white students, many living nearby, were permitted to transfer to another school as West Fulton became majority black, even though the school was not overcrowded. Transfers for whites who wished to avoid integration were easily obtained (*Atlanta Inquirer*, September 26, 1964; Bayor 1996, 234). There were even cases in which black students in desegregated schools were transferred back to overcrowded black schools (*Atlanta Inquirer*, September 25, 1965; Bayor 1996, 235). School desegregation in the 1960s was all smoke and mirrors and black students were shortchanged in their education, since tax dollars generally went with the white child. The city's image, however, was always protected and preserved. Atlanta's schools eventually were to function under black leadership, but years of neglect of the black child's needs had a pernicious effect on the city. Schools remained overcrowded in the 1960s and after, and segregated by race (in 1968, almost all black elementary students still attended all-black schools) and increasingly by class. As a result, schools often did not do the job of training their students for Atlanta's changing economy.

The clear loser here, aside from the black population, was Atlanta itself. Many well-educated black graduates of the Atlanta University Center colleges went elsewhere to find employment, since there were few outlets for their talents in Atlanta (Hefner 1971, 227–28; Bayor 1996, 114). The skills of many others went untapped.

Prosperity and Poverty

It was no surprise, then, that as Atlanta emerged as an example of Sunbelt prosperity during the 1960s and after, black participation in that prosperity was relatively small. Even the election of black mayors could not fully change the historical paradox of economic growth and black poverty. While city government jobs increased and the black middle class grew as a result of affirmative action and the Minority Business Enterprise program (designed to increase the percentage of city contracts gong to black firms), discrimination and resistance in the private sector to hiring blacks in skilled or upper level white collar positions persisted.

The number of black-owned firms in Atlanta did substantially increase by the 1980s, and Atlanta was home to four of the twenty largest black-owned companies in the country, but the legacy of discrimination remained evident. Many minority businesses still bumped up against racial barriers. There was still "exclusion of minorities from informal business networks" and a continuation of negative perceptions of minorities' abilities (Research Atlanta 1986; Bayor 1996, 123–24). Conditions had improved considerably, but problems remained.

For the black poor, much less had changed. The efforts of the black mayors had been directed at improving middle-class black employment. Priorities were still focused on enhancing the city's economic growth as a way of uplifting the poor. This trickle-down approach did not reach into the poorer neighborhoods. The percentage of Atlanta's blacks who were underemployed or unemployed remained substantial (Atlanta Region Area Development Profile 1983; Bayor 1996, 124).

It was not just the legacy of employment discrimination or the priorities of city government that resulted in continued high poverty levels; there were other historical factors as well. Atlanta's high unemployment rate was partly the result of a lack of skills among the city's poor in a job market made up increasingly of office, managerial, and technical positions. The unskilled and semiskilled jobs that were essential for lower-class survival in the past were now suburban-bound (see chapter 2). The manufacturing sector decreased sharply within the city in the 1970s and increased substantially in the suburbs (Atlanta Region Area Development Profile 1983; Bayor 1996, 124). The mismatch between the jobs in Atlanta and the skill levels of city dwellers was evident at times, such as in 1969, when the city's economy was strong but minority unemployment remained high. The suburban jobs would have been a source of employment except for two factors. The first was the housing discrimination evident in the suburbs, as illustrated by discriminatory mortgage policies and the refusal of suburban governments to build low-income public housing. These policies prevented many black families, particularly poorer ones, from entering that housing market. The second factor was the problem of commuting to suburban jobs.

Transportation Issues

Transportation problems also represent a long legacy of racial discrimination in Atlanta. The segregation enforced on the bus and streetcar lines into the late 1950s were a constant reminder to black Atlantans of their second-class status. The policy was to have blacks seat from rear to front with whites from the front to rear, with whites having first rights to any seat. The harassment of black passengers by white riders and conductors was all part of the effort to diminish black life. Black bus drivers were not hired until 1965 (Kuhn, Joye, and West 1990, 79–80, 82).

Although significant in their daily lives, the seating issue was not as important as the failure to provide transportation into black neighborhoods so that people could travel to work. As early as 1917, there is evidence of poor mass-transit service to black neighborhoods. The initial response to this neglect was the inauguration of black-owned and -generated bus lines, none of which could survive for long against the white power structure's opposition, which included the city council's refusal to allow the lines to operate (Porter 1974, 67–68; Bayor 1996, 188–89).

The lack of service to black areas was a problem for many years. In some cases this disregard resulted in new black areas not being served at all. Georgia Power Company, the owner of the transit lines, refused to extend its service into these neighborhoods during the 1940s and 1950s, thereby creating difficulties for blacks commuting into the downtown business district. In another case, the refusal to extend service was related to the effort to keep certain westside areas white. Not wishing to make it easier for blacks to travel throughout the west side and migrate into white sections, Georgia Power planned its line extensions with race in mind (Special Committee 1953; Bayor 1996, 189–90). The failure of suburban counties such as Cobb and Gwinnett to allow MARTA (Metropolitan Atlanta Rapid Transit Authority) expansion into their territory during the 1970s and after also suggests a racial motive. It makes little sense economically to hamper easy travel throughout the metro area. But a fixation on race explains much; racial concerns in this situation took precedence over economic considerations.

The earlier experience with race and mass transit made black leaders keenly aware of securing transit service when MARTA was being designed. As in the 1940s, transit was planned to serve the white business community and the white commuter.

Black leaders voiced their opposition to the neglect of the west side communities and of black areas south of downtown and of Perry Homes, a west side public housing project (Atlanta Summit Leadership Conference 1968; Bayor 1996, 192). Perry Homes, which was built in the 1950s, was a particularly isolated black housing project in the northwest part of the city and symbolized the harmful effect of poorly planned public housing site selection and the inadequacies of Atlanta's mass transit system. Additionally, there were complaints about MARTA's hiring policies.

After the 1968 defeat of the MARTA plan by public referendum (white suburbanites also voted no), the mass transit leadership agreed to consider black demands. The demands included rapid rail service to Perry Homes, giving priority to those most in need of mass transit and providing transportation from inner-city areas to major job concentrations, including in the suburbs. The MARTA board agreed to the development of an east-west line as an initial priority. This line would be most useful to the black community. Also, all routes would take into consideration the need of people to get to work or hospitals or shopping and provide the necessary crosstown transit lines. Perry Homes would be part of the planning process and would receive a rail line (although not until the 1990s and not all the way to Perry Homes). The new MARTA plan was passed in a referendum in 1971, with blacks providing strong support (MARTA meeting minutes 1971; Bayor 1996, 194–95). The plan was rejected in Cobb and Gwinnett counties, however, thereby preventing expansion into these largely white suburbs, where much of the new job development was taking place.

Neighborhoods and City Services

Nowhere is the Atlanta paradox more evident than in the slum neighborhoods that sit close to the gleaming skyscrapers that symbolize and proclaim the city's economic success. Historically, black neighborhoods, whether middle or lower class, have received the fewest services. City money always went to white areas first, particularly middle-class ones. The result was a long-term neglect of black sections of the city in regard to basic city services. Deprived for many decades, these neighborhoods could not readily recover even after black mayors gained control of the city's government. The lack of parks, playgrounds, paved and well-maintained streets in many sections, streetlights, and regular sanitation services created two Atlantas. Mayor Hartsfield acknowledged this problem when he noted that "you could always tell where the Negro sections started. Lights stopped, streets, sidewalks stopped" (Bayor 1996, 132).

It is difficult to determine exactly what effect all this deprivation had, but certainly a city that in 1954 had 128 parks for whites and 4 for blacks, and 18 white playgrounds and 3 black ones, helped set the stage for the Atlanta paradox (Atlanta Urban League 1954; Bayor 1996, 134). Black neighborhoods were separate but never treated equally. High densities, poor services, and uncaring city government took their toll. The inequities so clear in the Atlanta of today were, in every sense, based on historical neglect.

Various organizations such as the Atlanta Negro Voters League and the Atlanta Urban League had pressed city officials for years to upgrade black neighborhood services. It was only with the growth of black voting power and the threat of race riots, as had occurred in other cities during the 1960s, that city leaders began to respond. Summerhill and other south side communities started to receive attention when the Student Nonviolent Coordinating Committee (SNCC) took up their cause in the 1960s. In this "forgotten side of Atlanta," where neighborhood deterioration was a matter of public policy, there were a few meager efforts to improve the area, especially after a riot in Summerhill in September 1966 (SNCC 1963; Bayor 1996, 136–41). However, the problems in this part of the city reflected not just neglect based on race, which would be corrected with the growth of black political power, but also class bias and a limited view of city priorities.

Summerhill became significant and an object of city concern due to the riot, the fear of SNCC, the threat of more trouble that would tarnish the city's progressive race relations image, and rising black political strength (Bayor 1996, 136–43). Mayor Ivan Allen responded with some quick-fix solutions that had no long range impact on the community but had already proposed another "improvement" that forever stamped the neighborhood as expendable: the building of Atlanta–Fulton County Stadium in 1965 for the soon-to-arrive Atlanta Braves on land that was already cleared, rather than using that land for the construction of housing. Parking areas for the stadium destroyed even more housing in the area. Considering the problems this neighborhood faced, a stadium and parking lots were not what they needed. It did not answer the questions regarding recreational facilities, sanitation delivery, traffic lights, or housing code enforcement but did indicate what the city leaders considered a major priority. Atlanta was being rebuilt in the 1950s and 1960s with a stadium, civic center, highways, hotels, and office buildings all designed to make it more attractive to the recreational and business tourist and the middle-class suburban commuter. The city grew under the careful direction of its business elite, becoming a Sunbelt center. Many of its neighborhoods languished, however, and, regardless of federal government intervention through President Johnson's Great Society programs, remained eyesores for decades. But a different approach had been suggested.

SNCC and the Atlanta Summit Leadership Conference, a coalition of black organizations, envisioned a city that would vastly improve its poor communities. It was not impossible to create this city. Attention to housing code enforcement, a strong open-occupancy law, concern with revitalization of neighborhoods rather than just downtown commercial districts, a metrowide public housing site selection that placed tenants within easy reach of suburban and city jobs, a strong equal opportunity effort along with job training, and a serious attempt to improve the schools would have given Atlanta a different social profile. Instead, business-oriented change, as in many other cities, took a myopic course that led to an urban area pleasing to tourists, suburban commuters, and economic interests, but damaging to the majority of Atlanta's residents, who by the 1970s were African Americans.

The price for taking this turn in the road was high. As the Citizens Crime Commission of Atlanta stated in 1959, "A community is going to pay the price for decent housing and the good life whether or not it obtains these blessings. The price may be in terms of high welfare costs, high hospital charges, high police costs. . . . The community has the choice, however, of paying an equivalent amount of money and obtaining good housing and a decent community as preventive measures" (Bayor 1996, 127). That decent community never emerged. Temporary interest in improvements led back to permanent neglect. Summerhill, Vine City, Peoplestown, and other low-income black neighborhoods stand today as monuments to the failure of Atlanta's public policy.

Conclusion

Atlanta chose for years to favor its white and neglect its black citizens with housing, employment, schools, transportation, and other city services. Although this was not a sound economic strategy, it coexisted with an emphasis on enhancing the city's economy, supporting business interests, and establishing Atlanta as a Sunbelt center of business and tourist activity. The election of black mayors beginning in 1973 and continuing to the present day did not appreciably change the city's focus. Racism, of course, was attacked and efforts were made to open up the city's economic growth to the black community. Maynard Jackson also attempted to improve black neighborhoods. But the main priorities of the city's political and business leaders never shifted. What was good for business was seen as what was good for Atlanta. Left out of this equation were Atlanta's poor, who languished in schools that did not teach, in neighborhoods that remained run-down and neglected, in isolated low-income communities whose rising middle-class leaders headed for the suburbs, and in a city with fewer of the unskilled or semiskilled jobs they needed.

The city that was created was a gilded one. On the outside was gold in the form of skyscrapers, business growth, tourism, and a reputation for prosperity and progressivism. Just beneath the surface was the base metal of poverty and segregation—the problems created by Atlanta's history of racially discriminatory policy decisions.

References

Allen, Ivan, Jr., with Paul Hemphill. 1971. *Mayor: Notes on the Sixties.* New York: Simon & Schuster.

Atlanta Bureau of Planning. 1954. "Hartsfield to Clarke Donaldson." Atlanta Bureau of Planning Papers, Atlanta History Center.

Atlanta Committee for Cooperative Action. "The Role of the Unions." Eliza Paschall Papers. Box 17. Emory University Special Collections.

Atlanta Region Area Development Profile. 1983. "Central Atlanta Progress Papers." Box 1. Atlanta History Center.

Atlanta School of Social Work. 1933. "Thirteen Displaced Negro Workers." Prepared for Atlanta Urban League. National Urban League Papers. 4-D-27. Washington: Library of Congress.

Atlanta Summit Leadership Conference. 1968. "News Conference." Presentation at MARTA hearing. Mule to Marta Papers. Box 116. Atlanta History Center.

Atlanta Urban League. 1948. "A Supplemental Report on Public School Facilities for Negroes in Atlanta, Georgia, 1948." Grace Towns Hamilton Papers. Atlanta History Center.

———. 1954. "A Report on Parks and Recreational Facilities for Negroes in Atlanta, Georgia." Grace Towns Hamilton Papers. Atlanta History Center.

———. 1959. "Recommendations for Consideration on Employment, General Citizens Committee on Employment and Economic Opportunity." National Urban League–Southern Regional Office Papers. Box A 193. Washington: Library of Congress.

Bayor, Ronald H. 1996. *Race and the Shaping of Twentieth-Century Atlanta.* Chapel Hill: University of North Carolina Press.

Better Schools Atlanta. 1968. "Student Achievement in Atlanta Public Schools." Atlanta Public School Archives.

Calhoun, John H. 1985. Interview by author.

Council on Human Relations of Greater Atlanta. 1966. News Release. Southern Regional Council Papers. Atlanta University Center.

Douglas, Hamilton, Jr. 1961. "Housing the Million" report on Atlanta Housing (prepared for a group of Atlanta business leaders), January 10. Cecil Alexander Papers (privately held).

Flint, Barbara J. 1977. "Zoning and Residential Segregation: A Social and Physical History, 1910–1940." Ph.D. diss., University of Chicago.

Hefner, James A. 1971. "Black Employment in a Southern 'Progressive City': The Atlanta Experience." Ph.D. diss., University of Colorado.

Kuhn, Clifford, Harlon Joye, and E. Bernard West. 1990. *Living Atlanta: An Oral History of the City, 1914–1918.* Atlanta and Athens, Ga.: Atlanta Historical Society and the University of Georgia Press.

MARTA meeting minutes. 1971. Meeting between MARTA directors and Atlanta Coalition on Current Community Affairs. Mule to Marta Papers. Box 116. Atlanta History Center.

Mason, Lucy, comments. 1939. Commission on Interracial Cooperation Papers, May 12. Box 154. Atlanta University Center.

Mullis, Sharon Mitchell. 1976. "The Public Career of Grace Towns Hamilton: A Citizen Too Busy to Hate." Ph.D. diss., Emory University.

Porter, Michael L. 1974. "Black Atlanta: An Interdisciplinary Study of Blacks on the East Side of Atlanta, 1890–1930." Ph.D. diss., Emory University.

Racial Isolation in the Public Schools. 1967. A Report of the U.S. Commission on Civil Rights. Atlanta Public School Archives.

Report of Conferences with Officials of Southern Bell Telephone, A. T. and T. and Western Electric Companies. 1946. National Urban League–Southern Regional Office Papers. Box A 77. Washington: Library of Congress.

Research Atlanta. 1986. "The Impact of Local Government Programs to Encourage Minority Business Development."

SNCC. 1963. "The City Must Provide, South Atlanta: The Forgotten Community." SNCC Papers. Box 95. Martin Luther King, Jr., Center for Non-Violent Social Change.

Special Committee. 1953. Representing the Westside Committee for the Improvement of Transit Service to Mayor and City Council. A. T. Walden Papers. Atlanta History Center.

Stone, Clarence N. 1976. *Economic Growth and Neighborhood Discontent*. Chapel Hill: University of North Carolina Press.

Thompson, Robert A. 1986. Interview by author.

Thompson, Robert A., Hylan Lewis, and David McEntire. 1960. "Atlanta and Birmingham: A Comparative Study in Negro Housing." In *Studies in Housing and Minority Groups*, edited by Nathan Glazer and David McEntire. Berkeley: University of California Press.

Toward Equal Opportunity in Housing in Atlanta, Georgia. 1967, 1968. "A Report of the Georgia State Advisory Committee to the United States Commission on Civil Rights." Southern Regional Council Papers. Atlanta University Center.

4

RACIAL ATTITUDES AND PERCEPTIONS IN ATLANTA

*Obie Clayton Jr., Christopher R. Geller,
Sahadeo Patram, Travis Patton, and
David L. Sjoquist*

R ACE HAS always played an important role in Atlanta. Much of the character of the city is the result of policies driven by racial concerns. As discussed in chapter 3, in Atlanta the development of roads, the placement of public housing units, housing patterns, and the expansion of the city's boundaries were fueled, at least in part, by a desire to segregate blacks and to maintain white control of city government. One can trace the roots of the Atlanta paradox to a long history of suppression of blacks in Atlanta.

Despite this history, Atlanta has long had a relatively large black middle class and strong black leaders. In the 1960s, blacks gained political and economic strength without the violence that many other cities experienced. The white community saw it as in their interest to yield to the pressures for racial equality, believing that racial violence and disruptions would hurt the economic fortunes of the city. But it yielded power slowly and grudgingly.

Race is still a dominant factor in both the city of Atlanta and the metropolitan area. Policies, programs, and actions of government, business, and community groups are frequently seen through the lens of race. Because of the importance of race as a causal factor in explaining the degree of economic inequality in the Atlanta region, understanding racial attitudes and perceptions of both blacks and whites is of critical importance.

Attitudes about race and the degree of economic inequality are strongly intertwined. Douglas S. Massey and Nancy A. Denton (1993), for example, argue that residential segregation of blacks inevitably leads

59

to economic hardship for minorities. (See chapter 9 for a contrary opinion.) The degree of residential segregation depends on several forces, including the discriminatory behavior of real estate agents, apartment owners, and mortgage lenders. Of particular importance is how willing blacks and whites are to live in integrated neighborhoods. If, for example, many whites are unwilling to live in integrated neighborhoods, then it may not be possible to maintain integrated neighborhoods.

This chapter presents results pertaining to racial attitudes using the Greater Atlanta Neighborhood Study (GANS) survey. (See chapter 1's appendix for a discussion of the GANS.) Other chapters in this volume explore the consequences of racial attitudes for labor market and housing market outcomes. Our focus is on identifying factors that might explain differences in attitudes and perceptions between blacks and whites.

Opinions on Integration of Neighborhoods

Despite decades of legal efforts and other actions to integrate housing, blacks and whites still tend to live in separate and distinct areas of metropolitan Atlanta. Truman A. Hartshorn and Keith R. Ihlanfeldt (chapter 2) report that the Atlanta region remains highly segregated, although the level of segregation has decreased over the past twenty years. There are many possible reasons for this continued segregation. (See chapter 5 and Farley, Steeh, and Kryssan (1994) for a full discussion of these causes.)

First, it is possible that economic or class differences account for the geographic separation. But, as Massey and Denton (1993) point out, the degree of segregation does not differ by income level. A second explanation is that, despite fair housing laws and other policies, overt housing discrimination may have been replaced by more informal means of discrimination (see Yinger 1995 and Hunter and Walker 1996). It is also possible that residential patterns are the result of preferences to live in racially separate neighborhoods. If blacks and whites both desire to live in neighborhoods in which they are a majority, residential segregation will result.

Our focus is on the nature of the racial attitudes that underlie racial segregation. The (GANS) survey questions allow us to investigate such issues as the difference and similarities in preferences of blacks and whites to live in integrated communities, how these preferences differ by type of individual, and the implications for the future of geographic housing patterns. While the attitudes of whites have been extensively explored in national surveys, the attitudes of blacks have been largely ignored. Thus, the survey results provide information not only on preferences regarding racial composition of neighborhoods in Atlanta, but some of the first concerning the preferences of blacks.

Preferences of Blacks

Black respondents were shown five cards, each representing a neighborhood of different racial composition (figure 4.1), and were asked to imagine that they were looking for a home and had found one that they liked and could afford. They were then asked two questions concerning their preferences among the five neighborhoods, assuming that the same home could be found in each neighborhood. First, they were asked to rank the five neighborhoods from first to last choice. Second, they were asked which of the five neighborhoods they would be willing to move into.

Ranking of Neighborhoods   Table 4.1 shows the percentage of respondents who ranked each of the five neighborhoods first. Neighborhood C, which is 50 percent black, is the most preferred by blacks: 53.6 percent ranked it first. However, there is an inclination among blacks to want to live in a black neighborhood. Over 40 percent of Atlanta area black residents ranked Neighborhoods A and B first. Furthermore, among blacks who did not rank Neighborhood B first, 82.4 percent ranked it second. On the other hand, only 5.0 percent of blacks indicated a preference to live in a predominantly white area (Neighborhoods D and E); this response is consistent with other research that suggests that many blacks want to preserve a black identity (Demo and Hughes 1990).

Table 4.1 also presents the neighborhood preferences of blacks living in each of three Atlanta areas: the city, the southern suburbs, and the northern suburbs.[1] Blacks who live in the city are more likely to express a preference for blacker neighborhoods relative to those who live in the suburbs. There is essentially no difference in preferences between the two suburban areas.

To explore possible factors associated with the differences in neighborhood preferences by blacks, table 4.2 presents neighborhood preference by several respondent characteristics. The rankings of neighborhoods vary by socioeconomic characteristics of the respondent. Respondents who favor more integrated and whiter neighborhoods (Neighborhoods C, D, and E) tend to be younger, to have more education, and to have higher incomes than those who favor neighborhoods with a larger percentage of blacks (Neighborhoods A and B). There is no significant difference in preferences by gender.[2]

Those blacks who prefer more integrated or whiter neighborhoods

FIGURE 4.1   *Neighborhood Diagrams Used for Black Respondents*

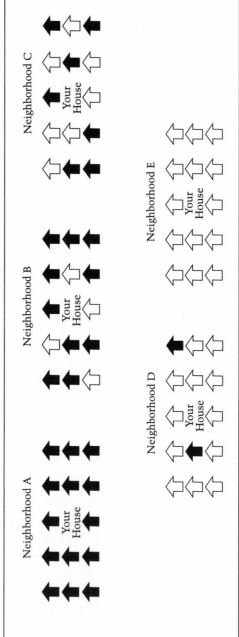

Source: Greater Atlanta Neighborhood Study 1994.

TABLE 4.1   *Blacks' First Choice of Neighborhood*

| | Neighborhood | | | | | |
	A	B	C	D	E	
Number of black homes out of fifteen	14	10	7	2	0	Total
Responses of all blacks	21.9%	19.6%	53.6%	2.4%	2.6%	100.1%
Responses of those living in city	28.3	26.4	41.1	2.6	1.6	100.0
Responses of those living in northern suburbs	20.9	13.2	61.4	4.4	0.0	99.9
Responses of those living in southern suburbs	18.4	18.0	58.0	1.5	4.1	100.0

Source: Greater Atlanta Neighborhood Study 1994. Results are weighted.

are more likely to live in neighborhoods in which the racial composition is less black. (Since the city is more highly segregated than the suburbs, this pattern might explain the preferences observed in table 4.1.) This suggests that while Atlanta's racial housing pattern is highly segregated, it is possible that the neighborhood preferences of blacks match the type of neighborhoods in which blacks actually live. To explore this, we determined the racial composition of the respondents' current neighborhood (census tract), but found that neighborhood preferences do not match the current residential patterns of blacks. More specifically, we found that 77.9 percent of blacks do not live in a neighborhood that matches their preferred racial composition.[3] At least part of the reason for this is that most blacks live in highly segregated neighborhoods. Thus, for most blacks who prefer even a modestly integrated neighborhood, their preferred neighborhood does not match the racial composition of their actual neighborhood. However, for the 16.4 percent of blacks in the sample who live in census tracts with 50 percent or fewer blacks, 58 percent prefer Neighborhoods A and B—which are more than 50 percent black. So, among blacks who live in more integrated communities, a majority prefer a more segregated neighborhood than the one in which they live.

Lawrence Bobo and Camile L. Zubrinsky (1996) suggest that confrontations with white prejudice lead to feelings of resignation and withdrawal. This suggests that neighborhood preferences of blacks may reflect experiences with and attitudes toward whites. For example, if a black has experienced discrimination, he or she may be less inclined to want to live in a majority white neighborhood. To explore this line

TABLE 4.2   *Blacks' First Choice of Neighborhood*

	Neighborhood					
	A	B	C	D	E	
Number of Black Homes Out of Fifteen	14	10	7	2	0	Total
Age						
Twenty-nine or less	16.3%	19.9%	58.7%	4.2%	0.9%	100.0%
Thirty to thirty-nine	19.7	21.4	54.7	2.0	2.0	99.8
Forty to forty-nine	21.9	20.7	53.4	0.7	3.3	100.0
Fifty to fifty-nine	23.7	14.9	51.2	2.2	7.9	99.9
Sixty +	32.8	16.9	47.8	2.0	0.3	99.8
Gender						
Female	20.7	20.4	54.7	1.7	2.4	99.9
Male	23.4	18.5	52.1	3.2	2.8	100.0
Education						
Less than high school	25.6	25.0	37.4	3.1	8.9	100.0
High school	28.5	20.2	47.4	1.8	2.1	100.0
More than high school	14.6	17.3	64.6	2.4	1.2	100.1
Family income						
Less than $20,000	26.3	20.1	48.2	2.1	3.3	100.0
$20,000 to $49,999	19.5	19.2	57.7	1.3	2.4	100.1
$50,000 or more	14.6	19.0	60.6	4.8	1.1	100.1
Percentage back in census tract						
Less than 25 percent	19.6	7.8	69.0	3.7	0.0	100.1
25 percent to 75 percent	19.5	26.4	54.1	0.0	0.0	100.0
Greater than 75 percent	23.3	22.6	47.4	2.4	4.2	99.9
White intelligence less black intelligence						
Less than 0	25.0	20.9	48.5	2.4	3.3	100.1
Equal to 0	24.6	18.6	52.2	2.9	1.6	99.9
Greater than 0	9.8	20.8	64.3	0.9	4.3	100.1

TABLE 4.2   *Continued*

	Neighborhood					
	A	B	C	D	E	
Number of Black Homes Out of Fifteen	14	10	7	2	0	Total
Political views						
Liberal (score < 4)	26.2	21.6	47.3	2.2	2.7	100.0
Moderate (score = 4)	11.9	17.1	68.1	0.5	2.4	100.0
Conservative (score > 4)	19.9	16.6	56.1	5.0	2.4	100.0
Blacks are accepted in Roswell-Alpharetta						
No	25.6	16.6	52.3	1.8	3.6	99.9
Yes	15.3	27.3	54.3	3.1	1.1	101.1
Experienced job discrimination						
Yes	16.5	29.3	51.4	2.8	0.0	100.0
No	18.9	19.6	56.5	2.2	2.8	100.0
Number of observations (unweighted)	252	168	350	24	16	810

Source: Greater Atlanta Neighborhood Study 1994. Results are weighted.

of thinking, we made use of several other questions from the GANS survey.

First, respondents were asked about their perception of the intelligence of blacks and whites. The question used a 7-point scale, with 1 being unintelligent and 7 being intelligent. We consider the response to this question an indication of racial prejudice, and thus, to the extent that blacks see blacks and whites as equally intelligent, blacks might prefer more integrated neighborhoods. To explore this hypothesis we created a variable, which is the difference between the respondent's perception (score) about whites' intelligence and blacks' intelligence (a positive number thus suggests that the respondent believes that whites are more intelligent than blacks.)

While 57 percent of respondents rated white and black intelligence equal, there are significant differences in the value of this variable by neighborhood preference. Consistent with the hypothesis, blacks who rated the intelligence of blacks and whites nearly equal preferred whiter neighborhoods, while those who rated black intelligence greater than white intelligence preferred blacker neighborhoods (table 4.2).

Second, we explored whether the political persuasion of respondents is reflected in neighborhood preferences. The GANS survey asked respondents to identify whether they were politically liberal or conservative on a 7-point scale, with 1 being extremely liberal. Our expectation is that more liberal respondents would favor integration. However, those who identified themselves as more liberal expressed a stronger preference for blacker neighborhoods than conservatives did, while moderates showed the strongest preference for integration.

Third, neighborhood preferences may reflect a respondent's belief that he or she would be accepted in a white community. Respondents were asked whether blacks would be accepted if they moved into certain communities. Six communities were identified, three of which are newer, largely white suburban communities, and three older, more integrated communities. (See the appendix to chapter 1 for a description of the six areas.) We used the responses for the area consisting of the cities of Roswell and Alpharetta, which represents a largely white northern suburban area, to measure belief about acceptance in a white community. Nearly 66 percent of blacks indicated they thought blacks would be unwelcome there. Respondents who thought blacks would not be accepted were more likely to prefer Neighborhood A. Essentially the same percentage chose either Neighborhoods A or B, however. Thus, there is no apparent relationship between a respondent thinking a black household will be accepted and the preference for racial composition of neighborhood.

Finally, respondents were asked whether in the past year they experienced racial discrimination at work. While we expected that individuals who had experienced discrimination (12.3 percent of the respondents) to favor blacker neighborhoods, there was in fact no such tendency, as table 4.2 shows.

Respondents were asked a follow-up question regarding the reason for their first choice of neighborhood. Most blacks (90.9 percent) who chose Neighborhood A gave as their reason that they wanted to be with other blacks. Eighty to 90 percent of blacks who selected Neighborhoods B and C gave as their reason that they wanted to be with different people or preferred the demographic mix. Blacks who selected Neighborhoods D and E also expressed a desire to be with different people or preferred the demographic mix, but 29 percent said they chose one of these two neighborhoods because they thought it would be a better neighborhood. These respondents appeared to associate a white neighborhood with being a better neighborhood, perhaps because white neighborhoods are thought to have better retailing and public services, including schools and public safety.

Willingness to Locate The second question concerning neighborhood preferences asked black respondents which of the five neighborhoods they were willing to move to. Black Atlantans showed a strong willingness to live in predominantly white areas. Nearly all blacks—90 to 100 percent—were willing to move into any of the integrated neighborhoods (Neighborhoods B, C, and D). About 18 percent were unwilling to move into an all-black neighborhood, but 52 percent were unwilling to move into an all-white neighborhood.

Discussion The results suggest that a majority of blacks are willing to live in any integrated neighborhood, that is, blacks appear to be open to the possibility of more integrated neighborhoods than currently exist.

The relationship between neighborhood preference and socioeconomic variables gives cause for optimism. Younger, more educated, and higher-income blacks expressed stronger preferences for integrated and whiter neighborhoods. If the larger preference among younger blacks for integrated neighborhoods reflects a cohort effect, and future generations retain a similar or even stronger preference for integrated neighborhoods, then over time we should find even greater openness to integrated neighborhoods among blacks as a whole. Furthermore, given increasing education and income levels, we might hope that in the future a larger percentage of blacks will express a preference to live in integrated neighborhoods.

There is no observed association between neighborhood preference and experience with past discrimination or view of acceptability in majority white communities. While 43.0 percent of blacks believed that one of the two racial groups has greater intelligence, 78.4 percent believed either that there is no difference in racial intelligence or that the races are nearly the same.[4]

These are encouraging results. Despite a history of racial oppression in Atlanta, blacks express an openness to continued and substantially increased residential integration. We turn now to white attitudes regarding the racial composition of neighborhoods.

Preferences of Whites

White residents were asked about their level of comfort with increasing levels of racial integration using cards similar to those used with black interviewees (see figure 4.2). The respondents were first presented a card

FIGURE 4.2 Neighborhood Diagrams Used for White Respondents

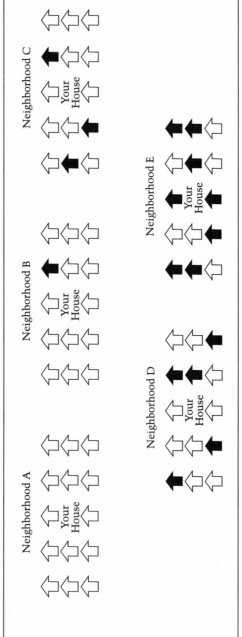

Source: Greater Atlanta Neighborhood Study 1994.

TABLE 4.3   *White Comfort by Maximum Number of Blacks in Neighborhood*

	Neighborhood					
	E	D	C	B	A	Total
Number of Black Homes Out of Fifteen	8	5	3	1	0	
Responses of all whites	37.8%	25.6%	22.8%	6.6%	7.1%	99.9%
Responses of those living in city	42.4	22.7	13.5	5.9	15.6	100.1
Responses of those living in northern suburbs	34.7	25.8	25.0	7.1	7.5	100.1
Responses of those living in southern suburbs	44.1	26.0	20.2	5.8	4.0	100.1
Number of observations (unweighted)	271	150	135	48	37	641

Source: Greater Atlanta Neighborhood Study 1994. Results are weighted.

showing a neighborhood with all white households, and then asked to imagine that they lived in that neighborhood and that one black family moved in. The respondents were asked their level of comfort with that change on a 5-point scale, ranging from very comfortable to very uncomfortable. If they replied that they were comfortable or very comfortable, they were shown the next card (with three black households) and asked again about their level of comfort. This process continued until the respondent replied that he or she was uncomfortable, or until a majority black composition was reached (with eight black households).

Given actual levels of segregation in the Atlanta area, a surprisingly high percentage of whites (see table 4.3) reported being comfortable with fairly high levels of integration, an observation that has also been made by Bobo and Zubrinsky (1996). Over 63 percent of white Atlanta area residents reported that they would be comfortable or very comfortable when the level of integration was 5 black households and 10 white households (Neighborhood D); 25.6 percent would be comfortable with no more than 5 blacks, while 37.8 percent would be comfortable with at least 8 blacks. (Thirty-six percent of whites expressed comfort with only 3 or fewer blacks.) About 75 percent of Atlanta area whites report being comfortable living in a neighborhood that reflects metropolitan Atlanta's racial composition of about 25 percent blacks.[5]

Regarding differences across the Atlanta metropolitan area, about 65 percent of white city residents, 70 percent of southern suburban residents, and 61 percent of northern suburban whites indicated that they would be comfortable or very comfortable with a level of integration of at least 5 black households (Neighborhood D). Comfort levels decreased as the number of black households in the hypothetical neighborhoods increased, with the level of comfort decreasing more rapidly in the suburbs (especially in the northern suburbs) in comparison to the city. About one out of five southern suburban whites and a fourth of whites in the city and northern suburbs would be uncomfortable when the level of integration reached a point where 25 percent of the neighborhood population was black.

It is commonly believed that among whites, younger, better-educated, and higher-income individuals are more likely to favor racial integration (Dyer, Vedlitz, and Worchel 1989), which is what we found for blacks. Age conforms to expectations to some degree; a higher percentage of elderly are comfortable with only 1 or 3 blacks, while a higher percentage of young whites are comfortable with at least 8 (see table 4.4). More educated whites have a tendency toward greater tolerance of black neighbors; compare the percentages of different education groups that are comfortable with Neighborhood E. We expected this among higher-income individuals as well, if for no other reason than the positive correlation between income and education. We found, however, that the least and the most tolerant whites are in the less than $20,000 income class. There is no significant difference by gender, although females may be more likely to be comfortable in a neighborhood with 8 or more blacks.[6]

Whites who live in census tracts with a higher percentage of blacks and those with a more liberal orientation are more inclined to feel comfortable with black neighbors. In addition, whites who consider black intelligence equal to white intelligence are more comfortable with black neighbors. Unlike blacks, whites who believe that blacks will be accepted in white communities such as Roswell-Alpharetta are more likely to be comfortable with integrated neighborhoods. This is an interesting pattern: whites who are more comfortable with blacks are more likely to believe not only that blacks are equal to whites but also that other whites are comfortable with blacks.

Discussion   These results are not as encouraging as those for blacks. A very high percentage of whites, 75 percent, are willing to live in a neighborhood that is reflective of the racial composition of the entire

TABLE 4.4   *White Comfort by Maximum Number of Blacks in Neighborhood*

	Neighborhood					
	E	D	C	B	A	
Number of Black Homes Out of Fifteen	8	5	3	1	0	Total
Age						
Twenty-nine or less	44.0%	26.3%	20.9%	6.7%	2.1%	100.0%
Thirty to thirty-nine	40.8	24.1	16.7	4.7	13.7	100.0
Forty to forty-nine	40.0	33.2	22.1	2.1	2.6	100.0
Fifty to fifty-nine	38.2	24.8	19.2	10.3	7.5	100.0
Sixty +	28.4	16.2	36.5	11.0	7.8	99.9
Gender						
Female	41.2	25.1	20.4	7.8	5.5	100.0
Male	34.3	26.2	25.4	5.4	8.7	100.0
Education						
Less than high school	29.8	31.8	18.5	12.3	7.6	100.0
High school	35.8	22.1	22.8	8.8	10.6	100.1
More than high school	39.6	27.6	23.6	4.5	4.6	99.9
Family income						
Less than $20,000	43.2	21.5	19.7	5.6	10.0	100.0
$20,000 to $49,999	37.1	22.2	24.5	5.6	10.5	99.9
$50,000 or more	34.0	31.1	24.3	8.1	2.4	99.9
Percentage black in census tract						
Less than 25 percent	36.5	25.9	23.3	6.8	7.5	100.0
25 percent to 75 percent	46.2	27.2	20.6	5.7	0.23	99.9
Greater than 75 percent	90.9	6.4	2.6	0.0	0.0	99.9
White intelligence less black intelligence						
Less than 0	26.6	21.9	33.1	7.7	10.6	99.9
Equal to 0	54.6	25.4	12.7	4.9	2.4	100.0
Greater than 0	25.2	26.7	29.7	8.0	10.5	100.1

(Table continues on p. 72.)

TABLE 4.4   *Continued*

	Neighborhood					
	E	D	C	B	A	
Number of Black Homes Out of Fifteen	8	5	3	1	0	Total
Political views						
Liberal (score < 4)	46.1	25.8	16.6	5.4	6.1	100
Moderate (score = 4)	31.6	19.5	29.2	9.1	10.6	100
Conservative (score > 4)	35.1	28.2	24.2	6.4	6.1	100
Number of observations (unweighted)	271	150	135	48	37	641

Source: Greater Atlanta Neighborhood Study 1994. Results are weighted.

metropolitan area. Only slightly more than a third would be comfortable living in a majority black neighborhood, however. While the questions posed to blacks and whites differed, it appears that relative to blacks, whites are less inclined to live in an integrated neighborhood.

As with blacks, the association of youth and higher education levels with a higher comfort level with living in an integrated neighborhood may bode well for the future, though this link is weaker for whites. Finally, whites view blacks in a less favorable light in terms of intelligence. Only 45.2 percent of whites rank black and white intelligence as equal, and 50.3 percent rank white intelligence higher than black intelligence.

Degree of Welcome

The GANS survey allows comparisons between white and black views on how welcome blacks would be in each of six areas of metropolitan Atlanta. If neighborhoods are to become racially integrated, then blacks must believe that they will be welcomed in currently white neighborhoods. We also consider the views of whites in order to judge the perceptions of whether blacks would be welcome.

Black and white interviewees were asked whether a black household would be welcomed or not welcomed (a neutral response was recorded as welcomed) in each of six residential areas of metropolitan Atlanta (see map 1.1). Blacks and whites agreed that blacks are substantially more welcomed in the three more centralized and southern areas—Midtown, Tri-Cities, and Decatur—than the three northern areas. But in general, whites were more likely to say that blacks were welcome than blacks were to say that they would be. The most extreme gap was for the Roswell-Alpharetta area, for which one-third of blacks thought their presence would be welcomed, compared with over half of whites. Even among residents of Roswell-Alpharetta and Norcross, a large percentages of whites (29.8 percent and 22.1 percent, respectively) believed that blacks were not welcome there.

While the general pattern of responses of blacks who reside in an area and blacks in general are the same, for the four areas that blacks considered the least welcoming, a larger percentage of blacks who resided in the area said the area was accepting of blacks than did nonresident blacks. Thus, having residential experience in an area is associated with more positive feelings for that area in terms of its acceptance of blacks. But not always: one-tenth to one-fourth of black residents in Decatur, Midtown, and Marietta-Smyrna believed that blacks were not welcome where they lived.

Conclusion

The results of the analysis are mildly encouraging. Both blacks and whites living in Atlanta appear to be open to living in neighborhoods with greater numbers of the other racial group than is currently the case. The association between positive attitudes toward integrated neighborhoods and age, income, and education suggests that residential segregation may continue to decrease over time. On the other hand, while blacks in Atlanta prefer integrated neighborhoods in comparison to all-white or all-black neighborhoods, they generally do not want to live in white neighborhoods. And whites prefer predominantly white areas, but they expressed a surprisingly high comfort level with black neighbors.

Stereotypes

Another aspect of the issue of racial inequality relates to the views each racial group holds about members of its own and other racial populations. Lawrence Bobo and James R. Kluegel (1996) argue that racial prejudice may be reflected in two main ways. The first is overt discrimination, such as was reflected in Jim Crow laws. The second they call laissez-faire racism, namely, blaming blacks themselves for their lower economic position. Bobo and Kluegel suggest that the importance of Jim Crow racism has declined, becoming inconsistent with American values. They argue that Jim Crow racism, but not laissez-faire racism, is reflected in the relationship between socioeconomic characteristics and willingness of whites to live in integrated neighborhoods. Laissez-faire racism, however, should be reflected in the perceptions and stereotypes that whites have of minorities. For example, we would expect to find that laissez-faire racists believe that blacks are less likely to be self-supporting or that they are less intelligent than whites. Believing blacks are not self-supporting is consistent with the belief that the lower economic position of blacks is due to their unwillingness to better themselves. Likewise, believing blacks are not as intelligent as whites is consistent with the belief that the lower economic position of blacks is due to their lack of ability.

A series of questions in the GANS survey explored these perceptions and stereotypes. Respondents were asked to rank whites and blacks on each of three characteristics: intelligence, the inclination to be self-supporting, and friendliness. Ratings were based on a 7-point scale. Intelligence ranges from (1) unintelligent to (7) intelligent; self-support from (1) "tends to prefer being on welfare" to (7) "tends to prefer to be self-supporting"; and friendliness from (1) "tends to be hard to get along with" to (7) "tends to be easy to get along with."

Table 4.5 presents the distribution of responses to these questions.[7] A couple of general points stand out. First, blacks and whites in Atlanta see themselves in very similar ways: the average score on intelligence, for example, was 5.13 for whites scoring whites and 4.75 for blacks scoring blacks. Second, Atlantans generally do not score other groups at the low end of the scale or themselves at the high end of the scale.

Level of Intelligence

The intelligence scores shown in the table are remarkable in that both blacks and whites consider all groups to have above average intelligence, the "Lake Wobegon" effect. Both whites and blacks rate the intelligence of other groups lower than their own group. On the other hand, very few respondents, either whites or blacks, responded with scores of 1 or 2 (unintelligent) for any of the groups.

We consider the opinions regarding intelligence as a basic measure of negative racial stereotyping, and therefore explore this variable in greater detail. Since the opinion of black intelligence is correlated with the individual's opinion of white intelligence, we consider the difference in the intelligence ratings. To the extent that whites rank black intelligence below white intelligence, we consider that an indicator that whites consider blacks inferior, even if whites view black intelligence as being above average. Among whites, 45.2 percent of the respondents

TABLE 4.5   *Racial Stereotyping*

	Intelligence							
	1: Unintelligent	2	3	4	5	6	7: Intelligent	Mean Score
Whites' view of								
Whites	0.3%	2.1%	2.9%	29.5%	24.7%	24.8%	15.7%	5.13
Blacks	1.3	3.4	17.9	45.0	14.9	9.2	8.3	4.29
Blacks' view of								
Whites	6.5	5.5	9.5	33.5	15.6	14.3	15.2	4.49
Blacks	3.3	5.2	5.9	35.3	18.7	12.2	19.5	4.75

	Self-Support							
	1: Welfare	2	3	4	5	6	7: Self-Support	Mean Score
Whites' view of								
Whites	0.5	0.5	2.7	14.8	11.2	33.2	37.0	5.83
Blacks	8.2	14.8	16.1	25.3	14.0	9.0	12.5	3.99
Blacks' view of								
Whites	2.6	1.4	6.0	24.1	13.8	18.6	33.4	5.34
Blacks	4.8	5.8	10.6	27.0	20.2	10.0	21.6	4.68

	Get Along							
	1: Hard	2	3	4	5	6	7: Easy	Mean Score
Whites' view of								
Whites	0.6	0.6	2.2	29.3	17.3	23.7	26.3	5.38
Blacks	2.5	7.0	10.7	35.9	18.6	13.8	11.5	4.48
Blacks' view of								
Whites	13.9	11.2	13.7	27.1	11.9	8.9	13.3	3.92
Blacks	3.3	3.4	9.1	36.1	13.7	17.8	16.6	4.73

Source: Greater Atlanta Neighborhood Study 1994. Results are weighted.

ranked white and black intelligence equal, while 50.3 percent ranked white intelligence higher than black intelligence. The latter percentage suggest that there is a widely held view among whites that blacks are inferior to whites.

A large percentage of younger whites rate black and white intelligence equal (see table 4.6), although a larger percentage of whites over sixty years of age rank black intelligence higher than white intelligence. Beyond that, there is no clear relationship between age and relative ranking of intelligence (the correlation is statistically insignificant, and the mean value of relative intelligence follows no particular pattern across age groups). There are no statistically significant differences in

TABLE 4.6   *White View of Relative Intelligence*

White Intelligence – Black Intelligence[a]	−1 or less	0	1	2	3 or more	Total
Age						
Twenty-nine or less	1.7%	60.3%	12.3%	12.9%	12.8%	100.0%
Thirty to thirty-nine	5.9	42.6	20.2	16.5	14.8	100.0
Forty to forty-nine	3.5	47.4	21.8	21.1	6.3	100.1
Fifty to fifty-nine	5.2	41.5	24.5	13.3	15.5	100.0
Sixty +	14.2	35.9	20.4	18.5	11.0	100.0
Gender						
Female	2.7	48.0	20.7	16.2	12.4	100.0
Male	9.5	42.4	19.9	17.2	11.0	100.0
Education						
Less than high school	10.0	31.3	29.0	19.0	10.6	99.9
High school	7.6	37.6	17.6	19.1	18.2	100.1
More than high school	4.7	51.1	21.6	15.0	7.6	100.0
Family income						
Less than $20,000	5.2	46.2	17.8	14.6	16.1	99.9
$20,000 to $49,999	3.0	44.2	24.4	17.2	11.3	100.1
$50,000 or more	8.7	45.1	19.6	17.8	8.8	100.0
Percentage black in census tract						
Less than 25 percent	6.3	43.5	21.0	17.4	11.8	100.0
25 percent to 75 percent	2.1	68.0	12.4	5.0	12.5	100.0
Greater than 75 percent	0.9	78.8	8.2	7.0	5.2	100.1
Political views						
Liberal (score < 4)	1.3	50.3	21.9	13.8	12.7	100.0
Moderate (score = 4)	7.3	45.0	17.4	19.3	11.0	100.0
Conservative (score > 4)	8.6	42.0	20.7	17.4	11.4	100.1
Number of observations (unweighted)	30	297	114	82	75	598

Source: Greater Atlanta Neighborhood Study 1994. Results are weighted.
[a]The difference in the respondent's rating of intelligence of whites and blacks.

the relative rankings by gender or income. Only for education is there a statistically significant difference in relative rankings, with more highly educated whites being much more likely to rank blacks and whites equal. Whites in more integrated areas (as measured by percent black in their census tract) and who are more liberal see blacks as being of more equal intelligence; for both variables, the correlation with relative ranking of intelligence is statistically significant. It is not clear, however, whether whites with less measured prejudice seek residences in integrated areas or that living in integrated areas results in less prejudice.

The literature on racial attitude focuses almost exclusively on white opinions. The GANS survey, however, asked the same perception questions of blacks, which allows interracial comparisons. The distribution by blacks of relative rankings of intelligence is different from that of whites. First, a substantially larger percentage of blacks (56.6 percent) rated black and white intelligence equal than did whites (45.2 percent), and blacks are more likely to rank white intelligence higher than are whites likely to rank blacks higher. Second, the association for blacks between relative intelligence and various variables differs somewhat from that found for whites (see table 4.7). Older blacks are more likely to rank intelligence of blacks and whites equal (the correlation between the ranking and age is positive and statistically significant). There is no significant difference in ranking by gender, education level, or income level, although higher-income blacks are more likely to rank black intelligence higher than white intelligence compared to blacks in other income levels. Blacks who live in more integrated neighborhoods (25 to 75 percent black) and blacks who are more liberal are more likely to rank intelligence equal.

These results are not very encouraging. The ranking by whites suggests that there is still substantial laissez-faire racism, and the analysis does not provide much encouragement that this will change much as the population ages and becomes more educated. For example, even among more highly educated whites, 44.2 percent rank white intelligence greater than black intelligence. Among blacks, there is evidence that they are more likely to rank black and white intelligence as equal. However, given the pattern of responses with respect to age, the trend could well be that blacks will, over time, increasingly rank black intelligence greater than white intelligence.

Means of Support

A second measure of racial stereotyping is related to views on self-support. Both blacks and whites in the GANS see whites as more self-supporting (table 4.5). Blacks reported that both groups were, on average,

TABLE 4.7   *Black View of Relative Intelligence*

White Intelligence − Black Intelligence[a]	−3 or less	−2 or −1	0	1 or 2	3 or more	Total
Age						
Twenty-nine or less	9.2%	10.7%	61.9%	14.0%	4.1%	100.0%
Thirty to thirty-nine	9.2	21.1	51.2	15.6	2.8	99.9
Forty to forty-nine	15.4	11.2	51.4	18.7	3.3	100.0
Fifty to fifty-nine	5.2	19.8	58.3	12.9	3.8	100.0
Sixty +	8.1	3.6	68.0	17.2	3.2	100.1
Gender						
Female	9.0	14.7	56.7	16.1	3.5	100.0
Male	10.6	13.3	57.0	15.7	3.5	100.1
Education						
Less than high school	12.6	9.6	58.1	13.6	6.1	100.0
High school	12.1	13.7	56.9	12.5	4.8	100.0
More than high school	5.7	16.0	57.5	19.5	1.4	100.1
Family income						
Less than $20,000	10.2	12.3	57.4	15.7	4.4	100.0
$20,000 to $49,999	9.5	12.2	54.3	20.3	3.8	100.1
$50,000 and more	8.4	21.2	60.2	9.3	0.8	99.9
Percentage black in census tract						
Less than 25 percent	4.6	9.5	59.1	23.8	3.0	100.0
25 percent to 75 percent	4.0	13.1	73.6	8.7	0.7	100.1
Greater than 75 percent	13.0	16.0	51.9	14.7	4.4	100.0
Political views						
Liberal (score < 4)	8.6	10.9	64.0	12.1	4.4	100.0
Moderate (score = 4)	10.3	17.4	49.7	18.8	3.7	99.9
Conservative (score > 4)	11.9	19.3	45.0	23.4	0.5	100.1
Number of observations (unweighted)	78	108	451	122	38	797

Source: Greater Atlanta Neighborhood Study 1994. Results weighted.
[a]The difference in the respondent's rating of intelligence of whites and blacks.

at least somewhat self-supporting (the mean scores are around 5.5). Whites gave blacks an average score of 3.99, suggesting that, on average, whites see blacks as having some preference to live off welfare. As with views of intelligence, there was strong correlation between each race's view of its own members' self-support and its view of the other race's self-support.

The correlation between relative self-support and relative intelligence for white respondents is positive and significant (0.449), which suggests that whites who hold one variation of laissez-faire racism tend to hold the other as well. Since the general pattern of relationships between responses to the issue of self-support and the characteristic variables listed in table 4.6 are essentially the same as for the intelligence variable, we do not present separate tables for self-support. There are, however, two differences in the results. First, for whites, there is a significant pattern between age and the relative ranking of self-support, with youth more likely to rate blacks and whites the same. Second, highly educated blacks rank black self-support higher than white self-support than do less educated blacks.

Getting Along with Others

The last question dealing with racial stereotype concerns perceptions of how easy it is to get along with members of racial groups. Both blacks and whites in Atlanta see their own group as easier to get along with than other groups. The pattern of responses (not presented) to this ranking is similar to that for the other two racial stereotype questions, with the exception that the rankings are positively associated with income but not age.

Conclusion

Clearly, many of Atlanta's whites and blacks have unfavorable opinions of blacks, especially with regard to their willingness to support themselves. However, the most severe of the laissez-faire prejudices seem weak; most whites rank black and white intelligence within 1 point of each other on a 7-point scale, and place blacks above average.

Age, gender, and income matter little with respect to white-held stereotypes. Education seems to play a major role in decreasing prejudice, but youthful opinions do not seem to reveal a revolution in progress. Rather, in light of the widespread belief that black intelligence is similar to that of whites, comparable opinions across age may indicate that those changes are reaching everyone. Black prejudices seem to shadow the white prejudices in that the forms are similar, but generally less severe.

The Zero-Sum Myth

Whites may be concerned that if blacks gain on some fronts, whites will lose. This competition could be one of the contributing factors leading to discrimination (Chesler 1976; Kinder and Sears 1981). We explore this possibility with the GANS, which asked respondents whether whites would lose if blacks gained with respect to jobs, housing, and political power.

Among whites, 30.5 percent agreed with the statement that "More good jobs for blacks means fewer good jobs for whites," while 27.0 percent agreed with the statement, "As more good housing and neighborhoods go to blacks, the fewer good houses and neighborhoods there will be for whites." Whites were even more prone to see black gains in local politics as causing white losses; 50.3 percent of whites agreed with the statement, "The more influence blacks have in local politics, the less influence whites will have in local politics." Less than 15 percent of blacks agreed with any of these statements.

Does the fear of loss from black gains drive racial prejudice? Most whites do not see competition between the races in economic areas, but a sizable minority do. The correlations of white views of relative intelligence and of self-support with the level of agreement with the statement that "More good jobs for blacks means fewer good jobs for whites" are 0.221 and 0.222, respectively (both are statistically significant). Thus, there appears to be some support for the view that fear of economic competition drives racial prejudice.

One form of Jim Crow prejudice is reflected in the view that blacks and whites are competitors, and therefore blacks must be subjugated (and isolated). With this form of prejudice, integration (as measured by percentage of blacks in the respondent's neighborhood) should correlate negatively with measures of competition, which it does significantly only for political competition (-0.137). We might expect that if whites view blacks as intelligent and hard-working (self-supporting), the fear of competition would be higher. We did not find this result; in fact, the opposite was true for all three measures of competition and both measures of prejudice. This result is consistent with other observations that whites fear competition from groups they consider inferior. So whites who fear competition also consider blacks inferior and isolate themselves from them.

Immigrants, Economic Opportunity, and Political Influence

The subject of immigration has aroused much public and scholarly controversy. Opinion polls (national and in the state of California) have revealed widespread anxieties among native-born American citizens about the impact of continued immigration. The concern focuses on two distinct sets of issues: economic issues, mostly the effects on the labor market prospects of native-born Americans, and issues of national identity and distribution of political influence.

This section examines perceptions regarding immigration in metropolitan Atlanta. Concerns among Atlanta residents regarding economic and political competition from current immigrants reflect more basic positions toward other groups that are not colored by black and white racism. This is particularly true in Atlanta, where the immigrant population is small, and where, presumably, the economic impact is weak. Thus, the analysis adds another dimension to the investigation.

Although Atlanta is international in outlook, most of the immigrants who came to the area before 1970 were "predominantly white, middle class, and could speak English well" (Dameron and Murphy 1996). These individuals blended well into Atlanta's black and white community and, according to C. E. Hill (1975) and Valerie Fennell (1977), did not resort to ethnicity for political or economic power.

Since the 1970s, new arrivals have been less likely to fit black-white racial labeling, less educated, less economically well off, speak little English, and have created a variety of ethnically based economic, political, and social organizations (Dameron and Murphy 1996). Further, the new wave is larger. The immigrant population in the Atlanta region increased from 40,564 in 1982 to 266,000 in 1995.

The demographic, social, and cultural changes that have developed as a result of the multicultural structure of the region create problems for Atlantans. Issues of interethnic conflict, competition, and communication have increased in recent years. Several articles in the *Atlanta Constitution* have alluded to the heightened tensions that have developed between the immigrant population and local residents.

Changes in the racial-ethnic composition of society have always produced strong negative response from the predominantly white society. Because of the underlying prejudice, whites are more likely to resent perceived encroachment on their political power and influence, and this is likely to be reflected in their perceptions about economic opportunities.

The GANS asked respondents their view of the effect of continued immigration on economic opportunity and political influence on the respondent's racial group. The replies were collapsed into three categories: more than now; no more or less than now; less than now.

Both whites and blacks perceived that immigration would lower their economic opportunities (see table 4.8). Among blacks, the economic consequences of immigration weighed more heavily than the ef-

TABLE 4.8   *Perceptions About Economic Opportunities, and*
            Political Influence by Race

	Economic Opportunities			Political Influence		
Perception	Black	White	Total	Black	White	Total
More than now	26.0%	8.5%	13.1%	25.0%	8.8%	13.0%
No more or less than now	25.1	39.0	35.3	33.4	35.4	34.9
Less than now	48.8	52.6	51.6	41.6	55.8	52.1
N	381	1071	1452	381	1074	1455

Source: Greater Atlanta Neighborhood Study 1994.

fects on political influence. Whites perceived a greater negative impact from immigration on their political influence than on their economic opportunities.

The percentage distributions by socioeconomic categories of those who responded that they would have less economic opportunities and less political influence are given in table 4.9. Also included are the percentage distributions on how subgroups in California voted on Proposition 187.[8] (The values are categorized differently from previous tables in order to compare the distribution with the California responses.) Although the California vote was directed at illegal aliens, it nevertheless speaks to the whole issue of immigration, both legal and illegal, and can be viewed as a referendum (at least of California residents) on the immigration issue.

The overall pattern of results showed that many Atlantans, regardless of race, gender, educational attainment, family income, political party identification, or political ideology believed that they would have less economic opportunities and less political influence if immigration continued at the present rate. The views of Atlantans are somewhat similar to those of Californians.

Group-interest theories (Jessor 1988; Kluegel and Smith 1983) provide possible explanations for Atlantans' responses to the immigration issues. Whites generally have higher family incomes, are likely to be more educated, and have lower unemployment rates than blacks. Yet, whites were more pessimistic than blacks about the impact of immigra-

TABLE 4.9   *Persons Who Feel That They Will Have Less Economic Opportunities, and Less Political Influence (GANS Data), and California's Yes Vote to Proposition 187*

Categories	GANS		California's Yes vote on
	Economic	Political	Proposition 187
Race			
Black	48.8%	41.6%	47.0%
White	52.6	55.8	63.0
Gender			
Male	49.4	56.7	60.0
Female	53.3	47.9	56.0
Education			
High school or less	56.3	57.4	66.0
Community college or associate's degree	47.5	44.0	62.0
Bachelor's degree or more	46.6	49.2	53.0
Family income			
Less than $20,000	52.5	53.3	53.0
$20,000 to $39,999	56.7	60.6	60.0
$40,000 to $59,999	52.4	52.8	59.0
$60,000 or more	51.0	38.9	58.0
Party affiliation			
Republican	54.7	61.2	78.0
Democrat	46.9	39.1	36.0
Independent	44.8	59.9	62.0
Political ideology			
Liberal	42.7	44.9	26.0
Moderate	61.2	54.0	55.0
Conservative	51.2	57.2	78.0

Source: Greater Atlanta Neighborhood Study 1994.

tion on their opportunities, especially political influence. Immigration has become a pivotal issue on the political landscape, and it would seem that whites are responding as a group and are driven by concerns about the impact of the erosion of their political power.

While group interest may also be driving blacks' responses (as seen from the higher percentages who feel that they would have less economic opportunities and less political influence), it is also possible that self-interest is a factor in their perceptions about immigration. T. R. Tyler (1980), T. R. Tyler and F. L. Cook (1984), and Alan I. Abramowitz and Jeffrey A. Segal (1986) have argued that personal experiences have powerful effects on attitudes and judgments.

The results conform to our expectations. Whites were more likely than blacks to perceive immigration as negatively impacting their political and economic opportunities. The results are consistent with our findings regarding white support of integrated neighborhoods and white stereotyping of other racial groups. Interestingly, the pattern emerged even though most respondents agreed that there was some discrimination that hurts the chances of Hispanics and Asians to get good-paying jobs.

Conclusion

Race relations have been perhaps the most pressing issue the Atlanta region needs to address (Atlanta Regional Commission 1994). While the GANS reveals that race still matters, the findings suggest that there is cause for optimism. First, whites in Atlanta were found to be more accepting of black neighbors than we expected based on actual residential segregation. Second, whites did not generally believe that the quality of their lives would be threatened by improvements blacks might make in the areas of housing, jobs, or neighborhood quality. However, we found that both blacks and whites felt threatened by immigration, which suggests that both sense a level of competition not felt from each other.

However, these same results suggest a continued presence of racial prejudice. But these attitudes are not strong enough to dominate white views as a whole. Blacks appear to have more moderated views than do whites in self-described politics and relative intelligence. As with whites, extreme views appear to decrease with education, but unlike whites, some of the black extreme views include an own-group inferiority stance.

The history of race relations discussed in the previous chapter and the nature of racial attitudes and perceptions discussed in this chapter are helpful in understanding of the role of race in Atlanta and in the continuation of the Atlanta paradox. Subsequent chapters go on to explore how race and racial attitudes play out in the housing and labor markets.

We thank Charles Jaret for helpful comments on an earlier version of this chapter.

Notes

1. The southern suburbs consisted of south Fulton County, DeKalb County south of I-20, and Douglas, Clayton, Fayette, Rockdale, and Henry counties. The northern suburbs were north Fulton County, DeKalb County north of I-20, and Gwinnett and Cobb counties.

2. Correlation coefficients between the choice of neighborhood and the socioeconomic variables listed in table 4.2 were calculated. The correlations with respect to age (-0.12), education (0.10), and income (0.18) had the expected sign and were significant. The correlation with gender was insignificant.

3. To calculate this percentage, we used the interval centered around the percent black in each of the five hypothetical neighborhoods to measure the preferred racial composition.

4. Fifty-seven percent believe intelligence is the same, 9.4 percent rank white intelligence 1 point higher on the scale, and 12.0 rank black intelligence 1 point higher on the scale.

5. This was calculated by adding the percentages for Neighborhoods A and B and assuming that half of those who were comfortable with Neighborhood C but not B would be comfortable in a neighborhood with four blacks.

6. The correlation coefficients between the level of comfort and these variables are insignificant.

7. Other surveys find that whites still endorse traditional stereotypes about blacks and Hispanics. That is, whites see blacks and Hispanics as more willing to live on welfare than are whites, more prone to violence, less intelligent, and less patriotic (Bobo and Kluegel 1991). Whites may simultaneously believe in the idea of racial equality and hold that blacks violate traditional American values about self-reliance, the work ethic, family stability, discipline, and individualism (Kinder and Sears 1981, p. 416).

8. Proposition 187 is intended to curb the economic hardships caused by the presence of illegal aliens in the state of California. The response categories for education in the California vote varied from that on GANS. The education categories for education in California were: High school or less; Some college, no degree; College graduate.

References

Abramowitz, Alan I., and Jeffrey A. Segal. 1986. "Determinants of the Outcomes of U.S. Senate Elections." *Journal of Politics* 50: 848–63.

Atlanta Regional Commission. 1994. *Vision 2020: A Shared Vision for the Atlanta Region*. Atlanta: Atlanta Regional Commission.

Bobo, Lawrence, and James R. Kluegel. 1991. "Opposition to Race-Targeting: Self-Interest, Stratification Ideology, or Racial Attitudes?" *American Sociological Review* 58: 443–64.

———. 1996. "Difference Between Black and Brown: Explanations of Racial Economic Inequality." Paper prepared for the American Association for Public Opinion Research.

Bobo, Lawrence, and Camile L. Zubrinsky. 1996. "Attitudes on Residential Integration: Perceived Status Differences, Mere In-Group Preferences, or Racial Prejudice." *Social Forces* 74(3): 883–909.

Chesler, Mark A. 1976. "Contemporary Sociological Theories of Racism." In *Towards the Elimination of Racism*, edited by Phyllis A. Kutz. Pergamon.

Dameron, Rebecca J., and Arthur D. Murphy. 1996. "Becoming an International City: Atlanta, 1970–1996." *Research Applications* 5(1). Atlanta, Ga.: Center for Applied Research in Anthropology, Georgia State University.

Demo, David H., and Michael Hughes. 1990. "Socialization and Racial Identity Among Black Americans." *Social Psychology Quarterly* 53(4): 364–74.

Dyer, James, Arnold Vedlitz, and Stephan Worchel. 1989. "Social Distance Among Racial and Ethnic Groups in Texas: Some Demographic Correlates." *Social Science Quarterly* 70(3): 607–16.

Farley, Reynolds, Charlotte Steeh, and Maria Krysan. 1994. "Stereotypes and Segregation: Neighborhoods in the Detroit Area." *American Journal of Sociology* 100: 750–80.

Fennell, Valerie. 1977. "International Atlanta and Ethnic Group Relations." *Urban Anthropology* 6(4): 345–54.

Hill, C. E. 1975. "Adaptation in Public and Private Behavior of Ethnic Groups in an American Urban Setting." *Urban Anthropology* 4(4): 333–47.

Hunter, William C., and Mary Beth Walker. 1996. "The Cultural Affinity Hypothesis and Mortgage Lending Decisions." *Journal of Real Estate Finance and Economics* 13(1): 57–70.

Jessor, Tom. 1988. "Personal Interest, Group Conflict, and Symbolic Group Affect: Explanations for Whites' Opposition to Racial Equality." Ph.D. diss., University of California.

Kinder, Donald R., and David O. Sears. 1981. "Prejudice and Politics: Symbolic Racism versus Racial Threats to the Good Life." *Journal of Personality and Social Psychology* 40(3): 414–31.

Kluegel, James R., and Eliot R. Smith. 1983. "Affirmative Action Attitudes: Effects of Self-Interest, Racial Affect, and Stratification Beliefs on Whites' Views." *Social Forces* 61:797–824.

Massey, Douglas S., and Nancy A. Denton. 1993. *American Apartheid: Segregation and the Making of the Underclass*. New York: Russell Sage Foundation.

Tyler, T. R. 1980. "The Impact of Directly and Indirectly Experienced

Events: The Origins of Crime-related Judgements and Behaviors." *Journal of Personality and Social Psychology* 39: 13–28.

Tyler, T. R., and F. L. Cook. 1984. "The Mass Media and Judgements of Risk: Distinguishing Impact on Personal and Societal Level Judgements." *Journal of Personality and Social Psychology* 47: 693–708.

Yinger, John. 1995. *Closed Doors, Opportunities Lost: The Continuing Cost of Housing Discrimination*. New York: Russell Sage Foundation.

5

BLACK-WHITE RESIDENTIAL SEGREGATION IN ATLANTA

Mark A. Thompson

W HILE the Atlanta metropolitan area has experienced rapid growth in population, income, and employment in recent years, the rewards have not been shared equally across the region. The inner-city core of Atlanta houses a disproportionate share of highly concentrated and persistent poverty, among blacks in particular.

One contributing factor to the Atlanta paradox of persistent inner-city poverty in a metropolitan area that has experienced robust growth may be the continuation of a high level of black-white residential segregation in the Atlanta metropolitan area. Additional evidence of the need to give consideration to housing segregation as a potential explanation for the Atlanta paradox lies in the fact that, outside the inner city, whites have located in large part in the northern suburbs of Atlanta (where employment and incomes have grown most rapidly), while a re-segregation of blacks has taken place in areas predominantly south and west of the city.

This chapter provides insights into the causes of residential segregation in Atlanta using data from the Greater Atlanta Neighborhood Study (see the appendix in chapter 1 for a discussion of the GANS data). A common measure of residential segregation between two racial groups is the dissimilarity index, which is the percentage of either racial group that must relocate to achieve complete integration. An index number of 0 indicates that each "neighborhood" within a metropolitan area has the same racial composition (full integration), while a value of 100 indicates complete segregation of the races. The dissimilarity index for the Atlanta metropolitan area based on the 1990 census was 67.7 (a significant improvement over the 1980 score of 76.2 reported in Douglas S. Massey and Nancy A. Denton [1989]). (Hartshorn and Ihlanfeldt [chapter 2] report a 1996 value of the index of 61.4 for the Atlanta Regional Commission planning area.) In 1990, Atlanta ranked 23rd out of the 44 metropolitan areas having populations in excess of one million; the average value of the dissimilarity index for the 44 largest metro areas in 1990 was 66.4.

In this chapter, I will provide a brief review of the problems resulting from residential segregation, followed by a review of notable trends in black-white residential segregation. My focus then turns to the possible causes of segregation in Atlanta. One thing that can be said with certainty is that there is no one factor or cause that can be singled out to explain residential segregation. Four potential (and probably interrelated) causes are explored, including the possibility that:

(1) residential segregation can be explained by racial differences in economic factors;

(2) racial differences in perceptions of and information about predominantly white suburban areas contribute to residential segregation;

(3) perceptions of blacks regarding institutional barriers in Atlanta's housing market preclude seeking housing in predominantly white suburban areas;

(4) racial differences in residential preferences exist, which prevent integration.

Notable Trends in Black-White Residential Segregation

Residential segregation of blacks and whites has not always existed. Prior to the turn of the twentieth century, integrated neighborhoods were commonplace in both northern and southern cities—even in those in which a high degree of segregation exists today. However, the size of the black population living in urban areas (particularly northern urban areas) was small. Between 1870 and 1970, a migratory shift of the majority of the black population occurred away from rural southern areas (where approximately 80 percent of blacks lived in 1870) to urban areas in both the north and south (where approximately 80 percent of blacks lived in 1970).

This shift elicited a response among whites, resulting in the development of black-white residential segregation. A segregated pattern of black-white residences was not coincidental, but came after intentional actions by whites to exclude blacks from residential opportunities in urban real estate markets. Between the turn of the century and the end of World War II, strategies for segregating blacks from whites included the subtle, such as restrictive covenants to a property deed preventing minority ownership (Committee on Civil Rights 1947), and the not so subtle, such as firebombing the homes of blacks who moved into white neighborhoods (Chicago Commission on Race Relations 1922). These intentional acts have been reinforced by an indifference among a majority of whites to the problems associated with residential segregation and the well-documented failure of public policy intended to alleviate it.

Residential segregation in America's cities continually increased until 1950, and generally stabilized at high levels for the next twenty years. Moderate declines in segregation occurred during the 1970s and continued through the 1980s. Reynolds Farley and William H. Frey (1994) report that the average value of the dissimilarity index for 232 metropolitan areas (those with a minimum of 20,000 blacks making up at least 3 percent of the population in 1990) declined from 69 in 1980 to 65 in 1990. The index fell in 83.6 percent of the metropolitan areas studied (194 out of the 232) and by five percentage points or more in 36.6 percent (85 out of the 232). In 1990, only four metropolitan areas had an index in excess of 85, down from fourteen in 1980.

Farley and Frey predict that residential segregation between whites and blacks will continue to decline as blacks migrate to southern and western metropolitan areas with a relatively young population that have experienced relatively strong growth in new housing construction. Despite this prediction, residential segregation indices between blacks and whites are expected to continue to be well in excess of similar Hispanic-white and Asian-white measures.

Residential Segregation in Atlanta

Chapter 3 makes clear that the development of racial segregation in Atlanta is the result of overt policies. Here we explore other reasons for the contemporary existence of housing segregation, through a consideration of four hypotheses.

Hypothesis 1: Economic Factors and Residential Segregation

When attempting to explain residential segregation, an often immediate response is that differences in economic factors between the races limit black residential choice. In other words, one might argue that blacks cannot afford to live in white suburban neighborhoods. A cursory review of household income data from the 1990 census seems to confirm that economic factors are a plausible explanation for residential segregation. In 1989, average household income for whites in the Atlanta metropolitan area was $56,300, compared with average household incomes for blacks at $31,753.

Despite differences in average household income, many blacks living in Atlanta are making monthly housing payments that would cover housing costs in an Atlanta suburb. Monthly owner costs reported in the 1990 census represent the sum of payments for mortgage(s), real estate taxes, property insurance, and utilities. A comparison of the reported owner costs for blacks living in the city and whites living in the suburbs is provided in figure 5.1. Census data on gross monthly rent (rent plus utilities) suggest that renting a residence in the suburbs is an economically feasible alternative for blacks living in the city. A comparison of the gross monthly rents for blacks living in the city and whites living in the suburbs is provided in figure 5.2.

As further evidence that economic factors are not a prime contributor to residential segregation, the dissimilarity index was calculated for households with reported 1989 incomes of less than $10,000 and greater than $100,000. For households with incomes of less than $10,000, the index was was 66.1. Black and white households with incomes greater than $100,000 had a much greater degree of racial segregation, with an index of 86.3. Thus, those blacks who presumably have the economic ability to purchase suburban homes are significantly more segregated than poor blacks are from poor whites.

It appears that renting a suburban residence is within the financial reach of many black city residents. While they may explain a small portion of residential segregation, racial differences in economic factors cannot be classified as a major contributor to the problem.

Hypothesis 2: Racial Differences in Perceptions and Information

Several survey questions in the GANS focus on particular neighborhoods or communities, which include Decatur, Tri-Cities, Midtown, Marietta-Norcross, Roswell-Alpharetta, and Norcross (see map 5.1). (The appendix to chapter 1 contains a short description of each of these areas.)

Housing Costs and Perceptions of Affordability Survey respondents to the GANS were asked to estimate the average home cost in each of six suburban areas. The responses allow determination of whether both races share similar information on housing costs and whether the information is accurate. Responses by location and race are provided in figure 5.3. Responses by location, race, and household income group are provided in table 5.1.

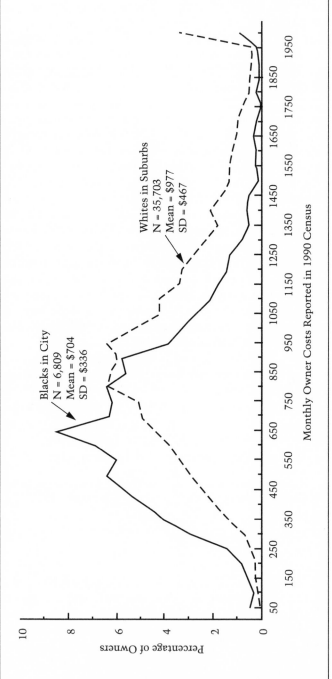

FIGURE 5.1   *Housing Costs for Blacks in the City of Atlanta and Whites in the Suburban Ring Monthly Housing Costs Reported by Owners*

Source: U.S. Department of Commerce 1993.

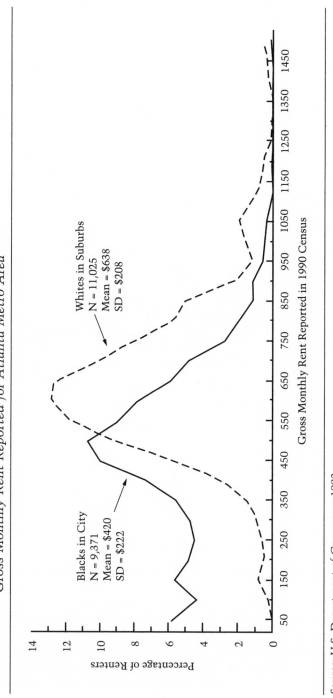

FIGURE 5.2   Housing Costs for Blacks in the City of Atlanta and Whites in the Suburban Ring
Gross Monthly Rent Reported for Atlanta Metro Area

Whites in Suburbs
N = 11,025
Mean = $638
SD = $208

Blacks in City
N = 9,371
Mean = $420
SD = $222

Percentage of Renters

Gross Monthly Rent Reported in 1990 Census

Source: U.S. Department of Commerce 1993.

MAP 5.1   *Atlanta*

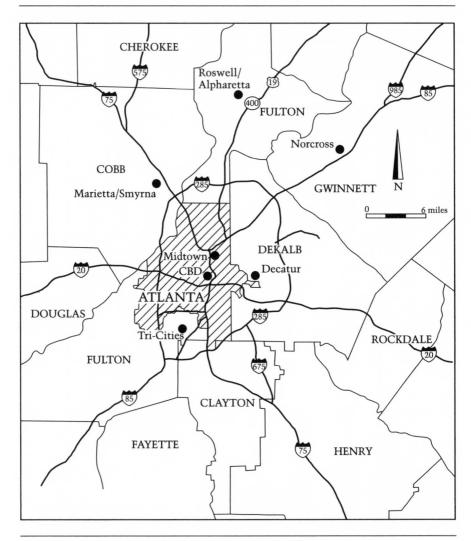

Source: Cartographic Research Laboratory, Department of Geography, Georgia State University, 1999.

The results for the full samples reveal that racial differences in mean responses are statistically significant for five of the six areas (Roswell-Alpharetta being the exception). Relative to whites, blacks undervalue average home costs in Decatur and Midtown. Blacks overvalued housing in Tri-Cities, Marietta-Smyrna, and Norcross. The rela-

(Text continues on p. 103.)

FIGURE 5.3   *Estimate of Average Home Value by Race*

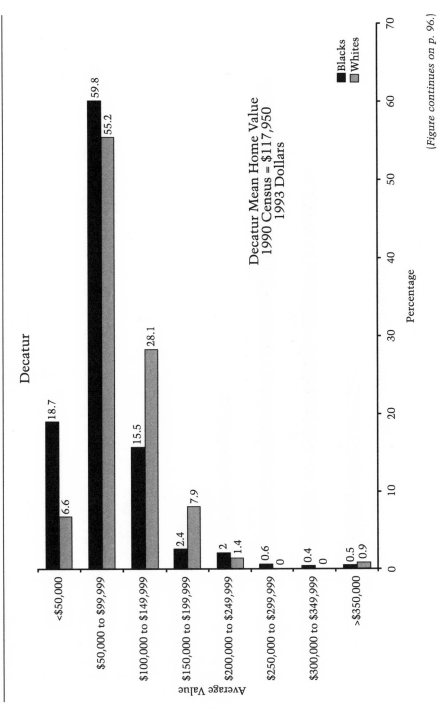

Decatur

(Figure continues on p. 96.)

FIGURE 5.3   *Continued*

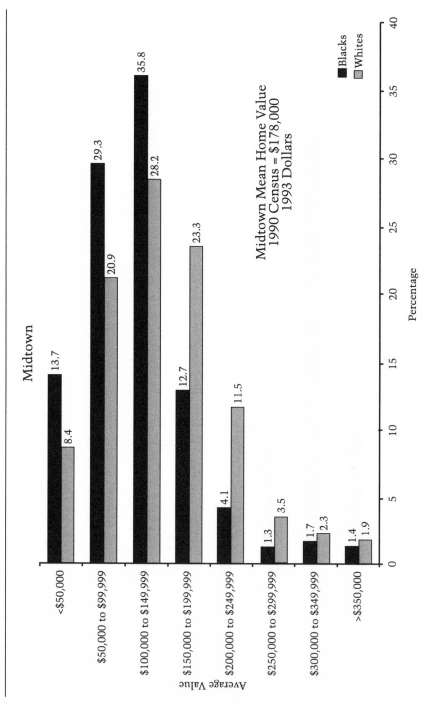

Midtown

Midtown Mean Home Value
1990 Census = $178,000
1993 Dollars

FIGURE 5.3   Continued

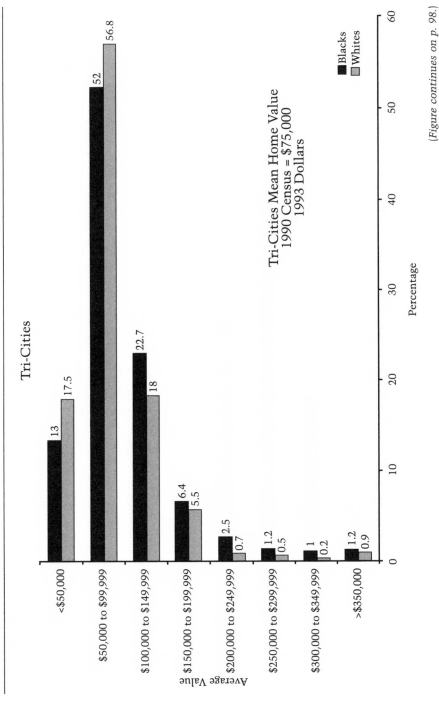

Tri-Cities

Tri-Cities Mean Home Value
1990 Census = $75,000
1993 Dollars

(Figure continues on p. 98.)

FIGURE 5.3   *Continued*

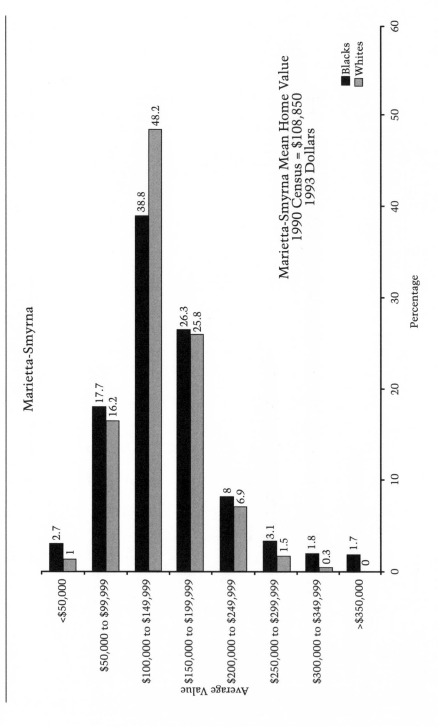

Marietta-Smyrna

Marietta-Smyrna Mean Home Value
1990 Census = $108,850
1993 Dollars

FIGURE 5.3   *Continued*

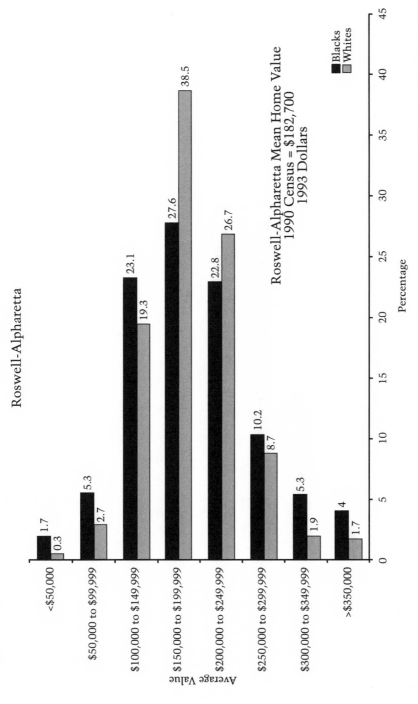

Roswell-Alpharetta

Average Value

<$50,000   Blacks 1.7   Whites 0.3
$50,000 to $99,999   Blacks 5.3   Whites 2.7
$100,000 to $149,999 Blacks 23.1   Whites 19.3
$150,000 to $199,999 Blacks 27.6   Whites 38.5
$200,000 to $249,999 Blacks 22.8   Whites 26.7
$250,000 to $299,999 Blacks 10.2   Whites 8.7
$300,000 to $349,999 Blacks 5.3   Whites 1.9
>$350,000   Blacks 4   Whites 1.7

Roswell-Alpharetta Mean Home Value
1990 Census = $182,700
1993 Dollars

Percentage

■ Blacks
□ Whites

(Figure continues on p. 100.)

FIGURE 5.3   Continued

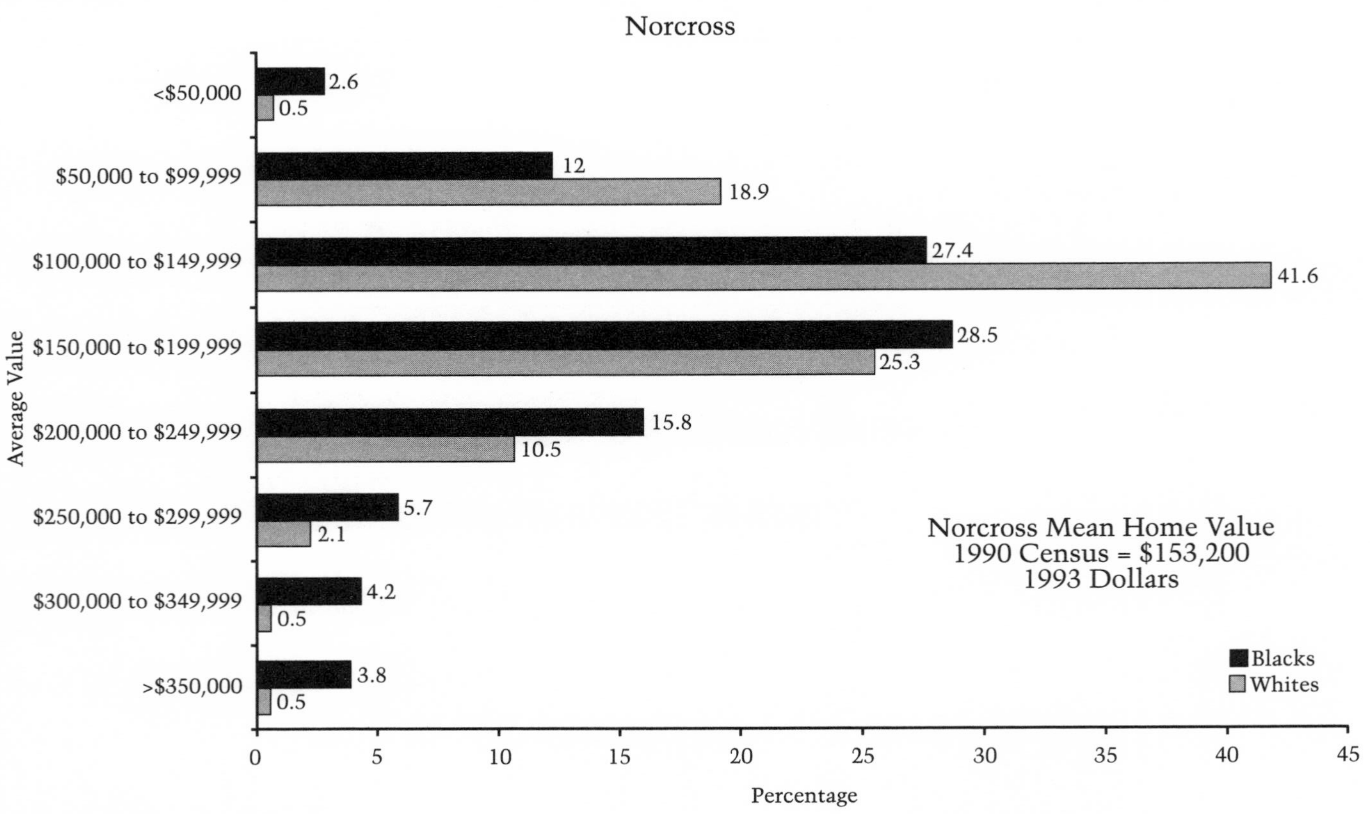

Norcross

Source: Greater Atlanta Neighborhood Study 1994.

TABLE 5.1   *Average Home Cost Estimates by Race, Location, and Income Group*

Decatur (39 Percent Black Population, 1990 Census)
Mean Home Value: $117,950, 1990 Census

Household Income Group	Mean Value of Price Category		Price Category with True Mean Home Value	Ratio of Mean Response to True Price Category	
	Black	White		Black	White
All respondents	2.15	2.46[a]	2	1.08	1.23
< $15,000	2.13	2.35[a]	2	1.07	1.18
$15,000–$29,999	2.42	2.1[a]	2	1.21	1.05
$30,000–$44,999	2.09	2.55[a]	2	1.05	1.28
$45,000–$59,999	2.54	2.56	2	1.27	1.28
>$60,000	2.57	2.43	2	1.29	1.22

Midtown (26.5 Percent Black Population, 1990 Census)
Mean Home Value: $178,000, 1990 Census

Household Income Group	Mean Value of Price Category		Price Category with True Mean Home Value	Ratio of Mean Response to True Price Category	
	Black	White		Black	White
All respondents	2.82	3.38[a]	4	.71	.85
< $15,000	2.69	3.04[a]	4	.67	.76
$15,000–$29,999	3.05	2.91	4	.76	.73
$30,000–$44,999	3.02	3.53[a]	4	.76	.88
$45,000–$59,999	3	3.65[a]	4	.75	.91
>$60,000	3.87	3.27[a]	4	.97	.82

Tri-Cities (64 Percent Black Population, 1990 Census)
Mean Home Value: $75,000, 1990 Census

Household Income Group	Mean Value of Price Category		Price Category with True Mean Home Value	Ratio of Mean Response to True Price Category	
	Black	White		Black	White
All respondents	2.47	2.22[a]	2	1.24	1.11
<$15,000	2.51	2.2[a]	2	1.26	1.1
$15,000–$29,999	2.32	2.42	2	1.16	1.21
$30,000–$44,999	2.38	2.2	2	1.19	1.1
$45,000–$59,999	2.6	2.09[a]	2	1.3	1.05
>$60,000	2.25	2.25	2	1.13	1.13

(Table continues on p. 102.)

TABLE 5.1   *Continued*

Marietta-Smyrna (18.5 Percent Black Population, 1990 Census) Mean Home Value: $108,850, 1990 Census

Household Income Group	Mean Value of Price Category		Price Category with True Mean Home Value	Ratio of Mean Response to True Price Category	
	Black	White		Black	White
All respondents	3.44	3.27[a]	3	1.15	1.09
< $15,000	3.44	3.21[a]	3	1.15	1.07
$15,000–$29,999	3.26	3.44	3	1.09	1.15
$30,000–$44,999	3.47	3.18	3	1.16	1.06
$45,000–$59,999	3.55	3.29	3	1.18	1.1
>$60,000	3.46	3.29	3	1.15	1.1

Roswell-Alpharetta (3.8 Percent Black Population, 1990 Census) Mean Home Value: $182,700, 1990 Census

Household Income Group	Mean Value of Price Category		Price Category with True Mean Home Value	Ratio of Mean Response to True Price Category	
	Black	White		Black	White
All respondents	4.37	4.31	4	1.09	1.08
< $15,000	4.38	4.31	4	1.1	1.08
$15,000–$29,999	4.23	4.39	4	1.06	1.1
$30,000–$44,999	4.24	4.23	4	1.06	1.06
$45,000–$59,999	4.5	4.41	4	1.13	1.1
>$60,000	4.37	4.21	4	1.09	1.05

Norcross (7.9 Percent Black Population, 1990 Census) Mean Home Value: $153,200, 1990 Census

Household Income Group	Mean Value of Price Category		Price Category with True Mean Home Value	Ratio of Mean Response to True Price Category	
	Black	White		Black	White
All respondents	3.96	3.37[a]	4	.99	.84
< $15,000	4.06	3.31[a]	4	1.02	.83
$15,000–$29,999	3.37	3.83[a]	4	.84	.96
$30,000–$44,999	3.89	3.29[a]	4	.97	.82
$45,000–$59,999	3.74	3.49	4	.94	.87
<$60,000	3.48	3.76	4	.87	.94

Source: Greater Atlanta Neighborhood Study 1994.
[a]Racial difference in means is statistically significant at the 5 percent level.

102

tive overvaluation of Tri-Cities homes by blacks is surprising, given that it is the area with the highest proportion of black residents. Blacks and whites slightly overvalued housing in Decatur, Tri-Cities, Marietta-Smyrna, and Roswell-Alpharetta, while both races undervalued housing in Midtown. The black mean response of home costs in Norcross is equal to the true price category, despite its having one of the lowest representations of blacks; whites undervalued home costs in Norcross.

Responses by household income group show some differences in estimation of value of homes. For all six areas, the under $15,000 income group gave responses comparable in nature to the full sample. The high-income group ($60,000+) shares similar, yet not accurate, price information for five of the six areas (there is no statistically significant racial difference in mean responses). The mean responses for Midtown are different, with high-income blacks displaying relatively more accurate information.

Survey respondents were also asked to indicate how many black families could afford to live in each of the geographic areas included in the survey. The proportion of whites and blacks that responded "almost all" or "many" black families could afford housing in each area is provided in figure 5.4.

Decatur and Tri-Cities are recognized as being affordable areas for blacks. Marietta-Smyrna was recognized by a majority of blacks and whites as being affordable, but not by the same proportion as Decatur, despite having a lower average home cost. Both races gave similar but less accurate information regarding black's abilities to afford a home in Midtown. Roswell-Alpharetta and Norcross are correctly viewed as being the least affordable areas for blacks. Including respondents who replied that "about half" of black families could afford housing did not change the assessment of relative affordability for each area.

Blacks view the predominantly white areas of Roswell-Alpharetta and Norcross as being the least affordable areas to buy a home. They view the areas with the highest proportion of blacks as being the most affordable (Decatur and Tri-Cities).

The evidence on perceptions of affordability suggests that segregation may be explained in part by the opinion among blacks that they cannot afford to live in the predominantly white areas.

Desirability of Suburban Areas   Another possible explanation for residential segregation may be that blacks simply don't view certain suburbs as desirable places to live. Survey respondents were asked to indicate for each geographic area whether it is a "very desirable," "somewhat desirable," "somewhat undesirable," or "very undesirable" place to live. Figure 5.5 shows the percentage of black and white respondents indicating that an area is very or somewhat desirable.

FIGURE 5.4 *Percentage of Respondents Indicating That Blacks Can Afford to Live in Select Locations*

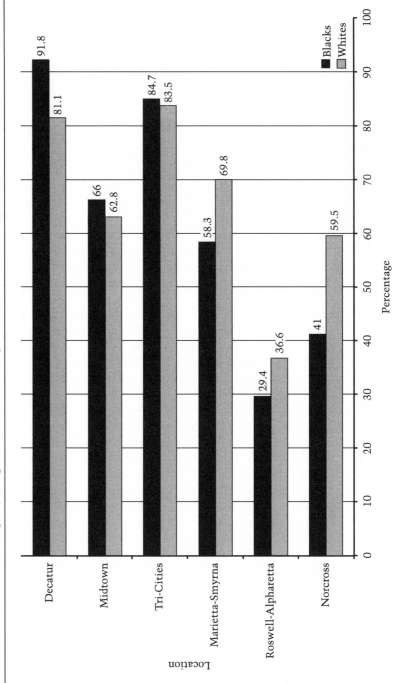

Source: Greater Atlanta Neighborhood Study 1994.

FIGURE 5.5   Percentage of Black and White Respondents Ranking Location as a "Very Desirable" or "Somewhat Desirable" Place to Reside

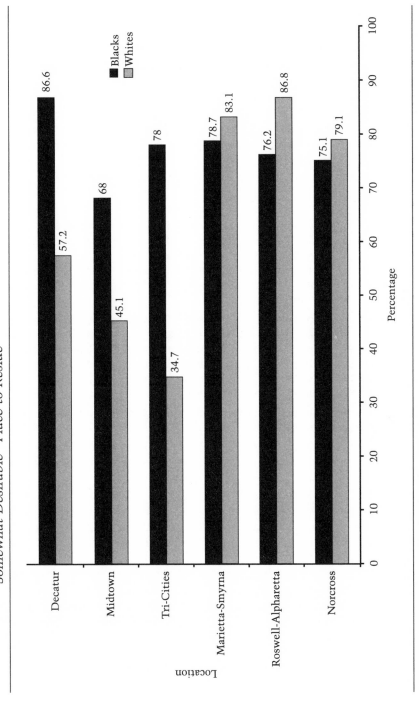

Source: Greater Atlanta Neighborhood Study 1994.
Note: Responses in all areas are statistically significantly different between races.

The desirability across locations did not differ much for blacks, with the exception of Decatur, which was clearly ranked highest. Given that a similar proportion of blacks viewed the remaining five areas as desirable, black evaluations of the suburbs did not appear to explain residential segregation in Atlanta.

Racial differences in the evaluation of the attractiveness of some areas clearly existed. Whites evaluated the fast-growing, predominantly white northern suburbs more highly than did blacks, while blacks evaluated the areas having a greater representation of blacks more highly than did whites.

Some interesting observations arise from the responses by income group (see table 5.2):

- The desirability of Decatur among blacks is relatively stable across income groups. However, the desirability of Decatur among whites falls steadily with increases in income; nearly 72 percent of white respondents with household incomes of $15,000 or less ranked Decatur as desirable, compared with only 42.2 percent from households with income of $60,000 or more.

- A similar observation is made for the Tri-Cities. Desirability among blacks is relatively stable across income groups, but declines among whites as income increases. Slightly more than half (52.3 percent) of white respondents from households with incomes of $15,000 or less ranked the Tri-Cities as desirable, compared with 16.2 percent from white households with incomes of $60,000 or more.

- Regardless of race, popularity of the northernmost areas is relatively stable across income groups.

- Midtown is ranked more highly by blacks than whites across income groups. However, it is rated the least desirable area by blacks for all income categories.

The popularity of the northern suburbs among whites is most likely attributable to the predominance of whites, rapid job growth, availability of newer housing, existence of higher-income families, and good quality schools. Decatur, Midtown, and Tri-Cities are probably not as highly ranked by whites because of a relatively high percentage of black residents, a lack of newer housing, and education quality below that in the northern suburbs. Blacks may give relatively high rankings to these areas because they are viewed as feasible alternatives to living in the central city, despite being older areas.

Attitudes of Existing Neighborhood Residents Toward a New Black Neighbor   Black families may avoid seeking housing in certain

TABLE 5.2   *Percentage of Respondents Ranking Location as a "Very Desirable" or "Somewhat Desirable" Place to Reside by Race and Income Group*

Decatur	Blacks	Whites	Marietta-Smyrna	Blacks	Whites
<$15,000	88.1	71.9	<$15,000	78.1	83.2
$15,001–$30,000	88.2	58.1	$15,001–$30,000	82.4	84.5
$30,001–$45,000	75.9	55.3	$30,001–$45,000	80.0	80.0
$45,001–$60,000	87.5	45.7	$45,001–$60,000	72.5	88.0
>$60,000	88.6	42.2	>$60,000	71.9	80.4

Midtown	Blacks	Whites	Roswell-Alpharetta	Blacks	Whites
<$15,000	70.6	52.3	<$15,000	77	85.4
$15,001–$30,000	70.2	46.3	$15,001–$30,000	77.9	84.8
$30,001–$45,000	58.8	36.7	$30,001–$45,000	73.1	87.3
$45,001–$60,000	64.9	51.5	$45,001–$60,000	71.8	80.8
>$60,000	57.1	36.1	>$60,000	74.2	89.4

Tri-Cities	Blacks	Whites	Norcross	Blacks	Whites
<$15,000	83.4	52.3	<$15,000	74.9	81.6
$15,001–$30,000	72.8	37.6	$15,001–$30,000	77.3	77.5
$30,001–$45,000	71.3	33	$30,001–$45,000	71.1	78.9
$45,001–$60,000	74.4	22.2	$45,001–$60,000	72.5	75.3
>$60,000	71.9	16.2	>$60,000	80.6	75.7

Source: Greater Atlanta Neighborhood Study 1994.

neighborhoods because they fear that white residents may be disturbed or upset by their arrival. Furthermore, they may fear the possible repercussions from upsetting white neighbors, ranging from a general sense that blacks are unwelcome to the potential for hostile acts. Survey respondents were asked to answer the following question about a particular area: "If a black family moved into that area, do you think they would be welcome, or do you think that people already living there would be upset?" Respondents were not given an opportunity to specify the degree of welcome.

Blacks and whites indicated that the residents in the three northern suburbs would be more likely to be upset by the arrival of a black family, compared with the three areas with a higher existing proportion of black residents (see figure 5.6). In five of the six locations, blacks saw the probability of an "upset" reaction to a black family moving in as being much higher than did whites. The exception was Decatur, the most integrated area of the six.

Summary Responses Regarding Perceptions and Information   Information on housing costs, black financial capabilities, the desirability

FIGURE 5.6   *Percentage of Respondents Indicating That Current Residents Would Be Upset If a Black Moved In, For Select Locations*

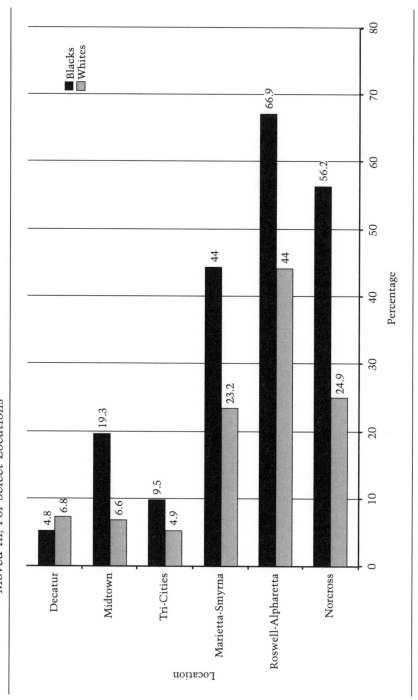

Source: Greater Atlanta Neighborhood Study 1994.
Note: The denominator for each percentage is the total black or white population.

of suburban areas, and the response of current suburban residents to new black neighbors was used to assess the hypothesis that racial differences in perceptions of and information about suburban areas contributes to residential segregation. Survey responses provide some support for the hypothesis. First, both races appear to share similar information by indicating that the predominantly white areas of Roswell-Alpharetta and Norcross were least affordable for blacks, and the areas with the highest proportions of black residents (Decatur and Tri-Cities) were most affordable. Second, while blacks view the three northern suburbs as being similarly desirable, a greater proportion of whites gave a "desirable" response to these locations. Desirability of the three areas with the greatest proportion of black residents is much greater among blacks in comparison with whites. Thus, racial differences in the perceived desirability of various locations provide some support for the hypothesis as well. Third, the hypothesis is supported by the feeling expressed by many blacks that current residents of the majority white suburbs would be upset by the entrance of a black family into the area.

Hypothesis 3: Perceptions Among Blacks Regarding Institutional Barriers in Atlanta's Housing Market

Another potential explanation for continuing residential segregation is a possible perception among blacks that institutional barriers exist that prevent them from feasibly seeking housing in predominantly white suburban areas. A question in the GANS asked how frequently (using a 4-point scale ranging from "very often" to "almost never") blacks "miss out" on good housing opportunities due to the practices of real estate agents, the practices of banks who lend money to purchase homes, and the actions of whites in terms of their willingness to sell or rent to blacks. Responses by race are provided in figure 5.7.

Relatively large racial differences in perceptions of institutional barriers for blacks exist. Regarding the possibility that whites will not sell or rent homes to blacks, 93 percent of blacks felt that this occurred "very often" or "sometimes," compared with 63.6 percent of whites. Blacks also perceived the practices of real estate agents as a more serious problem than did whites. Among blacks, 89 percent believed that blacks miss out on good housing because real estate agents will not show, rent, or sell homes to blacks. Only 48.6 percent of whites indicated the same. Discriminatory lenders are perceived as a problem by 91.1 percent of blacks, compared with only 49.2 percent of whites.

The large racial differences in perceptions regarding the existence of various institutional barriers may be explained by a feeling among

FIGURE 5.7   *Perceptions of Institutional Barriers Preventing Blacks from Getting Good Housing*

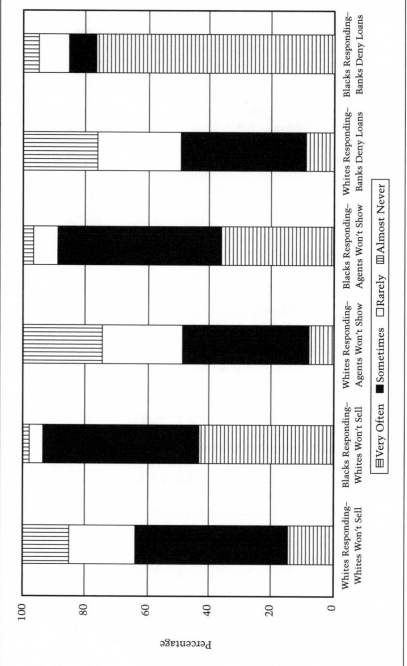

Source: Greater Atlanta Neighborhood Study 1994.

whites that public policy enacted to alleviate discrimination has been successful in breaking down these barriers. While whites are likely to agree that blacks confront discrimination from individual whites, they believe that protective laws prevent any large-scale or collective discrimination from limiting good housing opportunities.

Whether or not they are accurate, perceptions that institutional barriers exist will likely contribute to residential segregation. While many blacks may be able to afford residences in predominantly white suburban areas, they may avoid seeking housing there because they fear discrimination on as many as three fronts. If they find a nondiscriminatory real estate agent, they may face a discriminatory owner. If they do not encounter problems with a real estate agent or a property owner, they still face the possibility of problems with a discriminatory lender. Taken together, blacks may see these potential discriminatory acts as being formidable barriers to moving to the suburban ring. Whites, on the other hand, may not perceive institutional discrimination as a serious problem, and would likely not be supportive of new efforts to promote equal opportunity for blacks in the Atlanta metropolitan area housing market.

Hypothesis 4: Racial Differences in Residential Preferences

Chapter 4 of this volume contains an extensive discussion of racial differences in residential preferences using questions from the GANS. Given the coverage in the previous chapter, I provide only a condensed reference to that discussion.

Black Residential Preferences   The responses to questions seeking to determine the residential preferences of blacks suggest that blacks are willing to move into neighborhoods with a greater degree of integration in comparison with what currently exists. This is notably true among those blacks who are younger, more educated, and wealthier. Examples of this include the response that, in general, a majority of blacks express a preference for integrated, but majority black neighborhoods. Furthermore, an overwhelming number of respondents indicated that they would move into neighborhoods ranging from all black up to and including a neighborhood with a majority of whites. However, only about 50 percent indicated a willingness to move into an all white neighborhood, most indicating that they would not feel comfortable. The good news in these responses is that as education and income levels among blacks increase, greater residential integration may occur.

White Residential Preferences   Questions designed to determine the residential preferences of whites indicate that while whites are accepting of a greater degree of integration, whites exhibit a lower preference for integration relative to blacks. While greater than 90 percent of white respondents indicate that they would feel comfortable living in a neighborhood with one black household, the "comfort level" declines rapidly with increases in the proportion of black households in a neighborhood.

The responses by whites reveal that only a very few (less than 2 percent) would try to move out of a neighborhood with one black family. Again, the proportion of whites responding that they would move out of the neighborhood increases with increases in the proportion of black families living in that neighborhood. When whites were asked why they would try to move out of a particular neighborhood, concerns over falling property values was the reason most often expressed. A small proportion of whites indicated that they would not move into a neighborhood with one black household assuming that they had been looking for a house and found one that they could afford. Consistent with the other evidence concerning white residential preferences, the proportion of those who would not move into a particular neighborhood increases with increase in black representation.

Considering the response of blacks and whites regarding their residential preferences, it appears that blacks have a stronger willingness than do whites for living in integrated neighborhoods. While a mass exodus of whites would not occur as blacks move into their neighborhoods, the majority (more than 60 percent) of whites would not consider moving into a neighborhood that has an approximate equal number of black and white households. Given the response of whites, integration of neighborhoods does not appear to represent a stable equilibrium. The responses suggest that an expanding number of whites will leave neighborhoods as they become increasingly integrated, thus the number of integrated neighborhoods will be small.

Conclusion

Understanding the causes of residential segregation in Atlanta will put policy makers in a better position to take actions to continue the progress toward integration that took place during the 1980s. The potential for integration exists. The evidence suggests that economic factors are not a significant contributor to existing housing segregation in Atlanta. And there is no compelling evidence to suggest that segregation results from racial differences in information regarding average housing costs. There is evidence, however, suggesting that a feeling exists among many blacks that current residents of the predominantly white northern suburbs would be upset by new black residents. Black perceptions of the existence of institutional barriers to getting good housing provide an even stronger explanation for segregation. Differing residential preferences between blacks and whites also appear to play a role. It seems there is some hope for successful integration, however. While many whites expressed an unwillingness to move into a neighborhood with a mix of black and white households, a relatively small proportion would try to move out of a racially mixed neighborhood, even one with an equal number of blacks and whites.

To correct the problem of residential segregation in Atlanta and other metropolitan areas, Massey and Denton (1993) offer several possible policy options, all at the federal level. These include:

- Provision of increased funding from the U.S. Department of Housing and Urban Development (HUD) to local fair housing organizations to enhance the capability to investigate and prosecute individual housing discrimination complaints.
- Establishment of a HUD program to identify real estate brokers who commit discriminatory acts.
- Use existing data to monitor lenders and ensure compliance with fair housing laws.
- Expansion of HUD efforts to provide subsidized housing vouchers to blacks who get housing via the private market. This should be done in conjunction with a shift away from public housing construction in central cities, which reinforces segregation.
- Promotion of swift enforcement measures and judicial action against violators of the Fair Housing Act.
- Prosecution of perpetrators of hate crimes against blacks who move into white neighborhoods at the federal level under civil rights laws.
- Provision of wider minority access to multiple listing services that provide comprehensive listings of available properties for sale.
- Establishment of HUD training programs for realtors in fair housing practices and procedures.

Local efforts may also include training real estate agents and lenders in fair housing procedures and informing them of blacks' fears of discrimination. Additionally, there is a role for private organizations with a mission to help eliminate residential segregation (Freiberg 1993).

The devastating effects of residential segregation fall directly on blacks and indirectly, to one degree or another, on everyone. The information obtained through the Greater Atlanta Neighborhood Study sheds important light on the causes of residential segregation.

References

Bayor, Ronald H. 1996. *Race and the Shaping of Twentieth-Century Atlanta.* Chapel Hill and London: University of North Carolina Press.

Chicago Commission on Race Relations. 1922. *The Negro on Chicago: A Study of Race Relations and a Race Riot.* Chicago: University of Chicago.

Clay, Phillip L. 1979. "The Process of Black Suburbanization." *Urban Affairs Quarterly* 14(4): 405–24.

Committee on Civil Rights. 1947. *To Secure These Rights.* Washington: U.S. Government Printing Office.

Cutler, David M., and Edward L. Glaeser. 1997. "Are Ghettos Good or Bad?" *Quarterly Journal of Economics* 112(3): 827–72.

Darden, Joe T. 1995. "Black Residential Segregation Since the 1948 *Shelley v. Kraemer* Decision." *Journal of Black Studies* 25(6): 680–91.

Farley, Reynolds, and William H. Frey. 1994. "Changes in the Segregation of Whites from Blacks During the 1980s: Small Steps Toward a More Integrated Society." *American Sociological Review* 59: 23–45.

Freiberg, Fred. 1993. "Promoting Residential Integration: The Role of Private Fair Housing Groups." In *Housing Markets and Residential Mobility,* edited by G. Thomas Kingsley and Margery Austin Turner. Washington, D.C.: Urban Institute Press.

Holzer, Harry J. 1991. "The Spatial Mismatch Hypothesis: What Has the Evidence Shown?" *Urban Studies* 28: 105–22.

Ihlanfeldt, Keith R. 1992. *Job Accessibility and the Employment and School Enrollment of Teenagers.* Kalamazoo, Mich.: Upjohn Institute for Employment Research.

Ihlanfeldt, Keith R., and David L. Sjoquist. 1998. "The Spatial Mismatch Hypothesis: A Review of Recent Studies." *Housing Policy Debate* 9(4): 849–92.

Jencks, Christopher, and Susan E. Mayer. 1990a. "The Social Consequences of Growing Up in a Poor Neighborhood." In *Inner-City Poverty in the United States,* edited by Laurence E. Lynn, Jr., and Michael G. H. McGreary. Washington, D.C.: National Academy Press.

———. 1990b. "Residential Segregation, Job Proximity, and Black Job Opportunities." In *Inner-City Poverty in the United States,* edited by Laurence E. Lynn, Jr., and Michael G. H. McGreary. Washington, D.C.: National Academy Press.

Kain, John F. 1968. "Housing Segregation, Negro Employment, and Metropolitan Decentralization." *Quarterly Journal of Economics* 82: 175–97.

———. 1992. "The Spatial Mismatch Hypothesis Three Decades Later." *Housing Policy Debate.* Washington, D.C.: Fannie Mae.

Logan, John R., and Mark Schneider. 1984. "Racial Segregation and Racial Change in American Suburbs: 1970–1980." *Demography* 19: 874–88.

Massey, Douglas S., and Nancy A. Denton. 1989. "Hypersegregation in

U.S. Metropolitan Areas: Black and Hispanic Segregation Along Five Dimensions." *Demography* 26(3): 373–91.

———. 1993. *American Apartheid: Segregation and the Making of the Underclass*. Cambridge, Mass.: Harvard University Press.

Myrdal, Gunnar. 1944. *An American Dilemma: The Negro Population and Modern Democracy*. New York: Random House.

Orfeld, Gary. 1992. "Urban Schooling and the Perpetuation of Job Inequality in Metropolitan Chicago." In *Urban Labor Markets and Job Opportunity*, edited by George Peterson and Wayne Vrooman. Washington, D.C.: Urban Institute Press.

Schneider, Mark, and John R. Logan. 1982. "Suburban Racial Segregation and Black Access to Local Public Resources." *Social Science Quarterly* 63: 762–70.

Strahura, J. M. 1986. "Suburban Development, Black Suburbanization and the Civil Rights Movement Since World War II." *American Sociological Review* 51: 131–44.

Thompson, Mark A. 1997. "The Impact of Spatial Mismatch on Female Labor Force Participation." *Economic Development Quarterly* 11(2): 138–45.

U.S. Department of Commerce, Bureau of the Census. 1993. *Census of Population and Housing: 1990*. Public Use Microdata Samples. Washington: U.S. Government Printing Office.

Wilson, William Julius. 1987. *The Truly Disadvantaged: The Inner City, the Underclass, and Public Policy*. Chicago: University of Chicago Press.

6

THE GEOGRAPHIC MISMATCH BETWEEN JOBS AND HOUSING

Keith R. Ihlanfeldt and David L. Sjoquist

A AS EARLIER chapters have made clear, the Atlanta area has experienced substantial increases in employment, but mostly in the suburbs. Low-skilled blacks, however, have been confined largely to the central city. Thus, one possible explanation for the Atlanta paradox is the "spatial mismatch" that exists between the location of jobs and the residences of low-skilled minority workers.

This chapter focuses on the spatial mismatch hypothesis as a possible explanation for the Atlanta paradox. Most of the research is based on an analysis of data contained in the Greater Atlanta Neighborhood Study (see the appendix to chapter 1 for a description of GANS). The evidence includes an analysis of a special set of questions included in the GANS that deal with the factors that may account for the inability of blacks to secure suburban jobs.

Spatial Mismatch in Atlanta

Atlanta, which has a majority black central city, is a highly racially segregated community (Farley and Frey 1992), and the level and rate of low-skill job decentralization are among the highest in the nation (Kasarda 1985). (Chapter 2 provides evidence regarding the housing patterns of minorities and the spatial distribution of new jobs.) Moreover, in contrast to almost all other metropolitan areas, public transportation is virtually nonexistent within Atlanta's suburbs. Only three of the twenty counties that constitute the metro area have any public transportation.

There are at least four reasons why a lack of job access in the physical sense—that is, long distances to travel to get to available jobs—can result in poor labor market outcomes for minorities. These causes can also be seen as barriers to be overcome in order to reduce or eliminate the problems associated with spatial mismatch. First, poor job access may be associated with possible commuting difficulties. For inner-city, low-skilled workers, the additional cost associated with commuting to suburban jobs might exceed the benefits they would gain from doing so. Or, because of the absence of public transit, it may be impossible for inner-city, low-skilled workers to make the trip. Second, information about job openings and the ability to conduct effective job searches, may decrease the farther away one lives from the job site. (Chapter 10 discusses the job search process of lower-skilled minority workers.) Third, it is possible that suburban employers or suburban customers are more discriminatory against black workers than are central-city employers. For example, firms that practice racial discrimination may be more likely to be located in the suburbs, away from high concentrations of minority workers. Fourth is the problem of social distance. Inner-city minorities may be uncomfortable working in a suburban firm with a largely white, suburban workforce, or may fear that they will not be treated properly in such settings.

We now turn to a discussion of the evidence of a spatial mismatch problem in Atlanta, and the causes of and barriers to overcoming access to jobs.

The Existence of a
Spatial Mismatch Problem

One of the implications of the spatial mismatch hypothesis is that wage rates within the suburban labor market should rise above those paid in the central city. There are two possible reasons for this. First, if jobs (demand for workers) suburbanize to a greater extent than workers (labor supply), then there will exist a relative surplus of workers within the central city. The result will be downward pressure on wages in the central city and upward pressure in the suburbs. In addition, if employers are prejudiced, then the relatively large black labor supply in the central city will require a lower black-to-white wage ratio in the central city if employers are to hire blacks. If employers have a preference for hiring whites, then blacks will have to settle for lower wages in order to offset employers' aversion to hiring blacks (Becker 1971).

Analysis of intrametropolitan variations in earnings in Atlanta provides strong support for the notion that suburban employers in Atlanta pay higher wages (Ihlanfeldt 1988; Ihlanfeldt and Young 1994). It is important to recognize that the demography of particular suburban areas may differ markedly not only from the central city, but also from other suburban areas. In comparison to the south side of the city and the southern suburbs, the north side of the city and the northern suburbs are much more affluent, are considerably less black, and have experienced unprecedented job growth, both unskilled and skilled (see chapter 2). Restrictions on the residential and work locations of black and less-educated workers have resulted in wages that are markedly higher in the northern suburbs. For example, Ihlanfeldt and Young (1994) found that within the northern suburbs, fast-food restaurant workers earned about 20 percent more than their counterparts working in downtown Atlanta.

Black wages are also lower at establishments that draw more white customers, which lends support to the consumer discrimination hypothesis. That hypothesis argues that if white customers are less likely to frequent businesses with minority employees, then the business would hire only minority workers at lower wage rates in order to offset the loss in sales revenues (Becker 1971). What seems to happen, though, is that labor shortages in the northern suburbs have a positive effect on blacks' wages that more than offsets any negative effect resulting from customer discrimination.

There is no doubt that spatial mismatch is a problem in Atlanta. To develop policies that can effectively deal with it, factors accounting for its existence or persistence must be determined. We turn to a discussion of those factors.

Factors Accounting for Spatial Mismatch

Spatial mismatch can be eliminated by lower-skilled jobs coming back into the central city, by lower-skilled workers moving to the suburbs, or by lower-skilled workers commuting from the central city to suburban jobs. No evidence exists on why employers do not move into the city of Atlanta to take advantage of the relatively low wages paid to lower-skilled workers. Evidence does exist, however, on why residential relocation or reverse-commuting fail to eliminate Atlanta's spatial mismatch problem.

Beginning with commuting, as noted, there are several reasons why the number of central city blacks that travel to the suburbs to work may be too small to eliminate spatial mismatch: high commuting costs, poor information about suburban jobs, greater hiring discrimination in the suburbs, and social distance. Keith R. Ihlanfeldt and Madelyn V. Young (1996) have used their data on Atlanta's fast-food restaurant workers to analyze why the typical central city restaurant has a workforce that contains a higher percentage of blacks than the typical suburban restaurant. The following factors were considered: percent of customers who are white (to measure customer discrimination); race of the manager (to measure employer discrimination); whether the restaurant is within walking distance of a public transit stop; and the restaurant's distance from the center of the metro area (a proxy for distance from black residences).

Of these variables, transit appears to be the most important factor in explaining why more blacks do not have jobs in suburban fast-food restaurants. Thirty-five percent of the city-suburban difference in black employment share in these restaurants can be attributed to the greater likelihood that the suburban firms are not within walking distance of public transit. This result is not surprising, since inner-city blacks are heavily dependent on public transit. According to the 1990 census, 39 percent of the black households living within the city of Atlanta had no car at home for use by household members. Other important contributors to the city-suburban difference in black employment share are distance from downtown (explains 33 percent of the difference), race of the manager (15 percent), and percent of white customers (14 percent).

Another possible barrier that may explain the persistence of spatial mismatch, as noted, is that inner-city residents may have poor information about job opportunities farther from home (Ihlanfeldt 1997). Respondents in the household component of GANS were shown a map of the Atlanta region that identified six employment centers: Marietta-Smyrna, Roswell-Alpharetta, Norcross, Midtown, Decatur, and the Tri-Cities area (see map 1.1). The first three areas are major employment centers located in the northern suburbs, Midtown is a rapidly developing area just north of the central business district, and Decatur and the Tri-Cities area are in the southern suburbs. Respondents were asked two questions: "Which area has the fewest job opportunities or openings for a person without a college degree?" And, "Of these six areas, which one do you believe has the most job opportunities or openings for a person without a college degree?"

Three methods were employed to obtain "true" job availability rankings of the six areas: (1) managers of the five public employment offices located within the study area were separately interviewed and asked to rank the six areas in terms of the number of available jobs for people without college degrees; (2) employment data from the 1990 Public Use Microdata Sample (PUMS) and the Atlanta Regional Commission were used to compute the change in the number of jobs not requiring a college degree for each of the six areas for the three-year period preceding the GANS household survey, and; (3) the Multi-City Study of Urban Inequality Employer Survey was used to compute an average job vacancy rate for each area relevant to less educated workers. (See the

TABLE 6.1   *Rankings of Employment Centers Based on the Number
of Job Opportunities for Workers Without College
Degrees*

	Manager Number					Change in Jobs 1990 to 1993	Job Vacancy Rate
	(1)	(2)	(3)	(4)	(5)		
Roswell-Alpharetta	1	2	1	1	1	6501 (31.8)[a]	.117 [19][b]
Marietta-Smyrna	2	1	3	2	3	2967 (3.7)	.041 [54]
Norcross	3	3	2	3	2	3756 (7.8)	.007 [30]
Decatur	4	4	5	4	5	−582 (−9.0)	n.a.
Midtown	5	5	4	5	4	132 (0.6)	.002 [14]
Tri-Cities	6	6	6	6	6	−1420 (−6.0)	.005 [9]

Source: Interviews with managers of state employment offices and employment data from the Atlanta Regional Commission and the Multi-City Study of Urban Inequality Survey of Employers.
[a]Numbers in parentheses are percentage changes.
[b]The numbers in brackets are the number of sampled firms located in each area.

appendix to chapter 1 for a brief discussion of the Employer Survey.) The results from these methods are reported in table 6.1. The ranking of areas is remarkably similar across methods, with Roswell-Alpharetta having the most opportunities and the Tri-Cities area the fewest. As alluded to earlier, the northern suburbs of Atlanta have particularly rich employment opportunities for less educated workers. In addition to Roswell-Alpharetta, the other two northern suburban areas (Marietta-Smyrna and Norcross) are consistently ranked higher than the other areas.

The rankings of both black and white respondents differed markedly from the true rankings, indicating that both groups are poorly informed regarding the whereabouts of available jobs. For example, blacks most frequently listed Roswell-Alpharetta as having the fewest opportunities, when in fact it has the most opportunities, while whites most frequently ranked the Tri-Cities area as having the most opportunities, when in fact it has the fewest. Particularly revealing are the findings that only 19.9 percent of blacks and 27.1 percent of whites named a northern employment center as having the most opportunities, despite the phenomenal job growth that has occurred on the north side of the Atlanta region.

Another interesting finding is that neither educational level nor employment status has much of an effect on the respondent's knowledge of the labor market. Even among the group that has the most to gain from labor market information—namely, those who are unemployed and without bachelor's degrees—only 26.2 percent of blacks and 34.4 percent of whites are aware of the north side advantage.

To investigate why blacks are found to have somewhat poorer labor market information than whites, regression models were estimated in order to uncover the factors that might explain the respondent's knowledge of the labor market. Explanatory variables, which were selected based upon a theoretical model that relates knowledge acquisition to its costs and benefits, included the race, educational level, labor market experience, and sex of the respondent. Also included were the residential location of the respondent (city, northern suburbs, or southern suburbs) and the poverty rate of his or her neighborhood.

The regression results were used to develop an equation to explain differences in labor market knowledge between whites and blacks as a function of the racial differences in the mean values of the independent variables and their estimated coefficients. This equation reveals that *all* of the black-white difference in knowledge can be attributed to racial differences in residential location: blacks are 6.5 times more likely than whites to live within the central city (Ihlanfeldt 1997). The estimated coefficient on race in the knowledge equations is insignificant; thus race per se does not appear to play a role in explaining black-white differences. The results suggest that lack of information is an important cause of spatial mismatch.

Another possible barrier preventing blacks from taking suburban jobs is that they may be reluctant to search for a job in white areas because they believe they will not be socially accepted. The GANS is used to investigate this hypothesis (Sjoquist 1996). For the same six employment centers for which respondents were asked to assess the number of job opportunities, they were asked whether they had searched for a job in each area and whether they thought residents of the area would be upset if a black were to move in. It is necessary to infer that if the respondent thought that residents of an area would be upset if a black moved in, then the respondent would believe that a workplace in that neighborhood would not be a welcoming place for blacks, either.

Table 6.2 shows for each area the percentage of blacks who responded that the residents would be upset if a black household moved into the area, and the percentage indicating they had searched for work in the area. The sample is restricted to blacks with a high school degree or less who searched for a job within the previous year. Generally, the percentage of blacks who searched an area increases as the percentage of blacks who say that blacks would not be welcomed decreases. The numbers in the table support the hypothesis that the degree of social acceptability is a cause of the perpetuation of spatial mismatch.

TABLE 6.2   *Treatment of Blacks and Search Patterns*

(1) Job Site	(2) Percentage Saying Residents Would Be Upset	(3) Percentage Searched Job Site
Decatur	5.12	63.9
Tri-Cities	7.58	33.0
Midtown	21.80	48.4
Marietta-Smyrna	49.76	25.8
Norcross	61.06	20.6
Roswell-Alpharetta	73.68	30.9

Source: Greater Atlanta Neighborhood Study 1994.

To further explore the social-acceptance hypothesis, the same sample was used to estimate regression models that explained whether the respondent had searched for work in each of the six areas. Explanatory variables included the respondent's perception of the area's social acceptance of blacks, distance of the area from the respondent's home, and the respondent's assessment of the number of job opportunities in the area.

The measure of social acceptability is found to have a strong effect on whether an area is searched, providing strong support for the hypothesis that social acceptability is important in explaining spatial mismatch. Also as expected, blacks were found to have a lower probability of searching more distant areas and areas they felt would offer relatively few jobs for people without college degrees.

Another cause of spatial mismatch lies in employers' willingness to hire central-city minorities. The Employer Survey can be used to examine the factors that explain the racial composition of the workforce of the individual firm, which is similar to the analysis of Ihlanfeldt and Young (1996).

The Employer Survey for Atlanta includes a representative sample of 800 firms. Among the information obtained from the individual responsible for hiring at each firm were the characteristics of the most recently filled job in the establishment and the characteristics of the worker hired into that job. These data were employed to estimate the probability that the last worker hired was black (Holzer and Ihlanfeldt 1996). Following Ihlanfeldt and Young (1996), the explanatory variables included the firm's distance from a public transit stop, the distance the firm is located from the average black residence relative to the average white residence, the racial composition of the firm's customers, and the race of the respondent. An extensive set of firm-specific and job-specific independent variables was included as controls.

The regression results were used to analyze why blacks are less likely to be hired into a suburban than central city job opening. Roughly 34 percent of this difference is attributable to the relatively greater distances suburban firms are located from black in comparison to white residences. Also important are proximity to public transit (21 percent) and the race of the customers (18 percent). These results, obtained for a large and representative sample of Atlanta employers, are similar to those obtained using the sample of Atlanta fast-food restaurants (Ihlanfeldt and Young 1996). Both underscore the importance of hiring discrimination and poor proximity to public transit as barriers to greater employment of blacks among suburban firms.

To further understand the factors that limit black employment in high-growth suburban areas, a set of questions was included in the GANS that appeared only on the Atlanta Household Survey. These questions allow us to explore the permanency of the spatial mismatch. In particular, we can focus on why minorities tend not to move closer to suburban employment centers, and why they do not search or take jobs in these areas more often.

The set of questions begins with one asking respondents to name the areas with the fewest and the most job opportunities for people without a college degree. If the home of the respondent is not located in the area that he or she designates as having the most job opportunities, two sets of additional questions are asked. In the first, five possible reasons are offered for why the respondent may not wish to move to the area with the most opportunities (see table 6.3). Agreement with each reason is elicited using a 4-point scale: strongly agrees (1), somewhat agrees (2), moderately disagrees (3), or strongly disagrees (4). In the second set, respondents are asked: "If you were looking for a job and continued to live where you do now, would you take a job in _____?" listing the area that the respondent mentioned as having the most job opportunities. If the answer is no, agreement with three possible reasons for being unwilling to take a job in the area is elicited, where agreement is limited to a "yes" response (see table 6.4), but "yes" may be given to more than one reason.

Mean scores for the first set of questions are reported in table 6.3, broken down by race and the area designated as having the most opportunities. In light of the aforementioned differences in employment opportunity between the northern suburban areas (Marietta-Smyrna, Roswell-Alpharetta, and Norcross) and the other areas (Midtown, Decatur, and Tri-Cities), the results are discussed separately. Blacks most

TABLE 6.3   *Reasons for Not Wishing to Move to Area with Most Job Opportunities (Lower Score Indicates Higher Agreement)*

	Marietta-Symrna	Roswell-Alpharetta	Norcross	Midtown	Decatur	Tri-Cities
The cost of living is too high for me to move there						
Blacks	2.1	1.8	2.1	2.1	2.8	3.0
Whites	2.7	2.1	2.9	2.6	2.5	3.4
I wouldn't move there because I would be too far away from my friends and relatives						
Blacks	1.9	1.8	2.2	2.3	2.6	3.0
Whites	2.3	2.7	2.7	2.5	2.6	2.3
I wouldn't move there because public transit is not available there						
Blacks	2.0	2.0	1.9	3.2	3.2	3.1
Whites	2.7	3.3	3.1	3.5	3.2	3.4
I wouldn't move there because I wouldn't be accepted by residents						
Blacks	2.7	2.2	2.5	2.9	3.4	3.5
Whites	3.2	3.6	3.4	3.2	2.9	3.1
Moving there wouldn't make any difference in my getting one of the jobs there, or a better job						
Blacks	2.2	2.4	2.3	2.1	2.2	2.3
Whites	2.1	2.2	2.2	2.1	2.1	2.2

Source: Greater Atlanta Neighborhood Study 1994.

frequently agree with the following reasons for not moving to the northern suburbs: the cost of living is too high there, the areas are too far away from friends and relatives, and public transportation is not available. The level of agreement with these three reasons is pretty much the same. In contrast, whites are much less likely to agree with these reasons as explanations for their possible unwillingness to move to the northern suburbs. Also, while blacks agree less with the reason that not being socially accepted keeps them from moving, they do frequently cite this as a reason, especially for not moving to Roswell-Alpharetta. In

TABLE 6.4   Reasons for Not Taking a Job in Area with Most Job
            Opportunities (Percentage Indicating Agreement)

	Marietta-Smyrna	Roswell-Alpharetta	Norcross	Midtown	Decatur	Tri-Cities
The commuting time would be too long						
Blacks	78.6	100.0	84.2	70.4	66.7	50.0
Whites	100.0	80.0	100.0	70.0	85.7	80.0
You think employers would discriminate against you						
Blacks	38.5	50.0	44.4	36.0	22.2	37.5
Whites	00.0	00.0	00.0	00.0	14.3	4.5
There isn't good public transportation from your home to the area						
Blacks	78.6	90.0	78.9	53.8	87.5	37.5
Whites	75.0	20.0	25.0	35.0	14.3	24.4
Percentage who said they would continue to live where they do now and take a job in the area						
Blacks	57.1	59.3	61.7	80.3	83.3	86.7
Whites	68.8	68.8	80.6	71.8	64.0	57.1

Source: Greater Atlanta Neighborhood Study 1994.

contrast, very few whites agree that this reason keeps them from moving to the northern suburbs.

Regarding the other geographic areas, these reasons for not moving receive less agreement from blacks. This is particularly true for Decatur and the Tri-Cities areas. In contrast to the northern suburbs, blacks believe that the latter two areas offer a lower cost of living, greater proximity to friends and relatives, and less resistance to blacks moving in. These results are not surprising, since Decatur and the Tri-Cities areas contain higher fractions of black residents and lower-priced homes than the northern suburbs. Whites' levels of agreement with all these reasons varies little between the northern suburbs and the other areas.

Table 6.4 reports the percentages of blacks and whites who agreed with the reasons listed for not taking a job in the area they felt offered the most job opportunities, assuming that they continued to live where they do now. Once again, separate columns of responses are given for each of the six areas. Over 75 percent of the black respondents agreed that commuting time would be too long and that public transportation was inadequate for them to take a job in the northern suburbs. Smaller percentages, but still substantial in magnitude (40 to 50 percent), agreed that employer discrimination was keeping them from taking a job in the northern suburbs. Whites also felt that commuting time was a problem, but none agreed that discrimination was a factor and few agreed that their unwillingness to commute was related to poor public transit.

In comparison to the northern suburbs, blacks less frequently agreed that commuting time, employer discrimination, or poor public transit would keep them from taking a job in the other areas. White responses show little difference between north-side and other areas, except that some whites agreed they would not take a job in Decatur or the Tri-Cities area because of employer discrimination.

Black responses to the reasons listed for being unwilling to take a job in the northern suburbs reinforce the conclusion that a combination of barriers is responsible for the perpetuation of spatial mismatch. While poor information about suburban job openings may be an important factor, the results presented in table 6.4 indicate that, even among blacks who are well informed, concerns over commuting and employer discrimination keep them from taking suburban jobs.

The recent studies on Atlanta that have been conducted with GANS and Employer Survey data provide important new evidence on the factors perpetuating the spatial mismatch labor market disequilibrium. They suggest that a combination of barriers, rather than any single factor, keeps blacks from obtaining suburban jobs.

Conclusion

The problem of spatial mismatch in Atlanta is certainly one of the causes of the Atlanta paradox. Lower-skilled, central-city minorities have not benefited from the rapid economic growth experienced in Atlanta because they have limited access to these new job opportunities.

In this chapter, the focus has been on spatial variation in the employment and earnings of lower-skilled minorities. Another type of variation in employment and earnings that may be relevant to the Atlanta paradox is among workers with different levels of human capital. The next chapter takes up this issue.

References

Becker, Gary S. 1971. *The Economics of Discrimination.* Chicago: University of Chicago Press.

Farley, Reynolds, and William H. Frey. 1992. "Changes in the Segregation of Whites from Blacks During the 1980s: Small Steps Toward a More Residentially Integrated Society." Paper no. 92-257. Population Studies Center, University of Michigan.

Holzer, Harry J., and Keith R. Ihlanfeldt. 1996. "Spatial Factors and the Employment of Blacks at the Firm Level." *New England Economics Review*, Federal Reserve Bank of Boston. May/June, Special Issue:65–82.

Ihlanfeldt, Keith R. 1988. "Intra-Metropolitan Variation in Earnings and Labor Market Discrimination: An Econometric Analysis of the Atlanta Labor Market." *Southern Economic Journal* 55(1):123–40.

———. 1997. "Information on the Spatial Distribution of Job Opportunities Within Metropolitan Areas." *Journal of Urban Economics* 41:218–42.

Ihlanfeldt, Keith R. and Madelyn V. Young. 1994. "Housing Segregation and the Wages and Commutes of Urban Blacks: The Case of Atlanta Fast-Food Restaurant Workers." *Review of Economics and Statistics* (August):425–33.

———. 1996. "The Spatial Distribution of Black Employment Between the Central City and the Suburbs." *Economic Inquiry* 64:613–707.

Sjoquist, David L. 1996. "Spatial Mismatch and Social Acceptability." Working paper, Policy Research Center, Georgia State University.

7

EARNINGS INEQUALITY

Keith R. Ihlanfeldt and David L. Sjoquist

CCOMPANYING Atlanta's substantial growth in employment and
population has been substantial growth in income. Over the
past forty years, the ratio of median family income for the Atlanta MSA to that for the United States increased from near unity (1.02)
to 1.20 while the median income for black families in the city of Atlanta relative to the U.S. median family income for all families was essentially unchanged. This has led to substantial differences within the
Atlanta area in family income by geographic area and by race. Perhaps
most remarkable is the racial difference in median family income
within the city of Atlanta—$59,133 for white families but only $18,451
for black families in 1989. Also noteworthy is that at the metropolitan
level, the ratio of median black family income to median white family
income was essentially unchanged between 1979 and 1989. The persistence of substantial racial differences in income despite Atlanta's phenomenal growth in both employment and in real income constitute an
important dimension of the Atlanta paradox.

This chapter focuses on differences in earnings between Atlanta's
blacks and whites. Motivating our analysis are two concerns. First, for
both races, earnings comprise the largest single component of income;
therefore, understanding income inequality requires explaining racial
differences in the distribution of earnings. Second, an analysis of earnings rather than income is consistent with the general focus of this volume, which is on the functioning of the labor market rather than other
aspects of income determination.

One of the possible explanations for racial differences in earnings
lies in the human capital theory of earnings determination. Essentially,
this theory maintains that intergroup disparities in earnings can be attributed to group differences in the level of human capital endowments

(for example, education, training, and experience) and to group differences in how human capital attributes are valued by employers. The purpose of this chapter is to determine the extent to which differences in human capital endowments and in the market value of these endowments explain the level and persistence of racial differences in earnings in Atlanta.

Trends in the Level and Distribution of Earnings

This section has two purposes: to expand on the discussion in chapter 2 regarding changes in the distribution of earnings, and to explore, by simple comparisons with the United States and with other cities, how economic growth in Atlanta may have affected the distribution of earnings. Our hypothesis is that economic growth should have reduced earnings inequality, both within and across racial groups. This hypothesis is based on the premise that rapid employment growth increases the earnings of less skilled workers to a greater extent than more highly skilled workers—because the former experience greater increases in labor force participation, reductions in unemployment, and movement into relatively better-paying jobs. Empirical support for this hypothesis is provided by Timothy J. Bartik (1991, 1994), who finds that employment growth has the greatest effect on the earnings of workers who are young, black, or less educated.

Data

The analysis in this chapter is based on data from the 1980 and 1990 Public Use Microdata Samples (PUMS) and from the 1997 Current Population Survey. Earnings are measured by total earnings, including any self-employment earnings. In order to focus on those individuals who are most attached to the labor market, we restricted our analysis to people between twenty-five and fifty-four years of age with positive earnings.[1] All earnings are price-adjusted to 1994 dollars using the Consumer Price Index. The Public Use Microdata Samples do not separately identify the city of Atlanta. Thus, for our purposes, data for the city of Atlanta are an aggregation of those public use microdata areas (PUMAs) that either completely or substantially consist of city of Atlanta residents; this provides a geographic area that approximates the actual city to a high degree.[2] To obtain a larger sample size for 1997, we combined 1996 and 1997 observations from the Current Population Survey, with appropriate adjustment for inflation.[3]

Trends in Earnings Inequality

From the 1950s through the 1970s, the overall level of earnings inequality increased slightly in the United States. But during the 1980s, earnings grew much more slowly, and inequality in earnings increased much more rapidly than in the previous decades (Karoly 1992).[4] The change in the distribution of earnings was not uniform across all groups or earnings levels. For example, during the 1980s, the earnings of low-skilled workers and blacks suffered in both relative and real terms. There was also geographic variation in these trends across regions and metropolitan areas, as a result of differential shifts in the demand for and supply of workers of differing skills (Karoly and Klerman 1994). John Bound and Harry J. Holzer (1996) found that during the 1980s the decline in the relative wages for less-educated workers was greater in some areas (for example, the industrial centers of the Midwest) than in others.

In the Atlanta metropolitan region, mean real earnings increased from $30,553 in 1979 to $33,290 in 1989, and to $34,278 in 1997, or by 0.86 percent per year during the 1980s and 0.39 percent per year during the 1990s (see table 7.1).[5] During the period, the percentage of individuals in Atlanta with real earnings below $20,000 declined slightly, from 36.5 percent in 1979, to 33.4 percent in 1989, to 31.4 percent in 1997. However, despite this decline in the percentage of individuals at the lower end of the earnings distribution, inequality, as measured by the Gini coefficient, increased in Atlanta over the period, just as it had at the national level.[6] Thus, the economic growth experienced in Atlanta did increase earnings but did not overcome the national trend toward increased earnings inequality.

Much has been written about the causes of the growing national inequality in earnings. Frank Levy and Richard J. Murnane's (1992) extensive review of the literature provides a summary of the explanations for the growth in inequality both between groups and within groups.[7] In general terms, the growth in between-group inequality was the result of relative changes in earnings driven by the relative shifts in the demand for and supply of workers of differing age, experience, and educational levels. These shifts caused growing wage premiums for more educated, more experienced, and older workers.

The possible causes of the relative shifts in demand and supply are many, and there is still much debate as to the importance of each. Robert Kuttner (1983) and Barry Bluestone and Bennett Harrison (1986) argue that the deindustrialization of the U.S. economy during the 1980s resulted in a loss of middle-class jobs, as workers shifted from manufacturing to the service sector. Others have pointed out that the growth in inequality could not have been due solely to deindustrialization, since

TABLE 7.1   *Distribution of Earnings in Atlanta MSA (1994 Dollars)*

	Year		
Earnings Class	1979	1989	1997
0 to $10,000	0.158	0.137	0.102
$10,001 to $20,000	0.207	0.197	0.212
$20,001 to $30,000	0.225	0.230	0.235
$30,001 to $40,000	0.162	0.165	0.205
$40,001 to $50,000	0.103	0.111	0.088
Over $50,000	0.146	0.161	0.157
Mean earnings	$30,553	$33,290	$34,278
Gini coefficient	0.402	0.411	0.413

Source: U.S. Department of Commerce 1980, 1990, 1996, 1997.

earnings inequality was also growing within the manufacturing and service sectors (Grubb and Wilson 1989).

Racial Inequality

There are significant racial differences in the distribution of earnings in Atlanta (see table 7.2). In 1979, mean annual earnings of whites was 53.7 percent higher than for blacks. This reflects the fact that 52.5 percent of blacks had annual earnings of less than $20,000 (in 1994 dollars), compared with only 31.8 percent of whites; while nearly 30 percent of whites had earnings of $40,000 or more in 1979, compared with less than 10 percent of blacks. Despite the lower mean earnings for blacks, the Gini coefficients show that the earnings distribution was more equal for blacks than for whites in 1979.

Between 1979 and 1989, earnings of both blacks and whites in the Atlanta metro region increased in real terms: 8.5 percent for blacks and 10.7 percent for whites. As a result of this increase, the percentage of blacks with annual real earnings of less than $20,000 fell to 47.6 percent, and declined to 28.7 percent for whites. The estimated Gini coefficients indicate that the distribution of black earnings became slightly more equal during the decade, while for whites, earnings inequality increased slightly (see table 7.2). Despite the increase in black earnings, however, relative to white earnings they decreased from 65.0 percent to 63.7 percent.[8] Thus, while the dynamic economic growth in the Atlanta region did increase black earnings, it did not improve black earnings relative to white earnings; in fact, blacks lost ground relative to whites.

In the 1990s, black earnings increased 6.6 percent, while white earnings increased only 2.9 percent, and as a result black earnings rela-

TABLE 7.2   *Distribution of Earnings in Atlanta MSA, by Race (1994 Dollars)*

	Year					
	1979		1989		1997	
Earnings Class	Black	White	Black	White	Black	White
0 to $10,000	0.205	0.144	0.183	0.122	0.109	0.099
$10,001 to $20,000	0.320	0.174	0.293	0.165	0.315	0.172
$20,001 to $30,000	0.252	0.218	0.257	0.221	0.304	0.209
$30,001 to $40,000	0.125	0.169	0.146	0.171	0.178	0.215
$40,001 to $50,000	0.063	0.115	0.076	0.121	0.059	0.100
Over $50,000	0.035	0.179	0.044	0.199	0.360	0.205
Mean earnings	$21,631	$33,261	$23,463	$36,834	$25,009	$37,894
Gini coefficient	0.365	0.398	0.356	0.411	0.329	0.465

Source: U.S. Department of Commerce 1980, 1990.

tive to white earnings increased to 66.0 percent in 1997. The trend of reduced equality for whites and increased equality for blacks continued during the 1990s. Because of the small sample size for blacks in the Current Population Survey, the precision of the 1997 estimates is much lower than for the estimates based on census years. Thus, caution needs to be exercised in drawing too firm a conclusion regarding the magnitude of the relative improvement of Atlanta's blacks in the 1990s.

The decline in the relative position of Atlanta's blacks during the 1980s is consistent with what has been observed nationally. This decline comes after a protracted period in which the economic status of blacks improved relative to whites. For example, James Smith and Finis R. Welch (1986) show that between 1940 and 1980, the differential in wages between blacks and whites narrowed at an average rate of 0.71 percentage points per year. And Chinhui Juhn, Kevin M. Murphy, and Brooks Pierce (1993) report that the differential narrowed by 1.38 percentage points per year during the 1970s. During the 1980s, however, black earnings slipped relative to whites.

Racial Inequality by Gender

As is the case nationally, in Atlanta there are substantial differences in racial inequality in earnings between men and women (see tables 7.3 and 7.4).[9] For both 1979 and 1989, racial differences in mean earnings were much smaller for females than for males. In 1979, black female earnings were 90.0 percent of white female earnings (not quite parity), while black male earnings were 58.8 percent of white male earnings.

TABLE 7.3   *Distribution of Female Earnings in Atlanta MSA, by Race (1994 Dollars)*

Earnings Class	Year			
	1979		1989	
	Black	White	Black	White
0 to $10,000	0.254	0.255	0.212	0.203
$10,001 to $20,000	0.377	0.273	0.321	0.224
$20,001 to $30,000	0.232	0.281	0.258	0.269
$30,001 to $40,000	0.098	0.123	0.131	0.157
$40,001 to $50,000	0.027	0.042	0.054	0.082
Over $50,000	0.012	0.026	0.024	0.063
Mean earnings	$17,895	$19,873	$20,939	$24,707
Gini coefficient	0.363	0.373	0.349	0.375

Source: U.S. Department of Commerce 1980, 1990.

Nationally, black and white females had reached earnings parity by 1980, but black females, like black males, lost ground during the next decade (Anderson and Shapiro 1996). It is also the case that in Atlanta during the 1980s, black females lost ground relative to white females, with black female earnings falling to 84.7 percent of white female earnings. Black males also lost ground, with their earnings falling to 55.5 percent of white male earnings.

A second point is that gender differences in mean earnings are smaller for blacks than for whites. For example, in 1989, the ratio of female earnings to male earnings was 0.521 for whites but 0.796 for blacks. The latter figure reflects the fact that among blacks, earnings

TABLE 7.4   *Distribution of Male Earnings in Atlanta MSA, by Race (1994 Dollars)*

Earnings Class	Year			
	1979		1989	
	Black	White	Black	White
0 to 10,000	0.147	0.058	0.148	0.051
$10,001 to $20,000	0.250	0.097	0.262	0.114
$20,001 to $30,000	0.266	0.169	0.256	0.179
$30,001 to $40,000	0.177	0.206	0.164	0.183
$40,001 to $50,000	0.100	0.172	0.102	0.155
Over $50,000	0.060	0.298	0.068	0.318
Mean earnings	$25,680	$43,669	$26,299	$47,384
Gini coefficient	0.341	0.335	0.355	0.383

Source: U.S. Department of Commerce 1980, 1990.

increased much more rapidly for females than for males; in 1979, the ratio of female to male earnings for blacks was only 0.697.

During the 1980s, inequality in earnings in the United States increased for both males and females (Karoly 1992), but the increase was larger for males. In Atlanta, inequality of earnings increased for both black and white males and for white females; only black females experienced a decrease in inequality. The Gini coefficients (tables 7.3 and 7.4) indicate that racial earnings inequality in 1979 was greater for females than for males, while in 1989 just the opposite was true.

City Versus Suburban Comparisons

There are also spatial differences by place of residence in the level of earnings within the Atlanta region. As expected, earnings of blacks inside the city were lower than for blacks outside the city in both 1979 and 1989 (see table 7.5). These differences may reflect either better earnings opportunities in the suburbs in comparison to the central city, or the fact that higher-earning blacks may more frequently choose to live in the suburbs rather than the central city. During the 1980s, suburban black earnings increased slightly more than city black earnings, and thus there was a small rise in spatial inequality for blacks during the 1980s. Furthermore, in both years, earnings inequality for blacks within the city was higher than for blacks outside the city.

Table 7.6 presents equivalent data for whites. Due to a substantial increase in white earnings inside the city during the 1980s, white mean earnings went from near spatial equality to being substantially higher inside the city than in the suburbs. This change is the result, in part, of the loss of white middle-income families from the city and the small

TABLE 7.5   *Distribution of Black Earnings Inside and Outside City of Atlanta (1994 Dollars)*

	Year			
	1979		1989	
Earnings Class	Inside	Outside	Inside	Outside
0 to $10,000	0.235	0.166	0.146	0.270
$10,001 to $20,000	0.349	0.278	0.283	0.317
$20,001 to $30,000	0.233	0.266	0.271	0.222
$30,001 to $40,000	0.112	0.164	0.162	0.110
$40,001 to $50,000	0.047	0.079	0.086	0.053
Over $50,000	0.025	0.047	0.051	0.029
Mean earnings	$19,638	$23,906	$20,033	$24,799
Gini coefficient	0.375	0.347	0.401	0.336

Source: U.S. Department of Commerce 1980, 1990.

TABLE 7.6   *Distribution of White Earnings Inside and Outside City of Atlanta (1994 Dollars)*

	Year			
	1979		1989	
Earnings Class	Inside	Outside	Inside	Outside
0 to $10,000	0.162	0.142	0.107	0.122
$10,001 to $20,000	0.208	0.170	0.165	0.167
$20,001 to $30,000	0.214	0.219	0.194	0.226
$30,001 to $40,000	0.160	0.171	0.155	0.175
$40,001 to $50,000	0.084	0.118	0.116	0.121
Over $50,000	0.171	0.180	0.264	0.190
Mean earnings	$32,919	$33,300	$45,295	$36,218
Gini coefficient	0.440	0.393	0.468	0.405

Source: U.S. Department of Commerce 1980, 1990.

number of low-income whites in the city in 1979. The population now residing within the city of Atlanta can be largely characterized as high-income whites and low-income blacks.

Comparisons Across Metropolitan Areas

To explore whether the experience of Atlanta is similar to or different from that of other metropolitan areas, we selected for comparison six metropolitan areas that are similar in population size to Atlanta and for which the central city is identified in the Public Use Microdata Sample: Baltimore, Denver, Miami, New Orleans, Pittsburgh, and St. Louis. Obviously, this is neither a large nor a random sample, but it does reflect a variety of metropolitan areas of similar size and allow for some interesting comparisons.

Real mean earnings increased more rapidly between 1979 and 1989 in the Atlanta metro region than in any of the other six (see table 7.7). In fact, in five of the six comparison metropolitan regions, real earnings fell, the only exception being Baltimore. By 1989, mean earnings in the Atlanta metro region exceeded earnings in all of the other six. During the 1990s, however, real mean earnings in Atlanta increased at a rate faster than only three of the other metropolitan regions.

Earnings equality fell in all but one of the cities, Denver.[10] The increase in the Gini coefficient for Atlanta was essentially the same as for Baltimore, and smaller than for the other four regions. Thus, in terms of the level of and growth in real earnings and the increase in earnings inequality, Atlanta did somewhat better than the other six.

TABLE 7.7   *Earnings for Selected MSAs (1994 Dollars)*

| | Mean Earnings | | | Gini Coefficients | |
MSA	1979	1989	1997	1979	1989
Atlanta	$30,553	$33,290	$34,278	0.402	0.411
Baltimore	30,638	32,170	33,776	0.383	0.391
Denver	32,351	30,443	32,672	0.405	0.402
Miami	28,563	27,516	25,276	0.428	0.447
New Orleans	29,554	26,156	31,083	0.419	0.439
Pittsburgh	32,092	28,657	30,944	0.390	0.429
St. Louis	31,055	30,589	29,040	0.395	0.412

Source: U.S. Department of Commerce 1980, 1990, 1996, 1997.

Earnings for blacks in the Atlanta metro region increased substantially more during the 1980s than in the six comparison areas. In fact, black earnings fell in five of the areas (see table 7.8). Nevertheless, despite the large increase in the earnings of blacks in Atlanta, the ratio of black to white earnings fell, as it did in all areas except Pittsburgh. However, Atlanta's decline in the black/white ratio was small relative to the three areas experiencing the largest declines (Baltimore, St. Louis, and New Orleans). Among the seven metro regions, the change in the ratio of black to white earnings was unrelated to the change in the real earnings of blacks. For example, Pittsburgh, which had the second largest decrease in black earnings, experienced an increase in the black-white earnings ratio, while Baltimore, which had the second largest increase in real earnings, had the largest decrease in the black-white earnings ration.

As mentioned, there has been a decline in mean black earnings in the city of Atlanta relative to the suburbs. This is not unique to the Atlanta region (see table 7.9). However, with the exception of New Orleans—where black earnings inside the city increased relative to the suburbs—Atlanta experienced the smallest decline in the ratio of mean black earnings inside the city to mean black earnings outside the city.

Conclusion

Among the many findings described in this section, we believe two to be particularly noteworthy. First, since 1979, blacks in Atlanta have enjoyed rising real incomes, both absolutely and relative to blacks in our comparison metro regions. Second, despite these gains, both black males and black females lost ground to their white counterparts during the

TABLE 7.8   *Earnings of Blacks and Whites for Selected MSAs (1994 Dollars)*

| | Mean Earnings | | | | | |
| | 1979 | | | 1989 | | |
MSA	Blacks	Whites	Black/White	Blacks	Whites	Black/White
Atlanta	$21,631	$33,261	0.650	$23,463	$36,834	0.637
Baltimore	23,472	32,796	0.716	23,603	34,866	0.677
Denver	25,422	32,632	0.778	23,678	30,864	0.767
Miami	20,854	30,351	0.687	20,001	29,555	0.677
New Orleans	20,964	33,181	0.632	18,432	30,351	0.607
Pittsburgh	23,542	32,688	0.720	21,656	29,179	0.742
St. Louis	22,696	32,712	0.694	21,409	32,256	0.663

| | Gini Coefficients | | | | |
| | 1979 | | | 1989 | |
MSA	Blacks	Whites		Blacks	Whites
Atlanta	0.365	0.398		0.356	0.411
Baltimore	0.354	0.381		0.362	0.387
Denver	0.370	0.406		0.379	0.402
Miami	0.387	0.428		0.389	0.452
New Orleans	0.390	0.411		0.405	0.432
Pittsburgh	0.369	0.389		0.409	0.429
St. Louis	0.367	0.392		0.390	0.409

Source: U.S. Department of Commerce 1980, 1990.

1980s. These losses were nontrivial in magnitude. In each case, the ratio of black to white mean earnings declined about 5 percentage points during the 1980s. It therefore appears that economic growth in Atlanta did lead to improvement in black earnings, but it did not enable blacks to improve their position relative to whites. In the next section, we explore factors that might account for the rise in racial earnings inequality in Atlanta.

Variation in Earnings by Individual Characteristics

There are many ways of explaining racial and gender differences in earnings. Here we will explore the possibilities that they are related to (1) personal or human capital characteristics, such as age, experience, and education; (2) job- or employer-related characteristics, such as the industry of employment; and (3) unequal or discriminatory treatment in the

TABLE 7.9   *Earnings of Blacks Inside and Outside Central City (1994 Dollars)*

| | Mean Earnings | | | | | |
| | 1979 | | | 1989 | | |
MSA	Inside	Outside	Inside/ Outside	Inside	Outside	Inside/ Outside
Atlanta	$19,638	$23,906	0.821	$20,033	$24,799	0.816
Baltimore	21,807	27,690	0.788	21,040	28,338	0.742
Denver	24,541	28,020	0.876	21,897	26,490	0.827
Miami	17,346	22,452	0.773	14,486	21,537	0.673
New Orleans	20,838	21,445	0.972	18,509	18,162	1.019
Pittsburgh	21,910	25,383	0.863	20,129	27,444	0.733
St. Louis	20,109	25,783	0.779	17,459	25,041	0.697

| | Gini Coefficients | | | | |
| | 1979 | | | 1989 | |
MSA	Inside	Outside		Inside	Outside
Atlanta	0.375	0.347		0.401	0.336
Baltimore	0.359	0.326		0.365	0.358
Denver	0.376	0.354		0.393	0.396
Miami	0.372	0.388		0.408	0.392
New Orleans	0.391	0.388		0.409	0.374
Pittsburgh	0.378	0.369		0.419	0.354
St. Louis	0.383	0.338		0.407	0.336

Source: U.S. Department of Commerce 1980, 1990.

labor market. Thus, differences in earnings and changes in the distribution of earnings may be explained, at least in part, by differences in the value of these characteristics and by differences in the relative labor market returns to these characteristics.

Several authors have explained the growth in the racial earnings gap by the decrease over time in years of experience of blacks relative to whites and the increase in the rate of return to education, which favors whites, since on average they have more education than blacks (Card and Lemieux 1993). Francine D. Blau (1996) notes that gender differences in earnings have decreased nationally since the late 1970s, and Blau and Lawrence M. Kahn (1994, 1997) find that the gender earnings gap declined because of gains in the returns to occupations and industries dominated by females. Blau and Andrea H. Beller (1992) find that a significant factor explaining the decline in the earnings of black males relative to white males during the 1980s was a reduction in the annual time at work for blacks.

Other authors have emphasized the importance of occupation and industry in explaining both gender and racial earnings difference (Cunningham and Zalokar 1992; Anderson and Shapiro 1996). As noted in chapter 6, racial differences in earnings may also arise due to differences in the work locations of blacks and whites within metropolitan areas.

In addition to these observable characteristics, both the existence of and the trend in earnings differentials may be the result of labor market discrimination and generally unmeasured (or unobservable) characteristics, such as personality or drive. There are a number of authors who ascribe part, frequently a large part, of the earnings gap to discrimination in the labor market. (See, for example, Francine D. Blau and Marianne Ferber [1987]; David Neumark [1988]; Nan L. Maxwell [1994]; Andrew M. Gill [1994]; and Anderson and Shapiro [1996].) Andrew M. Gill (1994), for example, finds evidence that discrimination results in differential access to higher-paying occupations and that this contributes substantially to racial differences in earnings. Chinhui Juhn, Kevin M. Murphy, and Brooks Pierce (1993) and Francine D. Blau and Andrea H. Beller (1992) find that the slowed or reversed racial earnings and wage convergence during the 1980s for both males and females were associated with both measured and unmeasured skills.

We investigate the relationship between earnings and observable characteristics by considering the racial differences in earnings by gender across age, education, experience, job location, and industry categories. We begin by presenting simple tables for Atlanta relating mean earnings by categories of each of the characteristics. We then present estimated earnings equations. As with the analysis presented in the previous section, we restrict our sample to individuals with positive earnings who are between twenty-five and fifty-four years old.[11]

Earnings by Human Capital Characteristics

The typical relationship between earnings and age found in most studies is for earnings to increase with age until the individual is in his or her mid-forties, at which point workers, on average, become less productive and earnings begin to fall with age. This pattern was observed for blacks in both 1979 and 1989, but only in 1979 for whites (see table 7.10).

For all age categories, white earnings are larger than black earnings. The racial difference is most pronounced at older ages, as the black/white difference in age-earnings profiles would suggest. For example, for the youngest age category (twenty-five to twenty-nine years), the black-white earnings ratio in 1989 was 0.735, while the ratio was only 0.605 for the oldest age category (fifty to fifty-four years). The earnings of

TABLE 7.10   *Mean Earnings by Characteristics by Race*
             (1994 Dollars)

	Year					
	1979			1989		
Characteristics	Blacks	Whites	Black/ White	Blacks	Whites	Black/ White
Age						
Twenty-five to twenty-nine	$19,326	$24,187	79.9%	$18,943	$25,765	73.5%
Thirty to thirty-four	22,813	31,585	72.2	22,073	32,847	67.2
Thirty-five to thirty-nine	24,078	36,382	66.2	24,678	38,060	64.8
Forty to forty-four	22,434	37,761	59.4	27,281	42,931	63.5
Forty-five to forty-nine	22,002	39,618	55.5	27,193	44,059	61.7
Fifty to fifty-four	19,545	38,246	51.1	26,689	44,124	60.5
Education						
8th grade or less	17,071	22,888	74.6	19,130	20,919	91.4
Some high school	16,600	24,444	67.9	16,711	22,070	75.7
High school degree	20,625	27,652	74.6	19,668	26,372	74.6
Some college	22,729	31,685	71.7	23,429	32,794	71.4
Bachelor's degree or more	30,479	43,161	70.6	32,996	49,116	67.2
Experience (in years)						
Zero to four	21,722	25,936	87.1	23,998	28,942	82.9
Five to nine	21,682	28,716	75.5	21,134	30,719	68.8
Ten to fourteen	21,399	32,536	65.8	22,020	34,162	64.5
Fifteen to nineteen	23,580	35,882	65.7	23,890	39,655	60.2
Twenty to twenty-four	22,490	37,387	60.2	26,080	41,123	63.4
Twenty-five to twenty-nine	21,871	38,212	57.2	26,299	42,174	62.4
Thirty +	18,181	32,766	55.5	23,189	36,126	64.2

Source: U.S. Department of Commerce 1980, 1990.

blacks relative to whites declined nearly uniformly with age in both 1979 and 1989. However, the range of values of the black-white earnings ratio was smaller in 1989 than in 1979.

During the 1980s, earnings of whites increased for all age levels, but especially for older workers. For black workers, real earnings fell for younger workers, but increased for older workers. The increase in earnings for older black workers was larger in percentage terms than the increase experienced by older white workers. Thus, the largest relative gain in black earnings was observed in the older age categories. The decline in the 1980s in the overall black-white earnings ratio is thus driven by the relative earnings changes among younger (under forty years) workers.

As noted, human capital theory and the related empirical evidence suggests that education increases the productivity of workers, resulting in higher earnings. Juhn, Murphy, and Pierce (1993) and others have found that over the past fifteen to twenty years, there has been an increase in the returns to skills, as measured by education and training.[12] Since the returns to lower-skilled workers have declined relative to higher-skilled workers and since blacks are more likely to be lower-skilled, their relative earnings position has worsened (Juhn, Murphy, and Pierce 1993). Juhn, Murphy, and Pierce (1993) also found that educational quality accounted for half of the trend in the racial wage differential during the 1980s. This is consistent with Nan L. Maxwell (1994), who found that about two-thirds of the growth in the racial wage differential for young men was the result of differences in educational quality, as measured by basic skills. Jeff Grogger (1996), on the other hand, found that educational quality explained very little of the trend.

In Atlanta, earnings increase with education level for both racial groups for both years. Between years, the greatest gain in earnings for whites was found in the higher education categories (table 7.10). For example, earnings for those with a high school degree or less fell during the 1980s, while those with at least a bachelor's degree increased by 13.8 percent. As suggested by these changes for whites, the decrease in the racial earnings gap has been greatest among less educated, less skilled workers; but this is also partly due to the increase in earnings of less educated blacks. These findings are consistent with national trends.

In 1979, the black-white earnings ratio did not differ much by education level. The same was true for 1989, with the exception of the lowest education category, for which black earnings substantially improved relative to white earnings. For the higher education categories, black earnings either did not increase relative to white earnings, or, in the case of the highest category, fell slightly.

The earnings patterns by level of experience were very similar to those for the age categories. Given the relationship between age and our definition of labor market experience, this is not surprising.[13] The patterns observed in table 7.10 also apply separately to males and females (see table 7.11 and 7.12), although there are some differences in the mag-

TABLE 7.11   *Mean Earnings for Females by Race (1994 Dollars)*

Characteristics	1979 Blacks	1979 Whites	1979 Black/White	1989 Blacks	1989 Whites	1989 Black/White
Age						
Twenty-five to twenty-nine	$16,983	$19,052	89.1%	$16,995	$22,209	76.5%
Thirty to thirty-four	19,243	20,542	93.7	20,236	24,782	81.7
Thirty-five to thirty-nine	19,198	19,659	97.7	22,862	25,868	88.4
Forty to forty-four	18,073	19,825	91.2	23,275	26,543	87.7
Forty-five to forty-nine	16,594	20,394	81.4	24,041	24,870	96.7
Fifty to fifty-four	15,692	20,235	77.5	21,975	23,847	92.1
Education						
8th grade or less	10,730	12,594	85.2	17,431	12,469	139.8
Some high school	11,636	13,973	83.3	13,648	14,572	93.7
High school degree	16,993	18,742	90.7	17,059	19,846	86.0
Some college	19,300	20,029	96.4	20,645	23,898	86.4
Bachelor's degree or more	26,256	23,859	110.0	29,518	31,273	94.4
Experience (in years)						
Zero to four	21,301	20,919	101.8	21,702	26,520	81.8
Five to nine	18,839	20,359	92.5	18,787	24,955	75.3
Ten to fourteen	18,084	20,352	88.9	20,287	24,891	81.5
Fifteen to nineteen	18,826	19,115	98.5	22,139	25,288	87.5
Twenty to twenty-four	17,919	19,740	90.8	22,715	25,314	89.7
Twenty-five to twenty-nine	17,680	20,158	87.7	22,459	24,109	93.1
Thirty +	13,308	18,845	70.6	19,144	22,132	86.5

Source: U.S. Department of Commerce 1980, 1990.

TABLE 7.12   *Mean Earnings for Males by Race (1994 Dollars)*

| | Year | | | | | |
| | 1979 | | | 1989 | | |
Characteristics	Blacks	Whites	Black/ White	Blacks	Whites	Black/ White
Age						
Twenty-five to twenty nine	$22,111	$28,791	76.8%	$21,131	$29,093	72.6%
Thirty to thirty-four	26,698	40,170	66.5	24,119	39,464	61.1
Thirty-five to thirty-nine	28,824	48,657	59.2	26,944	48,921	55.1
Forty to forty-four	26,825	51,000	52.6	31,654	57,571	55.0
Forty-five to forty-nine	27,380	53,777	50.9	30,610	59,932	51.1
Fifty to fifty-four	24,152	51,088	47.3	31,244	60,838	51.4
Education						
8th grade or less	21,068	27,330	77.1	20,098	25,224	79.7
Some high school	21,546	32,390	66.5	19,296	27,920	69.1
High school degree	24,705	37,412	66.0	22,265	33,756	66.0
Some college	26,953	41,645	64.7	27,071	41,494	65.2
Bachelor's degree or more	35,596	53,439	66.6	37,687	61,702	61.1
Experience (in years)						
Zero to four	22,379	28,309	79.1	27,993	31,603	88.6
Five to nine	25,014	35,401	70.7	23,820	35,794	66.5
Ten to fourteen	25,171	41,895	60.1	23,918	41,882	57.1
Fifteen to nineteen	28,569	48,557	58.8	25,985	51,031	50.9
Twenty to twenty-four	26,862	50,750	52.9	29,881	55,168	54.2
Twenty-five to twenty-nine	26,231	51,278	51.2	30,591	58,116	52.6
Thirty +	22,867	43,988	52.0	26,852	49,648	54.1

Source: U.S. Department of Commerce 1980, 1990.

nitudes of the changes and there is a noticeable difference in changes in black-white earnings ratios by education level. For black males, only those with a college degree experienced a decline in their earnings relative to their white counterparts. In contrast, the earnings of black fe-

TABLE 7.13   *Mean Earnings by Industry*

Industry	1979			1989		
	Blacks	Whites	Black/ White	Blacks	Whites	Black/ White
Agriculture, for- estry, fishing	$11,625	$28,879	40.3%	$16,836	$33,668	50.0%
Mining	21,749	35,498	61.3	28,290	34,452	82.1
Construction	20,269	33,799	60.0	20,165	32,591	61.9
Manufacturing	23,076	38,213	60.4	25,340	40,572	62.5
Transportation, communication, public utilities	29,224	40,972	71.3	29,338	42,049	69.8
Wholesale trade	23,406	38,119	61.4	24,918	42,722	58.3
Retail trade	18,152	26,250	69.2	18,657	28,558	65.3
Finance, insurance, real estate	20,859	35,517	58.7	23,161	43,519	53.2
Business, repair services	17,127	32,451	52.8	19,584	35,366	55.4
Personal services	11,504	20,974	54.8	14,757	23,593	62.5
Entertainment or recreation	27,791	24,501	113.4	27,429	30,922	88.7
Professional services	20,148	28,452	70.8	24,335	35,805	68.0
Public administration	27,016	34,762	77.7	26,844	36,493	73.6
Military	16,469	28,446	57.9	26,677	40,410	66.0

Source: U.S. Department of Commerce 1980, 1990.

males with a high school degree, some college, or a college degree all declined relative to white females with the same level of education.

Earnings by Industry

As is true at the national level, in Atlanta there were sizable differences in earnings by industry for both racial groups in both years (see table 7.13). The variation across industries in the ratio of black to white earnings was substantially larger in 1979 in comparison to 1989, and the change between 1979 and 1989 in the earnings of blacks relative to whites varied considerably across industries, with declines in the black-white earnings ratios occurring in seven of the industries and increases in the ratio occurring in the other seven. In general, ratios tended to increase in industries employing large proportions of blue-collar workers and decrease in industries where white-collar workers predominate.

Earnings Equations

To explore in more detail the relationship between earnings and individual characteristics, earnings equations were estimated for each of the four race-gender groups for 1979 and 1989. The dependent variable is total annual earnings in thousands of dollars. The independent variables are those commonly found in estimated earnings equations, and include education, experience, experience squared, marital status, disability status, presence of a child under eighteen years of age in the family, and industry. Since age and experience are highly correlated, age was not included in the regression equations.

Table 7.14 presents the results for 1979 and table 7.15 contains the results for 1989. The coefficients are generally statistically significant and of the expected sign. In particular, the results imply that earnings increase with the level of education and at increasing rates and increase initially with the level of experience but then decrease.[14]

A comparison of the estimated coefficients for whites and blacks reveals that in 1979 the estimated education and experience coefficients were substantially larger for white in comparison to black males (only the difference in the coefficients on School2 is not statistically significant). For example, the coefficients for a high school education are 14.41 for white males and 1.76 for black males. Thus, the return from graduating from high school *among those who had attended high school* is $6,670 in additional annual earnings for white males but only $4,240 for black males (where the returns equal the difference in coefficients for School4 and School3 times $1,000). Thus, individual human capital characteristics affect the level of earnings, but the marketplace does not appear to value these characteristics as highly for black males as it does for white males. The industry coefficients are also somewhat larger for white than black males, although only two of the seven differences are statistically significant. (The excluded category is Agricultural, Forestry, Fishing, and Mining.)[15] The estimated coefficients on being married, having a disability, and having a child under the age of eighteen are all significantly larger in absolute magnitude in the white male than in the black male regression.

For females, the estimated coefficients for 1979 on the education and experience variables are either essentially the same or slightly larger for blacks in comparison with whites, and none of the differences are statistically significant. For example, the increases in annual earnings from a high school degree are $3,194 for whites and $3,810 for blacks, which are essentially the same values. These results are consistent with the relatively small racial difference in earnings for females in 1979 (table 7.2). As was true for males, the married, disability, and child vari-

145

TABLE 7.14   *Estimated Earnings Equations, 1979 (t-Statistics in Parentheses)*

Variables	White Males	Black Males	White Females	Black Females
Constant	−28.52[c]	−0.22	14.97[c]	4.02
	(7.65)	(0.06)	(4.98)	(0.90)
School2[a]	1.09	−2.33	−2.40	−1.27
(5th–8th grade)	(0.35)	(1.08)	(0.91)	(0.58)
School3	7.74[c]	−2.48	0.004	−0.24
(9th–12th grade)	(2.54)	(1.15)	(0.002)	(0.11)
School4	14.41[c]	1.76	3.19	3.57
(High school degree)	(4.74)	(0.81)	(1.25)	(1.64)
School5	22.72[c]	5.71	4.83	6.07
(Some post–high school)	(7.44)	(2.56)	(1.89)	(2.75)
School6	35.75[c]	12.55	8.43	13.23
(College degree)	(11.66)	(5.30)	(3.28)	(5.84)
School7	41.71[c]	18.68	11.36	16.81
(Graduate work)	(13.55)	(7.78)	(4.42)	(7.43)
Experience	2.77[c]	1.16	0.67	0.72
	(24.61)	(8.22)	(9.96)	(7.18)
Experienced squared	−0.05[c]	−0.02	−0.01	−0.01
	(16.46)	(6.93)	(8.20)	(5.98)
Married	8.13[c]	4.88	−3.68[c]	0.10
(yes = 1)	(12.91)	(7.04)	(12.74)	(0.26)
Disability	−9.57[c]	−6.51	−6.01[c]	−2.61
(yes = 1)	(9.07)	(5.94)	(8.96)	(2.80)
Under18	3.07[c]	0.75	−4.78[c]	−0.95
(yes = 1)	(5.63)	(1.12)	(16.17)	(2.24)
Construction[b]	6.46	5.41	−1.79	−0.74
	(2.79)	(1.92)	(0.94)	(0.17)
Manufacturing	10.79	9.64	1.06	4.04
	(4.78)	(3.48)	(0.64)	(1.03)
Transportation, communication, public utilities	13.46	11.92	6.40	11.39
	(5.90)	(4.28)	(3.87)	(2.88)
Trade	8.20	6.51	−3.13	1.18
	(3.64)	(2.34)	(1.93)	(0.30)
Finance, insurance, real estate	12.52[c]	4.75	−0.18	3.60
	(5.33)	(1.57)	(0.11)	(0.91)
Service	6.34	4.24	−3.77	0.12
	(2.81)	(1.52)	(2.35)	(0.03)
Public administration	4.58[c]	11.86	2.50	4.96
	(1.93)	(4.09)	(1.49)	(1.25)
N	13,419	3,469	10,543	3,794
R^2	0.245	0.178	0.154	0.204

Source: Authors' tabulations.
[a]Reference category for the education dummy variables is less than a 5th-grade education.
[b]Reference category for the industry dummy variables is agriculture, forestry, fishing, and mining.
[c]Racial difference in coefficients is statistically significant.

TABLE 7.15   *Estimated Earnings Equations, 1989 (t-Statistics in Parentheses)*

Variables	White Males	Black Males	White Females	Black Females
Constant	−27.83[c]	−1.56	10.01	6.29
	(5.01)	(0.43)	(2.59)	(1.63)
School2[a]	−0.08	1.50	−6.62	−5.55
(5th–8th grade)	(0.02)	(0.46)	(1.19)	(1.89)
School3	6.84	1.77	−4.66	−7.21
(9th–12th grade)	(1.34)	(0.59)	(1.38)	(2.83)
School4	14.12	5.50	−0.20	−3.77
(High school degree)	(2.78)	(1.82)	(0.06)	(1.48)
School5	23.41[c]	11.63	3.79	0.67
(Some post–high school)	(4.61)	(3.82)	(1.13)	(0.26)
School6	40.16[c]	19.50	10.08	8.10
(College degree)	(7.89)	(6.32)	(3.00)	(3.14)
School7	55.98[c]	32.52	17.07	17.27
(Graduate work)	(10.94)	(10.16)	(5.04)	(6.57)
Experience	2.77[c]	0.82	1.16	1.09
	(19.43)	(6.41)	(15.42)	(12.79)
Experience Squared	−0.04[c]	−0.01	−0.03[c]	−0.02
	(11.21)	(3.22)	(13.27)	(8.96)
Married	8.86[c]	4.78	−3.24[c]	0.40
(yes = 1)	(12.88)	(8.28)	(10.20)	(1.16)
Disability	−11.05[c]	−5.76	−6.20	−6.51
(yes = 1)	(8.03)	(5.40)	(7.57)	(7.68)
Under18	4.13	0.60	−5.57[c]	−1.99
(yes = 1)	(6.56)	(1.06)	(17.29)	(5.50)
Construction[b]	−0.92	0.89	3.96	2.58
	(0.38)	(0.42)	(1.88)	(0.70)
Manufacturing	4.92	7.49	7.12	4.23
	(2.08)	(3.61)	(3.74)	(1.28)
Transportation, communication, public utilities	6.22	8.05	10.07	9.17
	(2.61)	(3.88)	(5.27)	(3.00)
Trade	14.56[c]	1.68	7.17	3.92
	(5.91)	(0.73)	(3.79)	(1.28)
Finance, insurance, real estate	3.70	3.12	1.62	1.66
	(1.58)	(1.52)	(0.86)	(0.54)
Service	3.11	2.06	1.07	1.14
	(1.33)	(1.01)	(0.58)	(0.37)
Public administration	−6.06[c]	3.86	6.90	4.37
	(2.35)	(1.76)	(3.50)	(1.42)
N	17,976	5,159	16,027	6,077
R^2	0.243	0.215	0.154	0.238

Source: Authors' tabulations.
[a] Reference category for the education dummy variables is less than a 5th-grade education.
[b] Reference category for the industry dummy variables is agriculture, forestry, fishing, and mining.
[c] Racial difference in coefficients is statistically significant.

ables all have estimated coefficients that are significantly larger in absolute magnitude for white females than for black females. None of the estimated coefficients on the industry variables are significantly different between the two female groups.

The 1989 pattern of racial differences in estimated coefficients is highly similar to that found in 1979 for both males and females (table 7.15). However, there is one important difference: the racial differences in the education coefficients for males are larger for 1979 than for 1989. For example, the ratio of black male to white male coefficients on School6 (college degree) is 0.35 for 1979 and 0.49 for 1989. A comparison of the results for 1979 and 1989 also shows that for all groups, the returns to education fell for low levels of education relative to higher levels of education, a pattern observed nationally.

While there are racial differences in the returns to individual characteristics, differences in earnings can also be due to differences across individuals in the values of these characteristics. For example, if blacks have lower levels of education, then even if blacks and whites with the same education are rewarded the same, there will be differences in earnings. We can use the results from the estimated regression equations to decompose the racial differences in mean earnings into the portion that can be attributed to racial differences in the value of individual characteristics and the portion that can be attributed to racial differences in estimated coefficients. This is accomplished using the Blinder decomposition technique (Blinder 1973).

Table 7.16 shows for each year the percentages of racial differences in mean earnings by gender that are due to differences in individual characteristics and to differences in estimated coefficients. For both years, the importance of the racial differences in endowments is less than that for the differences in coefficients. The difference in the importance of characteristics versus coefficients is substantially smaller for males than females. There is essentially no change between 1979 and 1989 in the relative importance of the two effects.

The differences in mean earnings attributable to the differences in coefficients have been associated with racial discrimination—that is, racial differences due to market returns to endowments (Corcoran and Duncan 1979). The results shown in table 7.16 certainly suggest that discrimination may be an important factor in explaining earnings differences in Atlanta. On the other hand, differences in endowments are also very important. Since we have not measured all the potential characteristics that might affect earnings, we have to be careful in drawing conclusions about the level of discrimination. In particular, omitted variables may be a cause of at least some of the racial differences in coefficients. Most important, unmeasured differences in the quality of

TABLE 7.16   *Decomposition Analysis*

Year	Gender	Racial Difference in Mean Earnings	Differences Due to Endowments		Differences Due to Coefficients	
1979	Male	$17,989	$8,532	47.4%	$9,472	52.6%
1979	Female	1,978	783	39.6	1,195	60.4
1989	Male	21,085	10,288	48.8	10,797	51.2
1989	Female	3,768	1,408	37.4	2,360	62.6

Source: Authors tabulations.

schools attended by blacks and whites may affect the differential returns to educational achievement.

Changes in the Distribution of Characteristics

The preceding analysis shows that racial differences in earnings are due, in part, to racial differences in the value of observable characteristics and racial differences in the market return to these characteristics—that is, in the estimated coefficients. Similarly, the change in earnings between 1979 and 1989 may be attributed to changes in the value of characteristics and changes in the regression coefficients. To explore this issue, we first show how the distributions of education, experience, and industry of employment changed in the decade of the 1980s for Atlanta workers.

Table 7.17 presents the distribution of education, experience, and industry of employment by race-gender groupings for 1979 and 1989. The percentages of blacks with less than a high school degree, which are much higher than the corresponding percentages for whites, decreased during the 1980s. In contrast, the percentages of whites with less than a high school degree remained essentially unchanged. There were also increases in the percentages of blacks relative to whites with at least some college. These relative improvements in the educational achievement of blacks lead to the expectation that black earnings should have improved relative to white earnings during the 1980s for both males and females.

The pattern of change in experience is the same for each race-gender group; the combined percentage in each of the three experience categories between fifteen and twenty-nine years increased, while the combined percentage in the three experience categories between one and fourteen years decreased. The relative increase in the total percentage in the categories between fifteen and twenty-nine years was larger for

TABLE 7.17   *Distribution by Level of Characteristic (Percentage)*

	Black Male		Black Female		White Male		White Female	
	1979	1989	1979	1989	1979	1989	1979	1989
Education								
8th grade or less	11.8	2.8	6.8	1.4	4.9	1.7	2.8	1.0
Some high school	9.1	15.3	8.3	11.5	4.2	7.0	4.2	6.3
High school graduate	40.9	32.2	42.0	28.5	26.0	20.0	37.5	26.1
Some college	20.2	29.4	22.7	34.2	23.5	28.4	26.5	31.9
Bachelor's or more	18.1	20.3	20.1	24.4	41.4	42.9	29.0	34.8
Experience (years)								
1 to 4	2.7	1.8	3.8	2.8	5.0	3.2	5.4	4.0
5 to 9	19.7	18.9	21.3	19.2	19.3	16.8	19.9	17.0
10 to 14	25.0	23.6	26.2	22.9	20.7	20.9	20.5	20.0
15 to 19 years	16.9	19.6	16.4	20.8	17.0	19.7	16.5	17.9
20 to 24 years	13.8	16.2	12.2	16.3	13.7	16.9	13.3	17.3
25 to 29	9.3	9.9	8.9	9.8	11.8	12.6	10.9	12.7
Over 30	12.7	10.1	11.3	8.2	12.6	9.8	13.5	11.1
Industry								
Agriculture, forestry, fishing	0.7	1.4	0.2	0.3	0.8	1.2	0.5	0.5
Mining	0.2	0.2	0.1	0.0	0.1	0.1	0.1	0.1
Construction	11.6	10.0	0.8	0.6	9.3	11.3	1.5	1.9
Manufacturing	20.9	15.6	12.6	8.8	20.3	15.3	11.3	9.1
Transportation, communication, public utilities	18.3	16.7	8.7	11.6	13.9	13.3	8.0	8.3
Wholesale trade	6.2	6.8	2.3	3.1	8.9	9.7	5.6	5.9
Retail trade	11.7	12.9	12.5	14.5	12.5	13.0	15.4	15.1
Finance, insurance, real estate	4.1	4.6	7.9	10.1	7.5	7.9	11.4	12.3
Business or repair services	4.7	8.3	4.9	6.2	6.5	7.3	5.9	6.6
Personal services	2.8	3.5	10.2	6.2	1.6	1.5	3.5	3.1
Entertainment or recreation	0.8	1.0	0.6	0.7	0.9	1.1	1.0	1.1
Professional services	10.8	10.8	30.7	29.1	11.5	13.1	29.8	31.7
Public administration	7.1	7.4	8.5	8.7	6.1	4.7	6.1	4.2
Military	0.1	0.8	0.0	0.2	0.0	0.7	0.0	0.1

Source: U.S. Department of Commerce 1980, 1990.

black females than for white females, but smaller for black males than for white males. The former suggests that the black-white earnings ratio for females should have increased, while the latter is consistent with the observation that the ratio fell for males.

There are generally small differences in each of the two years in the racial distribution across industries, but large gender differences. There are no large racial differences in the changes that occurred between 1979 and 1989 in the allocation across industries.

As noted, the change in mean earnings between 1979 and 1989 can be separated into the effect of changes in the level of individual characteristics and the effect of changes in the market value of these characteristics. To estimate the change in earnings due to changes in the level of the characteristics (see table 7.18), we predict earnings for 1989 using the coefficients from the 1979 earnings equations but employ the 1989 values of the characteristics. The difference between 1979 actual earnings (column 1) and the predicted earnings (column 2) yields an estimate of the effect on earnings from the change in characteristics. For all race-gender groups, the predicted 1989 earnings are greater than actual 1979 mean earnings (column 5), which indicates that changes in characteristics enhanced the earnings of all groups. These results are consistent with the increase in education and experience among all groups documented in table 7.17. The relatively small difference between actual and predicted earnings for black males appears to be the result of a sizable decrease between 1979 and 1989 in the percentage of black males who were married. Recall that being married increases male earnings.

The difference between the predicted 1989 earnings (column 2) and the actual 1989 earnings (column 3) measures the effect of changes in the returns to individual characteristics, that is, the effect of the changes in coefficients. The differences are shown in column 6. All four race-gender groups experienced an increase in earnings due to changes in the returns to characteristics. However, the change for black males is very small ($26).

Columns 5 and 6 of table 7.18 thus decompose the change in mean actual earnings (column 4) into the portion associated with the change in characteristics and the portion associated with changes in coefficients. For example, for white females, characteristic improvements resulted in a predicted increase in earnings of $976 ($20,849 − $19,873), while the improvement in returns led to an increase of $3,858 ($24,707 − $20,849). Thus, of the $4,843 increase in actual earnings (column 4), 20.2 percent is due to the improvements in characteristics, while 79.8 percent is due to improvement in the market return to those characteristics.

The numbers in table 7.18 can also be employed to gauge the roles played by changes in characteristics and coefficients in explaining the growth in earnings inequality between the races. The ratio of black to white earnings for males is slightly smaller for the 1989 predicted earnings as compared to the ratio for 1979 actual earnings, while just the

TABLE 7.18   *Change in Earnings Due to Changes in Characteristics and in Returns to Characteristics (1994 Dollars)*

Gender-Race Group	(1) Mean Actual Earnings (1979)	(2) Mean Predicted 1989 Earnings[a]	(3) Mean Actual Earnings (1989)	(4) Change in Actual Earnings (3)-(1)	(5) Change Due to Change in Characteristics (2)-(1)	(6) Change Due to Change in Coefficients (3)-(2)
White Males	$43,669	$45,198	$47,384	$3,715	$1,529	$2,186
Black Males	25,680	26,273	26,299	619	593	26
Black/White	0.588	0.581	0.555			
White Females	$19,873	$20,849	$24,707	$4,834	$976	$3,858
Black Females	17,895	19,558	20,939	3,044	1,663	1,381
Black/White	0.900	0.938	0.847			

Source: Authors' tabulations.
[a] Estimated using coefficients from 1979 earnings equations (table 17.4) and 1989 values of characteristics.

opposite is true for females. This indicates that changes in the characteristics of blacks in comparison to those experienced by whites reduced the relative earnings of black males, but improved the relative earnings of black females.

A comparison of the ratio of black to white 1989 predicted earnings to the ratio of 1989 actual earnings shows how coefficient changes affected changes in the black to white earnings ratio. The predicted earnings ratio is larger than the actual earnings ratio for both males and females. This indicates that changes in the estimated coefficients for blacks in comparison to the changes in the coefficients estimated for whites caused declines in the relative earnings of blacks, regardless of gender.

The findings reported in this section suggest that during the 1980s, black male earnings declined relative to white male earnings because of both changes in personal characteristics and changes in the market returns to these characteristics. The adverse effect of characteristics changes on relative black earnings occurred despite the narrowing of the educational differential between black and white males over the decade. Among females, changes in characteristics worked toward reducing earnings inequality. In particular, changes in both education and experience were greater for black females than for white females. However, the positive effect of characteristics changes was dominated by the negative effect of changes in the returns to characteristics, resulting in black females also losing ground to their white counterparts.

Conclusion

In many ways the Atlanta metropolitan region reflects changes in earnings that have occurred at the national level: slow growth in real earnings, an increase in overall inequality, greater earnings differences between city and suburban residents, and a decline in black earnings relative to those of whites. These findings suggest there may be nothing at all paradoxical about the Atlanta experience.

On the other hand, a number of the facts that are presented in this chapter and in chapter 2 suggest that the earnings of Atlanta's blacks should not have declined but rather should have improved relative to white earnings during the 1980s. First, there were favorable changes in the human capital of blacks—education improved relative to whites for both black males and black females, and black females also experienced a relative improvement in labor market experience. Second, Timothy J. Bartik (1991) and Richard Freeman (1991) have provided strong evidence in support of the proposition that city employment growth increases the real earnings of blacks to a greater extent than whites. This is because black workers experience relatively larger benefits from promotion to higher-paying jobs. According to Bartik's results, faster local growth has a 20 percent greater effect on black earnings (in comparison to the average). Given the magnitude of this effect, one would have expected that the Atlanta economy's remarkable employment growth should have substantively and dramatically reduced racial disparities in earnings. These are our reasons for believing that Atlanta's experience is unique and aptly characterized as a paradox.

Special thanks to Dagney Faulk for her very helpful assistance.

Notes

1. Many studies of inequality consider wage rates rather than earnings, which depend on both wages and hours of work. We focus on earnings rather than wage rates because we are interested in the total labor market outcome, that is, both hours worked and wage rates. Several studies have found that the growth in earnings inequality during the 1980s was driven by growing differences in wage rates rather than hours worked (Levy and Murnane 1992, 1,351). There are many ways in which earnings can be measured, for example, earnings from self-employment are included in some studies but not others. Lynn A. Karoly (1993) provides a good discussion of the data and methodological issues involved in measuring earnings and earnings inequality.

2. PUMAs are collections of contiguous census tracts that contain a minimum population of 100,000 people.

3. To derive descriptive statistics from the Current Population Survey, the population weights were used. For blacks there were two outliers that were excluded from the calculations.

4. Lynn A. Karoly (1993) provides a comprehensive description of the growing inequality in wages and earnings in the United States among males and females.

5. Family income in Atlanta increased much more rapidly than did earnings per worker. In part this is due to an increase in the number of family members who worked; in 1979, 58.9 percent of families had two or more workers, while in 1989, 65.7 percent did.

6. The Gini coefficient is a measure of inequality ranging from 0 and 1; a value of zero implies perfect equality, and the larger the number, the greater the degree of inequality. See Frank Levy and Richard J. Murnane (1992) for a discussion of alternative measures of inequality.

7. Sheldon Danziger and Peter Gottschalk (1995) present a review focusing on the bottom of the income distribution (poverty) and public policies addressing the issue of income inequality. The 1998 *Economic Report of the President* contains a discussion of income inequality (Council of Economic Advisors 1998).

8. The Atlanta experience contrasts with evidence from a large sample of MSAs compiled by Timothy Bartik (1991), who finds that MSA employment growth increases the real earnings of both black and whites, but, as noted, the effect is greater for blacks.

9. The sample size for the CPS is too small to allow a breakout by race and gender. Therefore, the analysis in this section is restricted to the earnings data reported in the decennial censuses.

10. Given the small sample size of the CPS, it was not possible to calculate reliable Gini coefficients or split out earnings by race for 1996 to 1997, and thus we restrict the analysis to the PUMS data.

11. Given the small sample size of the CPS, we restrict the analysis to the PUMS data.

12. There is considerable debate regarding the reasons for this change; for example, see John Bound and George Johnson (1992), George Borjas and Valerie Ramey (1995), and Gregory Acs and Sheldon Danziger (1993).

13. Experience is measured as age minus years of education minus 6.

14. The reference education category is less than a fifth-grade education.

15. Note that several industries listed in table 7.13 were combined for the regression analysis.

References

Acs, Gregory, and Sheldon Danziger. 1993. "Educational Attainment, Industrial Structure, and Male Earnings Through the 1980s." *Journal of Human Resources* 28(3): 618–48.

Anderson, Deborah, and David Shapiro. 1996. "Racial Differences in Access to Higher-Paying Jobs and the Wage Gap Between Black and White Women." *Industrial and Labor Relations Review* 49(2): 273–86.

Bartik, Timothy J. 1991. *Who Benefits from State and Local Economic Development Policies?* Kalamazoo, Mich.: W. E. Upjohn Institute for Employment Research.

———. 1994. "The Effects of Metropolitan Job Growth on the Size Distribution of Family Income." *Journal of Regional Science* 34: 483–501.

Blau, Francine D. July 1996. "Where Are We in Economics of Gender? The Gender Pay Gap." NBER Working paper 5664. Cambridge, Mass.: National Bureau of Economic Research.

Blau, Francine D., and Andrea H. Beller. 1992. "Black-White Earnings over the 1970s and 1980s: Gender Differences in Trends." *Review of Economics and Statistics* 74(2): 276–86.

Blau, Francine D., and Marianne Ferber. 1987. "Discrimination: Empirical Evidence from the United States." *American Economic Review: Papers and Proceedings* 77(2): 316–20.

Blau, Francine D., and Lawrence M. Kahn. 1994. "Rising Wage Inequality and the U.S. Gender Gap." *American Economic Review* 84(2): 23–28.

———. 1997. "Swimming Upstream: Trends in the Gender Wage Differential in the 1980's." *Journal of Labor Economics* 15(1): 1–42.

Blinder, Alan S. 1973. "Wage Discrimination: Reduced Form and Structural Estimates." *Journal of Human Resources* 8(Fall): 436–55.

Bluestone, Barry, and Bennett Harrison. 1986. "The Great American Job Machine: The Proliferation of Low Wage Employment in the U.S." Study prepared for the Joint Economic Committee, U.S. Congress.

Borjas, George, and Valerie Ramey. 1995. "Foreign Competition, Market Power, and Wage Inequality: Theory and Evidence." *Quarterly Journal of Economics* 100(4): 1,075–1,110.

Bound, John, and Harry J. Holzer. 1996. "Demand Shifts, Population Adjustments, and Labor Market Outcomes During the 1980s." NBER Working paper 5685. Cambridge, Mass.: National Bureau of Economic Research.

Bound, John, and George Johnson. 1992. "Changes in the Structure of Wages in the 1980s: An Evaluation of Alternative Explanations." *American Economic Review* 82(3): 371–92.

Card, David, and Thomas Lemieux. 1993. "Wage Dispersion, Returns to

Skill, and Black-White Wage Differentials." NBER Working paper 4365. Cambridge, Mass.: National Bureau of Economic Research.

Corcoran, Mary, and Greg J. Duncan. 1979. "Work History, Labor Force Attachment, and Earnings Differences Between the Race and Sexes." *Journal of Human Resources* 14(1): 3–20.

Council of Economic Advisors. 1998. *Economic Report of the President.* Washington: U.S. Government Printing Office.

Cunningham, James, and Nadja Zalokar. 1992. "The Economic Progress of Black Women: 1940–1980: Occupational Distribution and Relative Wages." *Industrial and Labor Relations Review* 45(3): 540–55.

Danziger, Sheldon, and Peter Gottschalk. 1995. *America Unequal.* Cambridge, Mass.: Harvard University Press.

Freeman, Richard. 1991. "Employment and Earnings of Disadvantaged Young Men in a Labor Shortage Economy." In *The Urban Underclass*, edited by C. Jencks and P. Peterson. Washington, D.C.: Brookings Institution.

Gill, Andrew M. 1994. "Incorporating the Causes of Occupational Differences in Studies of Racial Wage Differentials." *Journal of Human Resources* 29(1): 20–41.

Grogger, Jeff. 1996. "Does School Quality Explain the Recent Black/White Wage Trend?" *Journal of Labor Economics* 14(2): 231–53.

Grubb, W. Norton, and Robert H. Wilson. 1989. "Sources of Increasing Inequality in Wages and Salaries, 1960–1980." *Monthly Labor Review* 112(4): 3–13.

Juhn, Chinhui, Kevin M. Murphy, and Brooks Pierce. 1993. "Wage Inequality and the Rise in Returns to Skill." *Journal of Political Economy* 101(3): 410–42.

Karoly, Lynn A. 1992. "Changes in the Distribution of Individual Earnings in the United States: 1967–1986." *Review of Economics and Statistics* 74(1): 107–15.

———. 1993. "The Trend in Inequality Among Families, Individuals, and Workers in the United States: A Twenty-Five-Year Perspective." In *Uneven Tides: Rising Inequality in America*, edited by Sheldon Danziger and Peter Gottschalk. New York: Russell Sage Foundation.

Karoly, Lynn, and Jacob Klerman. 1994. "Demographics, Sectoral Change, and Changing Relative Wages: A Regional Approach." DRU-795-NICHD. Santa Monica, Calif.: Rand Corporation.

Kuttner, Robert. 1983. "The Declining Middle." *Atlantic Monthly* (July), 60–69.

Levy, Frank, and Richard J. Murnane. 1992. "U.S. Earnings Levels and Earnings Inequality: A Review of Recent Trends and Proposed Explanations." *Journal of Economic Literature* 30(3): 1,333–81.

Maxwell, Nan L. 1994. "The Effect on Black-White Wage Differences of Differences in the Quantity and Quality of Education." *Industrial and Labor Relations Review* 47(2): 249–64.

Neumark, David. 1988. "Employers' Discriminatory Behavior and the

Estimation of Wage Discrimination." *Journal of Human Resources* 23(3): 279–95.

Smith, James, and Finis R. Welch. 1986. "Closing the Gap: Forty Years of Economic Progress for Blacks." R-3330-DOL. Santa Monica, Calif.: Rand Corporation.

U.S. Department of Commerce, Bureau of the Census. 1980. *Current Population Survey*. Public Use Microdata Sample. Washington: U.S. Government Printing Office.

———. 1990. *Current Population Survey*. Public Use Microdata Sample. Washington: U.S. Government Printing Office.

———. 1996. *Current Population Survey*. Washington: U.S. Government Printing Office (March).

———. 1997. *Current Population Survey*. Washington: U.S. Government Printing Office (March).

8

THE INTERSECTION OF GENDER AND RACE IN ATLANTA'S LABOR MARKET

Irene Browne and Leann M. Tigges

D URING the 1970s and 1980s, economic growth in Atlanta created expanding employment opportunities. Many of the new jobs created came to be occupied by women. Labor force participation steadily increased for both white and black women, from 47 percent in 1970 to 64 percent in 1990 among white women, and from 56 percent to 69 percent among black women. Despite this increased involvement in the labor force, the gender gap in earnings closed less than 2 percentage points in the 1980s for full-time workers. African American women, in particular, participated in the labor market in large numbers but had earnings insufficient to raise their families from poverty. These trends point to an especially sticky part of the Atlanta paradox: the continued high levels of poverty among African Americans in the labor force.

This chapter continues the focus on earnings inequality by examining the kinds and sources of disadvantage experienced by Atlanta's women workers. The problem of women's labor market disadvantage is especially crucial to the poor in Atlanta's African American community because 75 percent of poor black families in the Atlanta metropolitan area are headed by women (50 percent of metro Atlanta's poor white families are female-headed) (U.S. Department of Commerce 1992). The aim of this chapter is to understand how race and gender, sometimes singly and sometimes in combination, affect participants in Atlanta's labor market.

For poor and working-class black women, the disadvantages of being black and female combine with the deprivation arising from social class to create a situation of "multiple jeopardy" (King 1988). The concept of multiple jeopardy can be understood in at least two distinct ways. First, there is the notion that black women face multiple *sources* of disadvantage connected to their gender and their race. Because of their gender, black women are more likely than black or white men to be in low-paying female-dominated jobs and to sustain the bulk of responsibilities for child rearing and housework (England and Browne 1992; Hochschild 1989; Reskin and Padavic 1994). As African Americans, black women are more likely than white women or white men to be employed in low-paid jobs, to live in disadvantaged neighborhoods, and to confront racial stereotypes of employers and white coworkers (Feagin and Sikes 1994; Massey and Denton 1993; Moss and Tilly 1995).

Deborah King (1988) articulates a second meaning for the concept of multiple jeopardy. She argues that gender, race, and class combine in the labor market to produce oppressive conditions that are multiplicative in their *effects* on African American women. That is, race and gender are so intertwined that the effects of each are compounded. Thus, the negative effects of the respective sources of disadvantage on the labor market outcomes of African American women are experienced more intensely than just the addition of the negative effects of being black to the negative effects of being female.[1]

In this chapter, we investigate the labor market situation of African American women in Atlanta. We try to identify the processes that underlie disadvantage by gender and race in terms of both sources and effects. The Greater Atlanta Neighborhood Study (GANS) data allow us to look at three arenas in which gender and race in combination result in inequality: occupations, supervisory hierarchies, and family responsibilities. (See the appendix to chapter 1 for a discussion of GANS.) In our analyses of these arenas, we show that racial inequalities in the labor market play out differently for men and women, occurring through the gender and racial segregation of jobs, differential mobility opportunities, and child-care constraints. We also demonstrate that within the firm there is a gender hierarchy within race that maintains the advantage of men over co-ethnic women. After looking at these processes separately, we estimate their combined effect on wages. Although we do not find that African American women's wages suffer from the multiplicative *effects* of race and gender, their gender and race provide multiple *sources* of disadvantage, particularly through the demographic composition of occupations and supervisory hierarchies. We conclude the chapter by discussing the implications of our study for current theoretical formulations, empirical research, and public policy.

TABLE 8.1   *Median Earnings by Gender and Race, Atlanta SMSA, 1950 to 1990*[a]

	White Men	White Women	Black Men	Black Women	Gender Gap[b]		Race Gap[c]	
					Whites	Blacks	Men	Women
All workers								
1950	$2,801	$1,572	$1,457	$ 674	.56	.46	.52	.43
1960	4,745	1,957	2,286	979	.41	.43	.48	.50
1970	8,015	3,224	4,254	2,094	.40	.49	.53	.65
1980	14,862	6,822	8,333	5,177	.46	.62	.56	.76
1990	26,984	14,688	15,776	11,647	.54	.74	.58	.79
Full-time workers								
1980	19,353	11,329	12,259	9,154	.58	.75	.63	.81
1990	33,773	22,458	22,133	18,764	.66	.85	.66	.84

Source: U.S. Department of Commerce 1952, 1962, 1972, 1982, 1992.
[a]1950 to 1970 figures reported for workers fourteen and older; 1980 and 1990 figures are for workers sixteen and older. Income data for full-time, year-round workers available only for 1980 and 1990.
[b]Ratio of female to male earnings.
[c]Ratio of black to white earnings.

Wage Differences in Atlanta by Race and Gender, 1950 to 1990

Atlanta reflects the racial inequalities found throughout the United States. Within racial groups, significant wage discrepancies also fall along lines of gender. Table 8.1 reveals that African American women in Atlanta have consistently earned less than white women, African American men, and white men. However, the trend in median earnings since 1950 tells a hopeful story. The 1970s and 1980s saw a closing of the wage gap between African American women and white women, so that by 1990, black women earned 84 percent of white women's wages, compared with only 43 percent in 1950. The gender gap within race also closed, especially among blacks (see table). In addition, all groups gained relative to white men, although a substantial earnings gap remains. Among full-time workers in 1990, earnings of Atlanta's white women and black men averaged 66 percent of white men's income. It is striking that black women's annual earnings from full-time work in 1990 were only 56 percent of white men's.

Why do black women continue to occupy the bottom of the wage distribution? In particular, what are the processes that create disadvantage by race and gender in Atlanta's labor market, and are these processes *multiplicative* in their effects on outcomes for African American women, as King (1988) suggests? Economic theory would lead us to suspect that group differences in human capital explain group differences in wages (see chapter 7). If African American women have fewer years of schooling and employment experience than other groups of workers, then the presumed result will be lower productivity, which will be borne out in lower average wages. However, we know that African American women achieve slightly *more* years of schooling than African American men, and the black-white gap in experience is slight (England, Christopher, and Reid, 1999). There is some evidence that returns to human capital are higher for white males than for other groups, but these results are inconsistent across studies (England, Christopher and Reid, 1999). The literature identifies at least four additional sources of labor market disadvantage that could account for black women's lower earnings relative to black men and white women. These include job segregation, supervision and authority hierarchies, employer perceptions, and constraints arising from child-care responsibilities.

Considerable evidence exists to show that occupations and jobs are segregated by gender and race, with predominantly female and predominantly black jobs paying relatively low wages (England 1992; Tomaskovic-Devey 1994).[2] Several studies suggest that much of the gender gap within race is due to occupational sex segregation (Groshen 1991; Macpherson and Hirsch 1995; Petersen and Morgan 1995). Upward mobility in these jobs is often restricted as well, and the chances of promotion are limited (McGuire and Reskin 1993). Occupations and jobs are therefore segregated by gender and race in two ways: horizontally and vertically. Horizontal segregation situates race and sex groups in different kinds of occupations or different places within skill levels of an organization. Vertical segregation within an occupation or job puts groups in different positions of authority, responsibility, or pay.

Access to job rewards can also be hindered by employer perceptions based on gender and race. There is some evidence that employers invoke racial stereotypes when evaluating their workforce, to the detriment of African American workers (Moss and Tilly 1995; Neckerman and Kirschenman 1990). Employers may also hold assumptions that, because of child-care responsibilities, women workers are less attached to the labor force than are men, and thereby limit women's access to increases in pay and promotion. In addition to encountering employer beliefs about their problems with child care, mothers of small children also face actual work-family conflicts. Because they are more often single parents, African American women may be especially vulnerable to negative employer perceptions and constraints from child-care needs. With census and household survey data, we are able to explore three of these processes within Atlanta's labor market: occupational segregation, supervisory responsibilities, and child-care constraints.

Occupational Segregation by Gender and Race

The labor market is "gendered" in a least two important ways. First, women are concentrated in a relatively small number of occupations. Sex segregation is almost as high among African Americans as it is among whites. Fifty-five percent of white women and 53 percent of African American women would have to change occupations in order to achieve equal representation with men of their race in all occupational categories (Reskin and Cassirer 1994). Occupational segregation figures (usually computed with census data) actually mask the more extreme gender segregation of jobs that occurs within workplaces. James Baron and William Bielby found that within a firm, jobs are typically performed by one gender. The authors claim that "men and women shared job assignments in organizations so rarely that we could usually be certain that an apparent exception reflected coding or keypunch error. . . . We were amazed at the pervasiveness of women's concentration in organizational ghettos" (Baron and Bielby 1985, 235).

Second, occupational segregation lowers women's wages: the higher the percent female in an occupation, the lower the incumbents' earnings (England 1992). Debates continue over whether the "percent female" in an occupation depresses wages because female-dominated positions require fewer skills and human capital than male-dominated occupations, or because "women's work" is culturally devalued (England 1992; Tam 1997). Many of the jobs that women occupy in the labor market reflect women's roles in society, and are characterized by tasks involving nurturing, support, and caregiving (Reskin and Roos 1990; England et al. 1994; Kemp 1994). There is some evidence suggesting that women's jobs pay lower wages partly because these nurturing tasks are devalued compared to tasks usually performed by men that require equivalent levels of skill (England et al., 1994). The definition of what constitutes "skill" may therefore be gender-linked. Ronnie Steinberg (1990) shows that work performed by women was consistently evaluated as less skilled because evaluators failed to see the complexity in women's tasks and negatively evaluated the skills associated with dealing with children and bosses.

Occupations are segregated by race as well as by gender, and jobs that contain a disproportionate number of African Americans also tend to pay relatively lower wages (Tomaskovic-Devey 1994). Like the rest of the South before the civil rights movement, Atlanta's employers channeled blacks into manual jobs; African Americans were excluded from avenues of mobility such as trade unions. As Cynthia Lucas Hewitt demonstrates in chapter 9, although blacks currently represent about one-fourth of the population of the metropolitan area, it is not unusual to find jobs where the majority of the incumbents are black.

Patterns of Occupational Segregation by Gender and Race in Atlanta's Labor Market

What are the patterns of occupational segregation by gender and race in Atlanta, and how does this segregation affect wages? Census data from Atlanta show clearly that the labor market experiences of African American men and women have followed trajectories circumscribed by the gender and race segregation of the labor market (see figure 8.1). In 1950, 90 percent of black women and 78 percent of black men were employed in the low-skilled manual and service occupations. Black women especially were concentrated in one kind of work: as maids and housekeepers in private households. In Atlanta, almost half of employed black women were in household service jobs as late as 1960. The average earnings of African Americans in Atlanta reflected this occupational ghetto-ization (see table 8.1). Economic and political changes in the 1960s and 1970s cracked the foundation of rigid race segregation in men's and women's occupations. Black women made especially dramatic gains—out of private household employment and into the world of clerical work.

Unfortunately, the picture for African American women today is not as bright as the changes in occupational race segregation suggest. Black women continue to work in relatively few occupations within the broader occupational categories, and many of these do not pay well. For example, the top eight occupations of black women nationwide are cashier, secretary, elementary-school teacher, cook, janitor, cleaner, general office clerk, maid, and registered nurse. Together these occupations employ over one-fourth of black women workers (Reskin and Padavic 1994, 58). With 30 percent of their numbers in just eight occupational categories, white women are even more segregated than black women. However, their top occupations include some high-paying jobs, including salaried managers and administrators. Occupational segregation by race is much higher for poorly educated women than for college graduates (King 1992, 34).

Similarly, opportunities for African American men remain concentrated in lower-paid manual labor jobs. Nationally, about 11 percent of black men are either truck drivers or janitors, compared with 6 percent of white men (Reskin and Padavic 1994, 59). Data from the 1990 census (figure 8.1) show that almost half of Atlanta's black men held jobs as operatives or laborers, and in service occupations—a rate over twice as

FIGURE 8.1   *Occupational Distributions by Race and Gender, 1950 to 1990*

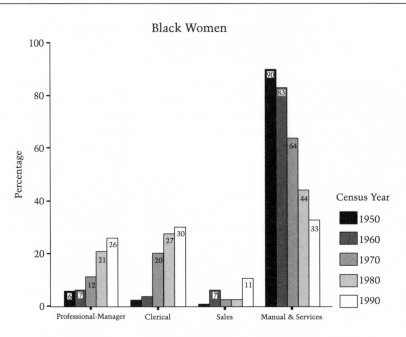

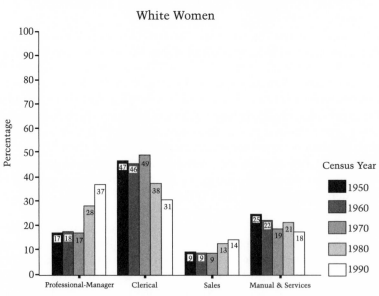

Source: Greater Atlanta Neighborhood Study 1994.

FIGURE 8.1   *Continued*

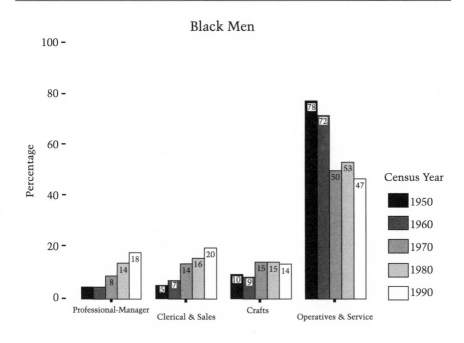

Black Men

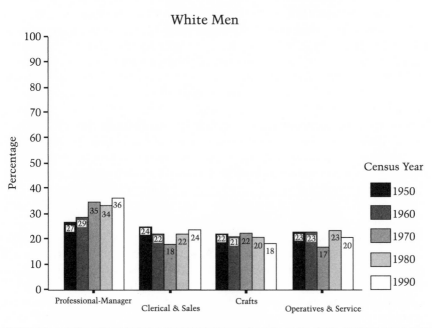

White Men

high as that of white men. In contrast, the representation of African American men in professional and managerial occupations, at 18 percent, was less than half that of white men.

Substantial segregation by race and sex within the workplace persists, as shown by responses to the GANS survey questions on race of co-workers and race and sex of supervisors. Respondents were asked, "What is the race and ethnicity of most of the employees doing the kind of work you do at [your current job] location?" Almost half of African American women and African American men (46 percent each) reported that the majority of their co-workers were also black (see table 8.2). We did not ask a question about the sex composition of jobs, so we must rely on census data to see the percent female in the respondent's occupation for the Atlanta metropolitan area. About 60 percent of black and of white women worked in female-dominated occupations (occupations with over 70 percent of incumbents female). Only 6 percent of African American women and 10 percent of white women worked in male-dominated occupations. In contrast, 13 percent of African American men and 8 percent of white men worked in female-dominated occupations.

To the extent that job segregation by gender and by race lowers wages, African American women will be facing a double set of disadvantageous job conditions. Indeed, segregated occupations and jobs are associated with reduced wages among our respondents. Table 8.3 shows that African American women who are employed full-time in female-dominated occupations earn $10,000 less than women employed in male-dominated occupations. The gap for white women is even larger. White women employed full-time in female-dominated occupations earn $15,000 less per year than white women employed in male-dominated occupations. African American men in female-dominated occupations earn $4,000 less than those in male-dominated occupations. (Although white men employed in female-dominated occupations show a large wage premium, our sample had only two cases in this category and so our ability to generalize from these data is extremely limited.)

Table 8.3 indicates that occupational and job segregation may operate differently for white men than for other groups. White men in the sample earn more if they are employed in predominantly female occupations and predominantly black jobs than if they are employed in positions where whites and men are the majority. As we noted earlier, these deviant patterns for white men may be the result of the small number of cases rather than unique processes. Another possible explanation is that white men who are in majority-female occupations or majority-black jobs actually maintain a certain advantage (Williams 1992). This would occur if occupations and jobs were vertically stratified as well as segregated horizontally, so that white males were more likely than other

TABLE 8.2   *Percentage of Workers in Female-Dominated Occupations and Majority-Black Jobs, by Race and Sex of Respondents*

	Black Women	White Women	Black Men	White Men
Occupation				
Female-dominated	59.0%	62.1%	12.7%	8.2%
(71 to 100 percent women)				
Gender-balanced	37.0	27.1	32.9	53.7
(31 to 70 percent women)				
Male-dominated	4.0	10.9	54.5	38.0
(0 to 30 percent women)				
Total occupations	100.0	100.0	100.0	100.0
	(N = 339)	(N = 164)	(N = 203)	(N = 166)
Race composition of job				
Majority black	46.0	6.7	45.8	15.1
Total jobs	N = 358	N = 188	N = 211	N = 182

Source: Greater Atlanta Neighborhood Study 1994.
Note: The table presents unweighted N's and weighted percentages.

TABLE 8.3   *Median Earnings of Full-Time Workers by Race, Gender, Sex Composition of Occupation, and Race Composition of Job*

	Black Women	White Women	Black Men	White Men
Total sample	$24,000	$29,000	$28,000	$35,000
	(N = 134)	(N = 90)	(N = 75)	(N = 65)
Sex composition of occupation				
Female-dominated	23,000	25,000	28,000	49,000
(71 to 100 percent women)	(N = 90)	(N = 44)	(N = 10)	(N = 2)
Male-dominated	33,000	40,000	32,000	28,000
(0 to 30 percent women)	(N = 4)	(N = 4)	(N = 35)	(N = 26)
Gender-balanced	26,000	30,000	28,000	41,000
(31 to 70 percent women)	(N = 45)	(N = 33)	(N = 30)	(N = 37)
Race composition of job				
Majority black	18,500	12,000	22,000	40,000
	(N = 57)	(N = 10)	(N = 26)	(N = 9)
Majority white or	25,000	30,000	37,000	34,000
balanced	(N = 77)	(N = 80)	(N = 49)	(N = 56)

Source: Greater Atlanta Neighborhood Study 1994.
Note: Table presents unweighted N's and weighted median earnings.

groups to occupy the *top* positions within an occupation, or possess more supervisory authority. We explore the question of the vertical stratification of occupations in the next section.

Job Supervision and Authority Hierarchies by Gender and Race

Jobs that are held primarily by women or African Americans carry other disadvantages in addition to their wage penalties. These jobs tend to offer fewer fringe benefits and less job security than jobs that are predominantly male or white (Browne et al. 1997; Nelson 1994; Tomaskovic-Devey 1994). Also, the opportunities for vertical mobility are often restricted in occupations in which women and African Americans are overrepresented (DiPrete and Soule 1988; Tomaskovic-Devey 1994). Even when women and African Americans enter fields dominated by white men, they may find their paths for advancement blocked. At the top of the occupational structure, this is referred to as the "glass ceiling."

A *Fortune* 500 study reported that a majority of male CEOs did not favor hiring a woman as their successor (Fisher 1992). These corporate heads stated that they want to be replaced by someone with the same perspective as themselves, a quality they are more likely to ascribe to a person of their same class, race, and gender. These reports are consistent with Rosabeth Moss Kanter's (1977) theory that to reduce the uncertainty in a corporate environment, individuals in positions of high authority seek to surround themselves with those who are similar in background and attitude, and they use gender, race, and class as cues of this similarity.

Answers to several questions on the GANS survey document black women's limited opportunities for promotion and authority. When asked if they had ever been promoted by their most recent employer, one-third of black women said yes, compared with 36 percent of white women, 39 percent of black men, and 43 percent of white men.

African Americans and women have fewer opportunities than white men for moving into jobs that wield authority, even if they are part of an internal labor market in which some jobs are connected to "job ladders" and opportunities for advancement are determined by the positions on the job ladder (Reskin and Ross 1992; Jacobs 1992). For instance, in a study of the federal civil service T. A. DiPrete and W. T. Soule (1988) found that predominantly female jobs were concentrated in the bottom tier of the organizational hierarchy, and were attached to job ladders with relatively low "ceilings." That is, the highest grade into which individuals could be promoted in female-dominated job ladders was relatively low compared to job ladders predominantly occupied by men. The

TABLE 8.4   *Supervisory Responsibilities by Race and Gender*

	Black Women	White Women	Black Men	White Men
Respondent is supervisor				
Yes	22.5%	26.1%	34.7%	43.4%
N	368	218	191	192
Authority (supervisors only)				
Hire and fire	31.0%	60.8%	40.2%	57.3%
Set pay	27.5%	45.3%	35.1%	55.0%
N	74	56	51	79

Source: Greater Atlanta Neighborhood Study 1994.
Note: Table presents unweighted N's and weighted percentages.

percent female in a job reduced the chances of mobility within the job ladder, and women were also less likely to be promoted across ladders into an upper-tier position, compared to men.

The GANS survey questions on supervisory authority in one's job show race and sex differences in who supervises and in how much responsibility they have (see table 8.4). Men were more likely to supervise other workers than were women. About one-fourth of black women and white women supervised another employee who was directly responsible to them. In contrast, 35 percent of black men and 43 percent of white men were supervisors. Among supervisors, white men were given more responsibility than other race-sex groups. Over half of white male supervisors had authority to hire and fire subordinates and to set their rate of pay. White women supervisors were as likely as white men to hire and fire subordinates, but were less likely to have authority to set wages (45 percent). African American supervisors, especially women, had less workplace power. Among black male supervisors, 40 percent had hiring authority and 35 percent could set pay. Only about 30 percent of black female supervisors had these kinds of responsibilities.

When women do find themselves in supervisory positions, they are most often supervising other women. In the workplaces of our Atlanta respondents, we found evidence that the gender hierarchy in authority relations occurs within a race hierarchy. Figure 8.2 charts the responses to questions asked to supervised workers; it shows the gender and race of supervised workers compared to the gender and race of their supervisors. The figure illustrates that blacks often have white supervisors, but whites rarely have black supervisors. There is also a gender hierarchy in supervision, so that women are supervised by men more often than men are supervised by women. Thus, white men are supervised primarily by other white men, and they also supervise all other groups.

FIGURE 8.2   *Gender and Race of Respondent by Gender and Race of Supervisor*

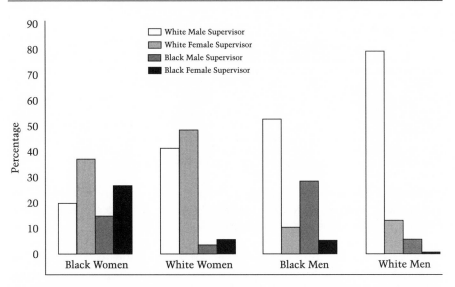

Source: Greater Atlanta Neighborhood Study 1994.
Note: For black women, N = 346; for white women, N = 194; for black men, N = 173; for white men, N = 162.
Numbers represent percent of respondents who report that they are supervised. For instance, 79 percent of all white men who are supervised in the workplace have a supervisor who is also a white man.

Approximately 80 percent of white men, 41 percent of white women, 53 percent of black men, and 19 percent of black women were supervised by white men. At the other extreme, African American women tend to supervise only other African American women. Virtually no white men, and only 1 in 20 white women and African American men, had a supervisor who was a black woman, compared with one-fourth of black women.

Looking at the figure, we also see the gender segregation of the labor market in lines of supervision. The most common pattern for all respondents is to be supervised by a white person of one's own gender. African American and white men are most often supervised by white men, and African American and white women are most often supervised by white women. The next most common supervisor depends on the race of the respondent. White women who are not supervised by the other white women are likely to be supervised by white men—they stay within their race category. African Americans, on the other hand, stay within their gender category. African American men who are not supervised by

TABLE 8.5   *Median Earnings of Full-Time Workers by Race and Gender of Supervisor*

	Women		Men	
	Black (N = 133)	White (N = 88)	Black (N = 74)	White (N = 65)
Supervisor is white man	$25,000 (N = 23)	$30,000 (N = 41)	$30,000 (N = 33)	$34,000 (N = 56)
Supervisor is white woman	21,000 (N = 60)	30,000 (N = 32)	37,000 (N = 8)	20,000 (N = 5)
Supervisor is black man	32,000 (N = 19)	—	24,000 (N = 21)	40,000 (N = 2)
Supervisor is black woman	18,000 (N = 24)	28,000 (N = 9)	27,000 (N = 3)	—
No supervisor	36,000 (N = 7)	30,000 (N = 6)	32,000 (N = 9)	48,000 (N = 2)

Source: Greater Atlanta Neighborhood Study 1994.
Note: Table presents unweighted N's and weighted percentages.

white men are likely to be supervised by other African American men, while African American women who are not supervised by white women are most likely supervised by other African American women.

The profiles of supervisors and supervised suggest that African American women have the most severely limited opportunities for job authority. If they are moved into supervisory positions, it is primarily to supervise other African American women. African American men and white women have slightly more opportunity for moving into positions of authority, as either group can acquire supervisory jobs over African American women as well as members of their own gender and race groups.

Is there a relationship between the race and gender of supervisor and wages? The results in table 8.5 suggest so, but the nature of the relation depends on the race and gender of the respondent. The table presents median annual earnings for respondents who were employed full-time, and reveals the following patterns. For black women and white men, higher annual earnings are associated with reporting to a male supervisor rather than a female supervisor. African American women supervised by white men earn an average of $25,000, while African American women supervised by black women earn $18,000. Supervision by African American men brings the highest annual wage premium to black women. The annual earnings of white women do not seem to be affected by the race and gender of their supervisors.

Our findings thus far indicate that gender and race together affect labor market outcomes on a number of levels, so that African American women face multiple sources of potential disadvantage. They are more likely than men to be in a female-dominated occupation, and they are more likely than whites to be in a majority-black occupation. They are also segregated vertically within occupations, so that it appears that those who are in supervisory positions are confined to wielding authority over other African American women; most do not have power to hire and fire or set the pay of their subordinates. The vertical segregation of occupations by race and gender carries wage consequences for black women as well. Positions where the next step in the ladder is occupied by a man receive higher annual earnings than positions where the immediate supervisor is female. It is possible, however, that this relationship simply reflects the preponderance of male supervisors in predominantly male occupations. We address this question with multivariate analyses. Before we turn to these analyses, however, we investigate whether child-care responsibilities may create an additional source of disadvantage for African American women.

Child-Care Responsibilities and Employment

Women's influx into the labor market over the past thirty years has not been accompanied by a great reduction in their responsibilities in the home. Although men now shoulder more of the domestic tasks than in the past, women are still responsible for the majority of housework and child care (Hochschild 1989). Shelton (1992) reports that women employed full-time spent an average of thirty-three hours a week on housework in 1987, compared to men's twenty hours. Arlie Russell Hochschild (1989) refers to this as women's "second shift." The second shift crosses race lines, although some researchers find that African American husbands spend more time than white husbands on household chores and child care (Ross 1987; Shelton and John 1993).

Children affect employment outcomes differently for women and men (Hayghe and Bianchi 1994). Women with children have lower rates of labor force participation, work fewer hours when they hold a job, and have lower wages than women without children (Presser and Baldwin 1980; Stolzenberg and Waite 1984). Because black women tend to have greater need for earned income, white women's employment rates are lower than black women's (Hayghe and Bianchi 1994). In contrast, having children increases men's probability of being employed at all and working year-round full-time (Hayghe and Bianchi 1994).

These gender differences in the relationship between children and employment do not necessarily indicate that mothers are discriminated against in the labor market. For instance, some women choose the path

FIGURE 8.3   *Absences, Lateness, and Changes in Hours Due to Child Care Concerns, by Gender and Race*

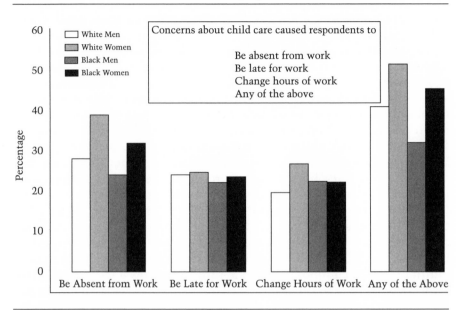

Source: Greater Atlanta Neighborhood Study 1994.
Note: For white men, N = 62; for white women, N = 97; for black men, N = 72; for black women, N = 148.
This table includes respondents who are employed and have children, and reports un-weighted N's and weighted percentages.

of motherhood and domesticity, preferring to remain out of the labor force or to work in part-time jobs (Gerson 1985; Heckman and Willis 1977). The option of homemaker is available to relatively few women, however, as wages for men have stagnated and more households require two wage earners (Levy 1996). Kathleen Gerson (1985) argues that many women face "hard choices" because the responsibilities of child care and success in the labor market are incompatible. An unequal division of labor in the household leads to unequal opportunities in the labor market. Our data from Atlanta show that both African American and white women raising children are indeed facing the hard choices that Gerson describes.

Among the parents in our sample, women were much more likely to report lost labor market opportunities due to concerns about child care. African American and white women were equally likely to report barriers to applying for a job arising from child-care concerns. About one-third of African American and white mothers reported that they did not apply for a job because of child-care concerns, compared to 14 and 11 percent of African American and white fathers, respectively. In the multivariate analyses of earnings, we assess whether these experiences help explain women's lower wages.

In in-depth interviews, employers expressed concern that responsibilities for children could hamper women's performance on the job, and that the assumed burden of single parenthood placed additional constraints on African American women (Kennelley 1999). Fortunately, the GANS survey allows us to see whether black mothers are more likely to report having had child care–related problems at work in the past year. Figure 8.3 illustrates how concerns with child care affect daily job-related performance, such a tardiness and absences. Although we find that women are more likely than men to report having had a problem with job schedules due to family responsibilities, the gender gap is not large. Mothers are more likely to say they were late for work or absent from their jobs, or that they had to shift their hours due to concerns with child care, but a substantial percentage of fathers experienced these difficulties as well. Among both African Americans and whites, about one-fourth of employed mothers and one-fifth of employed fathers were late for work sometime in the previous year due to concerns with child care. Absences from work were also a problem for mothers and fathers. About a third of the African American and white mothers, one-fourth of the white fathers, and one-fifth of the black fathers missed work at least once because of child-care concerns. Overall, child-care concerns led to a work absence, tardiness, or change in hours among half of African American and white mothers.

Gender, Race, and Job Rewards: Multivariate Analyses

It appears that there are multiple sources of potential disadvantage in the labor market for African American women, stemming from occupational and job segregation, authority hierarchies, and child-care responsibilities. The final step in our investigation involves assessing how these sources of disadvantage affect wages in a multivariate context. In order to have a sufficient number of cases to estimate the models, we include respondents employed full-time and part-time with nonmissing information on all the variables in our full model (Model III, table 8.6).

We begin by looking at whether these sources of potential disadvantage are producing disadvantage that is multiplicative in its effects on hourly wages of African American women.[3] Table 8.6 presents analyses of gender and race interactions at multiple levels, including the respon-

TABLE 8.6   *Regression of Hourly Earnings on Individual,*
Occupation, and Establishment Characteristics:
Interactions of Gender and Race for Total
Sample of Earners

	Model I	Model II	Model III
Individual and family variables			
Black (1 = yes)	−.190[a]	−.156[b]	−.161[b]
	(.073)	(.040)	(.041)
Woman (1 = yes)	−.132[a]	−.128[b]	−.145[b]
	(.112)	(.047)	(.043)
Black woman (1 = yes)	−.112	—	—
	(.092)		
Number of children	—	.004	.003
		(.019)	(.018)
Child-care constraints	—	−.042	−.045
		(.059)	(.058)
Human capital variables			
No high school diploma	—	−.596[b]	−.682[b]
		(.065)	(.063)
High school diploma only	—	−.310[b]	−.355[b]
		(−.047)	(.050)
Employment experience	—	.033[b]	.033[b]
		(.006)	(.006)
Experience squared	—	−.5E-3[b]	−.5E-3[b]
		(.2E-3)	(.2E-3)
Occupational and firm variables			
Occupation percentage black	—	−.818[b]	—
		(.205)	
Occupation percentage women	—	−.295[a]	—
		(.136)	
Occupation percentage black women	—	.480	—
		(.309)	
Supervisor male	—	—	.087
			(.073)
Supervisor white	—	—	.149[a]
			(.067)
Supervisor white man	—	—	−.054
			(.084)
Constant	2.444[b]	2.668[b]	2.191[b]
	(.050)	(.085)	(.087)
N	574	574	574
Adj. R^2	.087	.383	.363

Source: Greater Atlanta Neighborhood Study 1994.
[a]$p < .05$
[b]$p < .10$

dent's own characteristics, the demographic composition of those employed in the respondent's occupation, and the characteristics of the respondent's supervisor.

For our sample, hourly wages conform to the following pattern: mean earnings are lowest for black women, at $9.83 per hour, and highest for white men, at $15.21 per hour. Earnings for black men and white women are similar, at $12.74 per hour and $12.81 per hour, respectively.[4] Model I assesses whether black women pay an additional wage penalty for the combination of being black and female. That is, we test for an interaction in the effects of gender and race on hourly wages, without any controls for family, human capital, or job characteristics. We find from this model that there are two additive terms, but there is no statistically significant interaction. That is, although being black is associated with lower hourly earnings and being female is associated with earning less, gender and race do not combine to further lower the wages of African American women.

For Model II, we test for the effects of a race and gender interaction in the composition of the respondent's occupation, controlling for human capital and family characteristics. The findings are consistent with previous research, and demonstrate that as the percent female rises in an occupation, wages fall. Similarly, increases in the percent black in an occupation decreases hourly wages. However, the percent black female in an occupation does not significantly reduce wages when the additive effects are taken into account.

Model III reveals that the race of the supervisor is associated with wage differences, although the gender of the supervisor has no effect. Respondents who are supervised by a white individual earn about $0.15 more per hour compared to respondents whose supervisor is not white (among our Atlanta sample, this is almost always a black supervisor).

To summarize the findings in table 8.6, there are clear "direct effects" of gender and race at the level of the individual and the occupation, and a direct effect of race but not gender of the supervisor. There is no evidence in this sample for the interaction of gender and race on hourly wages. Therefore, we omit the interactions in the multivariate models predicting wages for men and women, which we present in table 8.7.

The results of the analysis show that among men and among women, blacks earn less than whites, even after controlling for human capital, family, occupation, and firm characteristics. The main variables of interest in table 8.7 are those that are unique to the GANS data: child-care constraints and characteristics of the supervisor. Child-care constraints do not appear to affect hourly wages for men or women. The supervisor variables reveal some novel findings, however. In particular, having a white supervisor raises wages for women but not for men. In addition, having "no supervisor" augments women's wages, but not men's. (We note that these analyses omit the self-employed.) From this model, we see clearly that gender and race operate together at the level of the supervisory hierarchy, suggesting that the concept of intersection of gender and race should be expanded to account for relations that have been virtually unexplored.[5]

There is also a relation between gender of the respondent and race composition of the occupation, suggesting again that the intersection of gender and race in the labor market is a complex process. We already noted in the discussion of table 8.6 that there is no "interaction" of percent black female in an occupation above the additive influences of race and gender composition. In the multivariate models presented in table 8.7, the inclusion of measures for occupational skill and job characteristics in the estimates eliminates the significant negative effect of percent female in an occupation on wages. The effect of race composition in an occupation remains significant only for men. Among Atlanta's employed men, working in an occupation that has many black men employed in it lowers wages, independent of the race of the respondent. Race composition of occupations does not significantly affect women's earnings. These occupation effects are net of the skill requirements within the occupation (captured by the "specific vocational training" variable).

The remainder of the results support findings from previous studies. Consistent with the research of David Maume (1985) and Richard B. Freeman and James L. Medoff (1984), we find that wages for both women and men are higher when they work in the public sector. For men, jobs covered by a collective-bargaining agreement also significantly increase wages. The benefits of unionization and government employment are greatest for the most disadvantaged groups. We also find that employment in a large establishment has positive effects on wages.

Conclusion

Our goal in this chapter has been to show how race and gender affect the position of African American women in Atlanta's labor market. Race inequalities in the labor market affect men and women differently, because they occur within a context of gender differences in workplace activities, organizations, and resources. These differences arise through the sex segregation of jobs and mobility opportunities, cultural ideas and perceptions about gender, and men's and women's divergent roles in the family. We examined the interaction of race and gender in three labor market dimensions: occupational segregation, authority hierarchies, and the constraints of child-care responsibilities. In turn, we investigated

TABLE 8.7   *Regression of Hourly Earnings on Individual,*
             Occupation, and Establishment Characteristics by Sex

	Women	Men
Individual and family variables		
Black (1 = yes)	−.165[b]	−.201[b]
	(.041)	(.066)
Number of children	−.007	.041
	(.024)	(.030)
Child-care constraints	.062	−.040
	(.060)	(.173)
Occupational and firm variables		
Occupation percentage white women	.115	−.110
	(.104)	(.161)
Occupation percentage black	−.254	−.391[a]
	(.146)	(.189)
Occupation training	.007[b]	.002
	(.002)	(.002)
Supervisor male	.012	.041
	(.042)	(.086)
Supervisor white	.087[a]	.048
	(.040)	(.070)
No supervisor	.257[b]	.003
	(.079)	(.136)
Establishment size (log)	.036[b]	.059[b]
	(.011)	(.018)
Collective bargaining	.132	.243[b]
	(.074)	(.083)
Public sector	.155[b]	.216[a]
	(.055)	(.104)
Full-time job	.236[b]	.182[a]
	(.044)	(.072)
Constant	1.774[b]	1.993[b]
	(.185)	(.200)
N	361	190
Adj. R^2	.589	.457

Source: Greater Atlanta Neighborhood Study 1994.
Note: The models in this table include control variables for human capital characteristics and industry. The human capital variables are: education, employment experience, and experience squared. Industry is coded as dummy variables indicating the 2-digit industry category from the SIC.
[a]$p < .05$
[b]$p < .10$

how race and gender segregation at work affect earnings. Through this process, we hope to make more visible the way labor market inequality by gender and race is embedded within the operation of the labor market itself, rather than being generated by external forces and brought into the labor market. Individuals' choices regarding employment are based on perceptions, preferences, and resources that are shaped by the structures of race, class, and gender. These choices then shape structure (Browne and England 1997).

The embeddedness of labor market inequality is also related to employers' perceptions. White employers and personnel managers raised in Atlanta were likely to have seen black women employed only as domestics or in other unskilled jobs. Does that lay a foundation for their beliefs about the typical African American woman worker today? Does this help explain why whites are unlikely to report having African American supervisors and why the only group with more than 6 percent of workers supervised by a black woman was comprised of black women? Employers' perceptions of African American women as single mothers who give higher priority to their children than their work (Kennelley 1999) may help explain black women's position at the end of the hiring queue. Child-care responsibilities caused considerable problems for employed parents, though more so for mothers than fathers.

We used multivariate analyses techniques to assess the importance for hourly pay of personal and family characteristics, occupational composition, and workplace conditions. The results show the continued significance of race for both women and for men. Women's wages are especially affected by the race segregation of supervisory hierarchies in the Atlanta area. A barrier to high wages for men in Atlanta came from working in occupations with more black male incumbents.

Finally, we want to emphasize the interconnectedness of disadvantages experienced by African American men and women. The lack of opportunities for black men affects the lives of black women because of the linkages between economic security and family structure, marriage rates, and the labor force participation of wives. Race continues to be an important determinant of labor market outcomes in Atlanta, but its effects operate within a gendered framework of opportunities and constraints. Theories of race need to be cognizant of gender and its meanings for the family, work, and community lives of minorities and majority populations. In addition, empirical studies need to incorporate gender- and race-relevant variables into models of labor market inequality. These models would go beyond identifying the sex and race of respondents to the consideration of factors such as the sex and race of co-workers and supervisors.

Our study offers several issues relevant for policymakers. First and foremost is the continued relevance of affirmative action in education and employment settings. Occupational segregation occurs because of the channeling of employers and the self-selection of workers. Affirmative action and antidiscrimination policies were shown by Augustin Kwasi Fosu (1992) to have been crucial to African American women's movement out of service occupations into "white women's occupations." Other researchers have argued that when women get access to men's jobs, they flock to them (Reskin and Padavic 1994). Government policies that require or reward nontraditional hiring seem essential, given the stereotypes exhibited by employers in Atlanta. Beyond hiring, employers must also be encouraged to promote women and minorities into supervisory positions—beyond those which involve supervising only workers of the same race and sex as the supervisor. Finally, since occupation is at least partially a matter of choice on the worker's part, government assistance for education and training needs to be made a priority to ensure that family economic circumstances do not determine access to skilled occupations.

We would like to thank Joya Misra for her insightful comments, and Gena Stanglein, Cheryl Seleski, Cynthia Ofstead, and Solon Simmons for their invaluable assistance.

Notes

1. Within the language of quantitative analysis, King's conception of multiple jeopardy implies an interaction term.

2. An "occupation" is a group of jobs that are broadly similar, such as registered nurse, real estate agent, or bank teller. A "job" is a particular kind of work, often particular to an organization or occupation. One person's job as a registered nurse may be in a geriatric ward of a large hospital, another may work in an emergency room, and another may be a school nurse.

3. We estimate hourly wages rather than annual wages for these models to circumvent the problem of the co-determination of hours and wages. That is, hours worked not only determine wages; they can also be determined *by* wages.

4. The means for hourly wage that we report are weighted and have been corrected for design effects.

5. We tested for whether the effect of having a white supervisor was different for blacks compared to whites by adding an interaction term (being a black respondent with a white supervisor versus not); the effect was not significant for either men or women.

References

Baron, James, and William Bielby. 1985. "Occupational Barriers to Gender Equality." In *Gender and the Life Course*, edited by Alice Rossi. New York: Aldine de Gruyter.

Becker, Gary. 1985. "Human Capital, Effort, and the Sexual Division of Labor." *Journal of Labor Economics* 3: S33–58.

Blau, Francine D., and Marianne A. Ferber. 1992. *The Economics of Women, Men, and Work*, 2nd ed. Englewood Cliffs, N.J.: Prentice-Hall.

Browne, Irene, and Paula England. 1997. "Oppression from Within and Without in Sociological Theories: An Application to Gender." In *Current Perspectives in Sociological Theory*, edited by Jennifer Lehman. Greenwich, Conn.: JAI Press.

Browne, Irene, Cynthia Hewitt, Leann Tigges, and Gary Green. 1997. "Segregated Jobs, Segregated Communities and Wages Among African Americans." Unpublished manuscript.

Corcoran, Mary, and Greg Duncan. 1979. "Work History, Labor Force Attachment, and Earnings Differences Between the Races and the Sexes." *Journal of Human Resources* 14: 3–20.

DiPrete, T. A., and W. T. Soule. 1988. "Gender and Promotion in Segmented Job Ladder Systems." *American Sociological Review* 53: 26–40.

England, Paula. 1982. "The Failure of Human Capital Theory to Explain Occupational Sex Segregation." *Journal of Human Resources* 17: 358–70.

———. 1992. *Comparable Worth: Theories and Evidence*. New York: Aldine de Gruyter.

England, Paula, and Irene Browne. 1992. "Internalization and Constraint in Women's Subordination." In *Current Perspectives in Social Theory*, edited by Ben Agger. Greenwich, Conn.: JAI Press.

England, Paula, Karen Christopher, and Lori Reid. 1999. "The Interaction of Gender and Race/Ethnicity in the Determination of Wage Disparities." In *Race, Gender and Economic Inequality: African American and Latina Women in the U.S. Labor Market*, edited by Irene Browne. New York: Russell Sage Foundation.

England, Paula, Melissa Herbert, Barbara Stanek Kilbourne, Lori Reid, and Lori McCreary Megdal. 1994. "The Gendered Valuation of Occupations and Skills: Earnings in 1980 Census Occupations." *Social Forces* 73(1): 65–99.

Epstein, Cynthia, F. 1989. "Workplace Boundaries: Conceptions and Creations." *Social Research* 56: 571–90.

Feagin, Joe, and Melvin Sikes. 1994. *Living With Racism*. Boston: Beacon Press.

Fisher, Anne B. 1992. "When Will Women Get to the Top?" *Fortune Magazine*. September 21, pp. 44–56.

Fosu, Augustin Kwasi. 1992. "Occupational Mobility of Black Women, 1958–1981: The Impact of Post–1964 Antidiscrimination Measures." *Industrial and Labor Relations Review* 45: 281–94.

Freeman, Richard B., and James L. Medoff. 1984. *What Do Unions Do?* New York: Basic Books.

Fulbright, Karen, 1985. "The Myth of the Double Advantage: Black Female Managers." *Review of Black Political Economy* 14: 33–45.

Gerson, Kathleen. 1985. *Hard Choices*. Berkeley: University of California Press.

Gill, Andrew M. 1994. "Incorporating the Causes of Occupational Differences in Studies of Racial Wage Differentials." *Journal of Human Resources* 29(1): 20–41.

Glass, Jennifer. 1990. "The Impact of Occupational Segregation on Working Conditions." *Social Forces* 68(3): 779–96.

Groshen, Erica. 1991. "The Structure of the Female/Male Wage Differential: Is It Who You Are, What You Do, or Where You Work?" *Journal of Human Resources* 26(3): 457–72.

Hartmann, Heidi. 1981. "The Family as the Locus of Gender, Class, and Political Struggle: The Example of Housework." *Signs: Journal of Women in Culture and Society* 6: 366–94.

Hayghe, Howard V., and Suzanne M. Bianchi. 1994. "Married Mothers' Work Patterns: The Job-Family Compromise." *Monthly Labor Review* 117(6): 24–30.

Heckman, James, and Robert Willis. 1977. "A Beta-logistic Model for the Analysis of Sequential Labor Force Participation by Married Women." *Journal of Political Economy* 85(1): 27–58.

Hochschild, Arlie Russell. 1989. *The Second Shift: Working Parents and the Revolution at Home*. New York: Viking Press.

Jacobs, Jerry. 1992. "Women's Entry in Management: Trends in Earnings, Authority, and Values Among Salaried Managers." *Administrative Science Quarterly* 37: 282–301.

Kanter, Rosabeth Moss. 1977. *Men and Women of the Corporation*. New York: Basic Books.

Kemp, Alice Abel. 1994. *Women's Work: Degraded and Devalued*. Englewood Cliffs, N.J.: Prentice-Hall.

Kennelley, Ivy Leigh. 1995. "'That Single Mother Element': How White Employers Typify Black Women." *Gender and Society* 13: 168–92.

King, Deborah. 1988. "Multiple Jeopardy, Multiple Consciousness: The Context of a Black Feminist Ideology." *Signs* 14(1): 42–72.

King, Mary C. 1992. "Occupational Segregation by Race and Sex, 1940–88." *Monthly Labor Review* 115(4): 30–37.

Levy, Frank. 1996. "Incomes and Income Inequality." In *State of the Union, America in the 1990s. Vol. 1: Economic Trends*, edited by Reynolds Farley. New York: Russell Sage Foundation.

McGuire, Gail M., and Barbara F. Reskin. 1993. "Authority Hierarchies at Work: The Impacts of Race and Sex." *Gender and Society* 7(4): 487–506.

Macpherson, David, and Barry Hirsch. 1995. "Wages and Gender Composition: Why Do Women's Jobs Pay Less?" *Journal of Labor Economics* 13(3): 426–71.

Massey, Douglas, and Nancy Denton. 1993. *American Apartheid: Seg-

regation and Making of the Underclass. Cambridge, Mass.: Harvard University Press.

Maume, David. 1985. "Government Participation in the Local Economy and Race- and Sex-Based Earnings Inequality." *Social Problems* 32: 285–97.

Moss, Phillip, and Chris Tilly. 1995. "Raised Hurdles for Black Men: Evidence from Interviews with Employers." Working paper #81. New York: Russell Sage Foundation.

Neckerman, Kathryn, and Joleen Kirschenman. 1990. "Hiring Strategies, Racial Bias, and Inner-City Workers: An Investigation of Employers' Hiring Decisions." *Social Problems* 38: 433–37.

Nelson, Joel. 1994. "Work and Benefits: The Multiple Problems of Service Sector Employment." *Social Problems* 41(2): 240–56.

Petersen, Trond, and Laurie Morgan. 1995. "Separate and Unequal: Occupation-Establishment Sex Segregation and the Gender Wage Gap." *American Journal of Sociology* 101(2): 329–65.

Polachek, Solomon. 1981. "Occupational Self-Selection: A Human Capital Approach to Sex Differences in Occupational Structure." *Review of Economics and Statistics* 58: 60–69.

Presser, Harriet, and Wendy Baldwin. 1980. "Child Care as a Constraint on Employment: Prevalence, Correlates, and Bearing on the Work and Fertility Nexus." *American Journal of Sociology* 85(5): 1,202–13.

Reskin, Barbara. 1988. "Bringing the Men Back In: Sex Differentiation and the Devaluation of Women's Work." *Gender and Society* 2(1): 58–81.

Reskin, Barbara, and Naomi Cassirer. 1994. "Segregating Workers: Occupational Segregation by Sex, Race, and Ethnicity." Paper presented at the Annual Meeting of the American Sociological Association. Los Angeles (August 6).

Reskin, Barbara, and Irene Padavic. 1994. *Women and Men at Work.* Thousand Oaks, Calif.: Pine Forge Press.

Reskin, Barbara, and Patricia Roos. 1990. *Job Queues, Gender Queues: Explaining Women's Inroads into Male Occupations.* Philadelphia: Temple University Press.

Reskin, Barbara, and Catherine Ross. 1992. "Job, Authority, and Earnings among Managers: The Continuing Significance of Sex." *Work and Occupations* 19: 342–65.

Ross, Catherine. 1987. "The Division of Labor at Home." *Social Forces* 65(3): 816–33.

Shelton, Beth Anne. 1992. *Women, Men and Time: Gender Differences in Paid Work, Housework and Leisure.* Westport, Conn.: Greenwood Press.

Shelton, Beth Anne, and Daphne John. 1993. "Ethnicity, Race, and Difference: A Comparison of White, Black, and Hispanic Men's Household Labor Time." In *Men, Work, and Family*, edited by Jane C. Hood. Newbury Park, Calif.: Sage.

Stack, Carol. 1975. *All Our Kin: Strategies for Survival in a Black Community*. New York: Harper & Row.

Steinberg, Ronnie. 1990. "Social Construction of Skill: Gender, Power and Comparable Worth." *Work and Occupations* 17: 449–82.

Stolzenberg, Ross, and Linda Waite. 1984. "Local Labor Markets, Children and Labor Force Participation of Wives." *Demography* 21(2): 157–70.

Tam, Tony. 1997. "Sex Segregation and Occupational Gender Inequality in the United States: Devaluation or Specialized Training?" *American Journal of Sociology* 102(6): 1,652–92.

Thurow, Lester. 1975. *Generating Inequality*. New York: Basic Books.

Tomaskovic-Devey, Donald. 1994. *Gender and Racial Inequality at Work: The Sources and Consequences of Job Segregation*. Ithaca, N.Y.: ILR Press.

U.S. Department of Commerce, Bureau of the Census. 1952. *1950 Census of Population and Housing*. Washington: U.S. Government Printing Office.

———. 1962. *1960 Census of Population and Housing*. Washington: U.S. Government Printing Office.

———. 1972. *1970 Census of Population and Housing*. Washington: U.S. Government Printing Office.

———. 1982. *1980 Census of Population and Housing*. Washington: U.S. Government Printing Office.

———. 1992a. *1990 Census of Population and Housing*. Washington: U.S. Government Printing Office.

———. 1992b. *1990 Census of Population and Housing*. Summary tape files 3A. Washington: U.S. Government Printing Office

Williams, Christine. 1989. *Gender Differences at Work: Women and Men in Nontraditional Occupations*. Berkeley: University of California Press.

———. 1992. "The Glass Escalator: Hidden Advantages for Men in the 'Female' professions." *Social Problems* 39(3): 253–67.

9

JOB SEGREGATION, ETHNIC HEGEMONY, AND EARNINGS INEQUALITY

Cynthia Lucas Hewitt

THIS chapter focuses on earnings inequality between blacks employed in a job with majority-white co-workers who do the same type of work and those employed in a job with majority-black co-workers. These two groups have been described as "assimilated" and "nonassimilated" black workers (Boston 1988). The attempt here is to understand the nature of majority-black jobs without assuming the negative connotations of the descriptive term *segregated*. Many studies of labor market outcomes for African Americans seek to explain restriction of blacks' access to jobs, and in labor market analyses the focus is generally on the degree to which African Americans have been assimilated into majority-white jobs. These theories tend to describe market outcomes only in their economic dimension. I extend the theoretical domain from the economic to political economy to show that the level of political power a group holds is an important factor in explaining the process of the racial concentration of jobs. Evidence from the study of Atlanta reveals that majority-black concentration within sectors of the labor market is the result not only of segregation but also of the more contemporary phenomenon of majority-black political power. Thus, in the latter case, majority-black concentration can be a causal factor in improved rather than diminished outcomes.

First, I will present the characteristics of African American jobs in Atlanta by racial composition, including a spatial analysis of the regional labor market and gender differences. Second, a brief historical summary highlights the labor market segmentation processes that yielded the described differences. Third, I propose that extending ethnic enterprise theory—in particular, the theory of ethnic hegemony contestation—will help explain better outcomes in some majority-black jobs. I will present results that support this analysis, then discuss the impact of African American political power on market inequality.

Earnings Outcomes in Segregated and Integrated Jobs

The focus of this study is on differences in job outcomes, particularly earnings, related to whether or not the respondent's co-workers at his or her current or most recent job were majority African American. In the Greater Atlanta Neighborhood Study (GANS), respondents were asked: "What is/was the race and ethnicity of most of the employees doing the kind of work you do/did at this location?" (See the appendix to chapter 1 for a discussion of GANS.) This question was used to categorize jobs into majority black and majority white. African Americans employed in majority-black jobs earned on average only 76 percent of what African Americans earned in majority-white jobs ($18,297 compared with $24,139; see table 9.1).

This gap is greater than the inequality in earnings between African Americans and whites (African American earnings average 86 percent of white earnings). More than half the black workers in Atlanta (57.9 percent) were employed in majority-black jobs, while 42 percent were employed in majority-white jobs. Only 1.5 percent reported job composition as "mixed black and white," and 3.4 percent reported "other" majority.

Majority-black jobs on average have fewer benefits such as paid sick leave and health insurance, formal training, and retirement plans (see

TABLE 9.1 *Descriptives for Analysis of African American Earnings by Job, Racial Majority Composition, and Other Variables*

Measure	Majority-White Job Composition N = 165	Majority-Black Job Composition N = 227	Standard Deviation
Mean earnings	$24,139[a]	$18,297[a]	11,846.94
Job racial majority distribution	42.1%	57.9%	
Percent female	58.8	67.8	—
Mean hours worked	40.7[b]	39.0[b]	8.95
Mean years education	13.5[a]	12.9[a]	2.23
Mean years experience	17.5	17.1	11.08
Mean years tenure	7.1	6.3	7.62
Mean days on-the-job training	36[a]	11[a]	84

Source: Greater Atlanta Neighborhood Study 1994.
[a]t-Test significant at .01.
[b]t-Test significant at .05.

186

TABLE 9.2   *Job Quality Descriptives for African American Workers by Job, Racial Majority Composition*

Percentage Reporting	Majority White Setting N = 165	Majority Black Setting N = 227
Formal training	41.7[a]	24.2[a]
Retirement plan	76.2[a]	50.7[a]
Paid sick leave	77.4[a]	57.7[a]
Health insurance for self	81.1[a]	60.8[a]
Health insurance for family	75.9[a]	55.9[a]
Discriminated against in past year	16.7	10.7
Others promoted faster due to race	31.5[b]	21.7[b]

Source: Greater Atlanta Neighborhood Study 1994.
[a]Pearson Test significant at the .01 level.
[b]Pearson Test significant at the .05 level.

table 9.2). In general, jobs with majority-black concentration display less quality outcomes in comparison to those with more balanced racial composition. However, there was less of a perception of social bias occurring where black co-workers were a majority, as seen in the fewer instances of the perception of having been discriminated against in the past year.

The three possible explanations for lower earnings related to majority-black job composition are preponderance of African Americans in majority-black jobs who may be low-skilled workers due to educational disadvantage; the spatial concentration of majority-black low-paid jobs in urban areas where African American workers experience labor market crowding; and the exclusion of African American workers from core sector industries and career ladders based on racial status.[1]

The first two explanations reflect a neoclassical economics orientation, and suggest either that blacks in majority-black jobs have less education on average and thus earn less, or that some spatial inhibition of the market restricts the supply of black labor or white labor to particular jobs. The average education level of blacks in majority-black jobs is less than in majority-white jobs (see table 9.1). The difference in education level is not sufficient to account for the large difference in earnings, however. (See chapter 7 for an analysis of the effect of education on earnings.) Further, as blacks make up only 30 percent of the low education population in the Atlanta metropolitan area, they should not comprise the majority in even low-skill jobs unless some other process of sorting is taking place (see table 9.3).

Another explanation for low earnings in majority-black jobs may be based on the idea that the Atlanta regional job market does not function as an integrated whole. The spatial mismatch hypothesis explains racial

TABLE 9.3   *Atlanta Area Lower Education Population by County and Race, 1990*

County (Percentage Black)	Black Population		White Population		Total	Adjusted
	Percentage High School or Lower	Number	Percentage High School or Lower	Number	Black Percentage of Total	Black Percentage of Total
Clayton (24 percent)	46.1	20,009	65.2	85,824	19	15
Cobb (10 percent)	51.4	22,695	32.7	128,342	15	12
DeKalb (42 percent)	62.5	144,016	31.7	92,731	61	49
Fulton (50 percent)	41.1	133,167	39.9	123,803	52	42
Gwinnett (5 percent)	39.8	7,234	39.5	126,633	5	4
Total for area	49.6	327,121	38.9	557,333	37	30

Source: U.S. Department of Commerce 1992; Department of Housing and Consumer Services 1994.

earnings gaps as the result of the inability of low-skilled inner-city workers to obtain employment in job-rich suburbs (see chapter 6 herein; Holzer 1992; Ihlanfeldt and Sjoquist 1989, 1990; Kasarda 1983, 1989). If workers holding majority-black jobs disproportionately reside in the inner city, then they may display lower earnings due to spatial mismatch factors.

The GANS data on average earnings by residential and work location provide tentative findings (given the small number of cases in some cells) for the analysis of earnings based on work location. According to the GANS data, the Atlanta African American population is concentrated residentially in a two-county area; over 90 percent of those with a high school education or lower reside in Fulton and DeKalb counties (see table 9.4). Place of residence is not strongly linked to place of work. For example, among the lower-education population the residential distribution of workers in majority-black and in majority-white jobs is basically the same—approximately 60 percent live in Fulton and somewhat above 30 percent live in DeKalb.[2]

The location of the respondent's job does relate directly to the racial composition of the job. The vast majority of jobs held by African Americans are located in Fulton County (59.9 percent) and DeKalb County (21.1 percent). In all areas except the northern suburbs, majority-black jobs predominate. Approximately 86.0 percent of those in majority-black jobs work in Fulton (including the central business district) or

TABLE 9.4   *Job and Residence Location by Education Level and Racial Composition of Job for African American Workers in the Atlanta MSA*

	Majority-Black Job	Majority-White Job	All Jobs
Work locations			
Work in	N = 93	N = 54	N = 47
Central business district[a]	12.9%	5.7%	8.2%
Fulton	64.5	51.9	59.9
DeKalb	21.5	20.4	21.1
Clayton	4.3	1.9	3.4
Northern suburbs	8.6	26.0	14.9
Total	100.0[b]	100.0	100.0[b]
Residential locations			
Reside in	N = 227	N = 165	N = 392
Fulton	54.2%	46.7%	51.0%
DeKalb	36.6	40.6	38.3
Clayton	.9	3.6	2.0
Northern suburbs	4.7	7.9	6.6
Total	100.0[c]	100.0[c]	100.0[c]
Less than high school education workforce			
Reside in	N = 132	N = 65	N = 197
Fulton	60.6%	61.5%	60.9%
DeKalb	34.8	30.8	33.5
Both counties	95.4	92.3	94.4

Source: Greater Atlanta Neighborhood Study 1994.
[a]Included in figures for Fulton and DeKalb as well.
[b]Henry County accounted for 1 percent of majority-white jobs.
[c]Douglas County accounted for six majority-white and one majority-black jobs; Fayette County accounted for one majority-white job (3.6 percent of majority-black jobs; 2.1 percent of all jobs).

DeKalb counties, compared with 72.3 percent of those with majority-white jobs. On the whole, no more than a third of Atlanta's black workers live and work in the same county, and the highest percentages of this group is found in northern suburban Cobb, not in counties home to older concentrated black communities.

In summary, there is evidence that majority-black jobs are found disproportionately in the urban center, and that they are the more common situation everywhere except the northern Atlanta suburbs. If crowding—the concentration of minority workers due to restrictions to their working elsewhere—is occurring, this may partially account for lower wages in majority-black jobs. The majority of black workers ap-

TABLE 9.5   *Mean Earnings of African American Workers by Job Composition, Job, and Residential Location*

	Work Locations					
	Majority-Black Job	N	Majority-White Job	N	All Jobs	N	Standard Deviation
Works in Central business						
district	$21,696	13	$20,700	5	21,419	18	10,145.13
Fulton[a]	18,052	60	19,100	28	18,392	88	10,911.49
DeKalb	13,935	20	21,621	11	16,662	31	8,023.04
Northern suburbs	17,690	8	17,911	14	17,831	22	8,234.14

Source: Greater Atlanta Neighborhood Study 1994.
[a]Fulton County outside of Atlanta has mean earnings of $17,053 (n = 47) for majority-black jobs and $18,752 (n = 23) for majority-white jobs, with an overall mean of $17,615 (S.D. = $11,034.38).

pear highly mobile, however, as they do not live and work in the same county.

Analysis of earnings by racial majority of the job and spatial location shows some notable interactions. Surprisingly, the finding of lower average earnings in majority-black jobs does not hold over the entire Atlanta labor market. Instead, for all African American workers, the highest average earnings ($21,696) were recorded for work in the central business district in a majority-black job, while work in a majority-white job in the central business district also yielded comparably high earnings ($20,700; see table 9.5). Average earnings in the northern suburbs were comparable for both compositions ($17,831), and were lower than for both job compositions in Fulton County ($18,392). The lowest average earnings for all job compositions was in DeKalb ($16,662), where extreme dichotomy of earnings by racial majority of job is seen. In DeKalb, employment in majority-white jobs yielded high average earnings as expected ($21,621), alongside the very lowest earnings for majority-black jobs ($13,935).

The relationship between spatial location of jobs and earnings does not explain lower earnings in majority-black jobs, since earnings have been found to be higher on average for African Americans employed in the urban center and in majority-black jobs in the central business district. In DeKalb County, however, spatial mismatch factors seem to explain a lot, as majority-black jobs are also somewhat concentrated there and pay much less than majority-white jobs. This is surprising, given that the conditions expected to generate the underclass effects of low human capital are much more prevalent in Fulton County (which contains the majority of the city of Atlanta) than in DeKalb. There appears a rather extreme dichotomy in what is occurring in Fulton and DeKalb counties, which is unexplained by spatial mismatch theory.

An analysis of gender differences by location is tentative because of the small sample size. A discrepancy in the number of men willing to report their place of business (57) and the number of women (92) suggests that some nonreporting bias may be in effect as well. However, analysis of earnings by job location and gender shows that earnings among African American women tend to follow the aggregate pattern, but are slightly more extreme in that they have the highest average income ($27,700) in the central business district (see table 9.6). African American men, however, earned more on average in majority-white jobs in all occupations. The pattern of higher earnings in Fulton County and the northern suburbs and very low earnings in DeKalb County continues to hold. The differences by gender suggest that status factors operating to benefit women may be particularly important in Fulton County, since earnings could have been affected by two low-status rankings: race and gender (see chapters 7 and 8).

The Historical Record: Labor Market Segmentation

Labor market segmentation theories offer another way of understanding majority-black jobs. Neo-Marxist theoretical approaches, such as split-labor market theory and dual economy theory, stress the importance of monopoly by unions and firms of labor or commodity markets, so that they control conditions within them and are able to demand high prices. Central to the development of this power is the ability to use state power, or politics, to effect the closure of particular market opportunities. A historical analysis of the creation of majority-black jobs and integrated majority-white jobs illuminates how the exercise of political power over markets has functioned as a major factor of racial status (chapter 3 herein; Bayor 1996; Pomerantz 1996; Harmon 1996; Stone 1989; Holmes 1995, 1994, 1993; Orfield and Askhinaze 1991).

Abundant evidence tells the story of white workers and employers collaborating in relegating African Americans to low-wage jobs (Bayor 1996; Butler 1991; Pomerantz 1996; Foner 1974). For example:

> By the end of the 1950s there were still numerous jobs closed to blacks— for example, certain city jobs, including positions as firemen or building inspectors. . . . In the private sector, blacks could not get positions as truck

TABLE 9.6   *Mean Earnings of African American Workers by Job Composition, Gender, and Location*

	Women					
	Majority-Black Job	N	Majority-White Job	N	All Jobs	N
All locations	$16,671	64	$17,871	28	$17,036	92
Work in						
Central Business district	27,700	5	23,000	1	26,917	6
Fulton	17,921	38	16,866	10	17,701	48
DeKalb	13,751	16	24,340	7	16,973	23
Northern suburbs	18,517	7	15,356	9	16,739	16
	Men					
All locations	$17,354	29	$20,148	28	$18,727	57
Work in						
Central business district	17,944	8	20,125	4	18,670	12
Fulton	18,308	22	20,341	18	19,223	40
DeKalb	14,673	4	16,864	4	15,768	8
Northern suburbs	11,902	1	22,511	5	20,743	6

Source: Greater Atlanta Neighborhood Study 1994.

drivers on bread, milk, beer, and candy delivery routes; office workers and clerks in department stores and pharmacies; auto mechanics; workers at Southern Bell and Western Union; and skilled workers at Atlanta Steel Company. Even in federally sponsored work, black craftsmen lost out. [Bayor 1996, 111]

Where unionization was achieved, African Americans were generally restricted from union membership benefits (Bayor 1996, 111).

As well, blacks and whites were generally paid different wages for the same work (Frisbie and Neidert 1977). To the extent that majority-black jobs are those that historically have been race-typed, it is expected that earnings of such jobs will be lower.

Another explanation may be drawn from dual economy theory. Dual economy theory posits the existence of two market sectors: primary and secondary. Primary industries are those with greater power to amass surplus and thus greater leeway in providing returns to labor, which also becomes empowered by the conditions of the primary industry. They are characterized by monopolistic position within the market, high capital concentration and large scale of operations, and thus high productivity and surplus generation. Often their power begins with government sponsorship of a sort, through assignment of franchises or other regulation, extremely lucrative contracts, and assistance in maintaining market share (Hodson 1983; Hodson and Kaufman 1982). Race, as a measure of social status, generally became one line of demarcation, such that a firm with a majority of minority workers was considered part of the secondary sector (Portes and Bach 1985; Model 1987).

The picture of labor market segmentation is more complex today. Successful industrial unionization in many industries has resulted in greater racial equality due to more formalized universalistic employment conditions. Indeed, black workers have come to have the highest percentage of union members of any racial group (U.S. Department of Labor 1994), particularly within industrial unions, while African Americans employed in the service economy are subject to more exclusionary processes (Szafran 1982; Mueller, Parcel, and Tanaka 1989).

To explore dual economic theory, we assigned the industry in which a GANS respondent worked to one of forty-six major industries, and grouped them as either primary- or secondary-sector (based on the classification of Hodson [1983]). Approximately 74 percent of African American jobs in Atlanta were in the secondary sector, while 81 percent of majority-black jobs were in the secondary sector, as opposed to 65 percent of majority-white jobs (see figure 9.1). Organizational descriptives show that majority-black jobs have fewer of the characteristics that are associated with the primary sector (table 9.7).

Integrated Jobs and Class Shifts

Along with considering the historic placement of majority-black jobs at the bottom of the earnings hierarchy, we must also look at the assimilation of African Americans into integrated jobs, that is, majority-white jobs. This integration resulted not only in higher earnings vis-à-vis white workers, but in greater inequality between African Americans in majority-white jobs and those in majority-black jobs. The current vogue is to assert that lower-class blacks did not benefit from the opening of markets resulting from political power gained and political principles won in the civil rights movement (Wilson 1987; Dawson 1994), and to imply that benefits accrued only to the elite. There is much evidence to the contrary, however, supported by the case of Atlanta.

Integration of jobs largely began at the bottom of the job status hierarchy and worked upward to more elite and powerful positions. Basic working-class jobs were opened to blacks through civil rights struggles from the New Deal coalition era up to the 1970s (Cross 1984; Quadagno 1994). Fair Employment Practices legislation of the New Deal and desegregation of assembly line jobs by Executive Order 8802 in 1941 began the process. In Atlanta, municipal employment gains by African Ameri-

FIGURE 9.1   *Distribution of Jobs Held by Blacks by Industrial Sector*

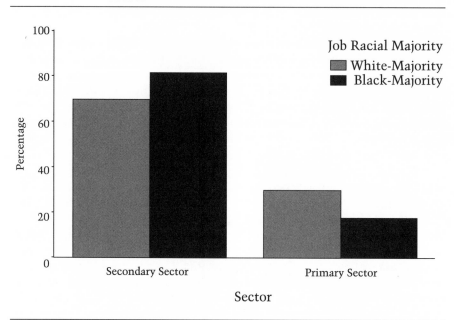

Source: Greater Atlanta Neighborhood Study 1994.

cans began about 1962, and by 1964 Atlanta for the first time employed African American brickmasons, building mechanics, switchboard operators, clerk typists, waste-collection drivers, pollution-control operators, and supervisors. Following targeting by civil rights groups, private in-

TABLE 9.7   *Organizational Descriptives of Jobs of African Americans by Racial Majority Composition*

Measure	Majority-White Job Composition N = 165	Majority-Black Job Composition N = 227
Percentage primary sector jobs	39.9**	17.7**
Percentage unionized	12.1	18.1
Percentage large firms	52.7**	39.2**
Percentage small firms	14.5*	23.8**
Percentage government jobs	21.2	19.8
Percentage high skilled	6.6	5.5
Percentage with authority	7.9	9.7

Source: Greater Atlanta Neighborhood Study 1994.
**Pearson Test significant at .01.
*Pearson Test significant at .05.

TABLE 9.8   *Desegregation Chronology for Atlanta, 1948 to 1980*

1948	First black policeman hired; by 1959, only 40 hired
1961	Southern Bell promotes first two blacks to mechanics level (no white-collar jobs)
1963	City sanitation department, forced by protests, hires first two black truck drivers (supervisors)
1964	First four black mechanics at city water works
1967	Nondiscrimination clause states companies engaged with city work must not discriminate
1969	First black firemen hired
1969	1969 to 1973: city government affirmative action raises black employees from 22 to 44 percent
1970	City jobs 38 percent black but only 9 percent white collar, 70 percent low-income (sanitation, janitor, and maid)
1970	Court-ordered Atlanta public school faculty desegregation
1971	Some formerly segregated craft union apprenticeships secured by blacks
1972	Equal Employment Opportunities Act passed
1972	First blacks hired by MARTA in semiskilled and higher positions
1972	1972 to 1978: black professional positions in city increase from 19.2 to 42.25 percent; managers from 13.5 to 32.6 percent
1973	1973 to 1978: city funds to black contractors increase from 2 percent to 33 percent
1974	Police and firemen struggle for promotion of blacks to chief and lieutenant
1979	Blacks hold only 3 of 458 positions on boards of 53 top Atlanta firms
1979	Banks appoint first black directors after Jackson threatens to remove city funds
1980	Hartsfield Airport construction completed with 25 percent of fees to black contractors

Sources: Bayor 1996; Harmon 1996; Pomerantz 1996; Stone 1989.

dustry began to follow suit (Harmon 1996, 185). Desegregation of craft, construction, and skilled jobs was forced through in the 1960s when black workers, prepared by training programs of the War on Poverty, were continually denied jobs; setasides and contract compliance grew in the antipoverty-program backlash of the 1970s, when black capitalism and self-help emerged as possible alternatives (Quadagno 1995). The history of job desegregation in Atlanta clearly mirrors this process, as shown in table 9.8.

Earl Black and Merle Black (1987) analyze the political and social changes connected to the changing demographic and industrial organization of the south and the rise of middle-class society. Among African Americans, there has been a rapid decline of what Black and Black define as the traditional lower class (nonindustrial laborers, private household workers, and agricultural workers), from 35 percent in 1960 to approximately 4 percent in 1980—with a corresponding rise in the new middle class (white-collar workers), from approximately 9 percent in 1960 to 32 percent in 1980 (see figure 9.2).[3]

Among African American women this is particularly evident, as 50 to 60 percent had been employed in traditional black low-class jobs from 1950 to 1960, while by 1980 less than 8 percent were. Rapid increases led to approximately 40 percent of African Americans being employed in new middle-class occupations and 50 percent in the working class by 1980. These jobs were filled largely not by an existing elite or middle-class African Americans, but rather by African Americans escaping historic lower-class work or shifting from blue-collar work.

An analysis of census data of occupational distribution by race in Atlanta in 1960 shows that African American men and women were most underrepresented in manager, official, and administrator jobs; sales jobs; professional and technical jobs; and craft and foremen jobs (see table 9.9).

African American men held less than one-tenth of the expected number of manager, official, and administrator positions, given their proportion in the labor force. On the other hand, they comprised 88 percent of the household laborer positions, almost four times the amount expected by their labor force proportion. Similar figures pertained for laborer positions. The inequality in the racial occupational distribution can be gauged by the index of dissimilarity, which measures the proportion of workers who would have to switch jobs to bring about an equitable racial distribution within each occupation (Tomaskovic-Devey 1993).[4] An index of dissimilarity computed for 1960 reveals that approximately 50 percent of men and 61 percent of women would have had to change jobs in order to achieve racial equality across occupations. Table 9.10 provides the same analysis for 1990.

While black overrepresentation in private household and laborer occupations has decreased, African American men and women are still approximately two and a half times more prevalent in these occupations.

The biggest shift for African American women has been out of private household work—which accounted for 45.7 percent of their jobs as late as 1960 but only 1.8 percent in 1990—and into clerical work, which was virtually closed to them in 1960 (employing 3.8 percent of African American women but 45 percent of white women). In 1990, roughly equivalent proportions of black and white women—31.5 and 30.3 percent, respectively—were employed in clerical jobs. Sales occupations show a similar pattern of initial closure to African American women, who held less than 10 percent of the expected number of positions, given the number of blacks in the labor force, and came to hold approximately 82 percent of expected positions by 1990.

FIGURE 9.2   *Black Class Shifts*

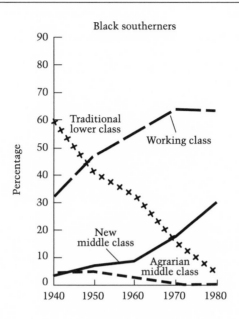

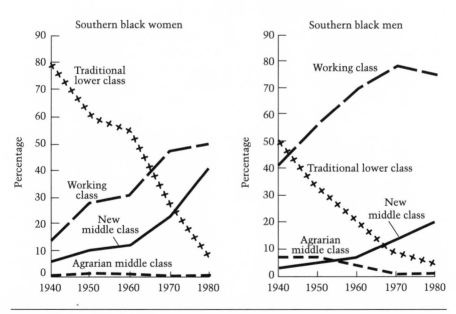

Source: Black and Black 1987.

TABLE 9.9   Atlanta Metro Area Occupational Distribution by Race and Sex, 1960

	Total Employed	Black		White		Percentage of Total Occupation		Multiple of Black Over/Under-Representation	Index of Dissimilarity
		Number	Occupational Distribution (Percentage)	Number	Occupational Distribution (Percentage)	Black	White		
Men									
Professional and technical	25,008	1,299	2.8	23,709	12.9	5.2	94.8	0.25	50.24
Managers, officials, proprietors	30,385	577	1.2	29,808	16.3	1.9	98.1	0.09	
Clerical	21,307	2,797	6.0	18,510	10.1	13.1	86.9	0.64	
Sales	22,815	614	1.3	22,201	12.1	2.7	97.3	0.13	
Craftsmen, foremen	39,893	4,042	8.6	35,851	19.6	10.1	89.9	0.49	
Operatives	41,239	12,189	26.0	29,050	15.9	29.6	70.4	1.44	
Private household	748	658	1.4	90	0.0	88.0	12.0	4.29	
Service	17,644	10,947	23.4	6,697	3.7	62.0	38.0	3.03	
Farm labor	1,148	383	0.8	765	0.4	33.4	66.6	1.63	
Laborers	15,664	9,797	20.9	5,867	3.2	62.5	37.5	3.05	
Not reported	12,782	3,346	7.1	9,436	5.2	26.2	73.8	1.28	
Total	228,633	46,813	99.6	183,116	99.4	20.4	79.6	0.99	
Women									
Professional and technical	15,282	2,171	5.9	13,111	13.2	14.2	85.8	0.53	61.36
Managers officials, proprietors	4,442	230	0.6	4,212	4.2	5.2	94.8	0.19	
Clerical	46,081	1,381	3.8	44,700	45.0	3.0	97.0	0.11	
Sales	9,287	243	0.7	9,044	9.1	2.6	97.4	0.10	
Craftsmen, foremen	1,542	210	0.6	1,332	1.3	13.6	86.4	0.50	
Operatives	16,070	4,389	11.9	11,681	11.8	27.3	72.7	1.01	
Private Household	19,191	16,794	45.7	2,397	2.4	87.5	12.5	3.24	
Service	15,228	8,679	23.6	6,549	6.6	57.0	43.0	2.11	
Farm labor	181	30	0.1	151	0.2	16.6	83.4	0.61	
Laborers	555	389	1.1	166	0.2	70.1	29.9	2.60	
Not reported	8,263	2,250	6.1	6,013	6.0	27.2	72.8	1.01	
Total	136,122	36,782	100.0	99,398	100.0	27.0	73.0	1.00	
Total population	364,755	83,595		282,514		22.9	77.5		

Source: U.S. Department of Commerce 1962.

TABLE 9.10 Atlanta Metro Area Occupational Distribution by Race and Sex, 1990

	Total Employed	Black		White		Percentage of Total Occupation		Multiple of Black Over-/Under-Representation	Index of Dissimilarity
		Number	Occupational Distribution (Percentage)	Number	Occupational Distribution (Percentage)	Black	White		
Men									
Professional and technical	109,400	14,555	9.9%	91,009	18.8%	13.3%	83.2%	0.59	
Managers, officials, proprietors	116,092	12,813	8.7	100,484	20.8	11.0	86.6	0.49	
Clerical	55,691	18,791	12.8	35,644	7.4	33.7	64.0	1.49	
Sales	99,976	11,442	7.8	86,331	17.9	11.4	86.4	0.51	
Craftsmen, foremen	99,378	19,957	13.5	75,521	15.6	20.1	76.0	0.89	
Operatives	68,512	27,858	18.9	38,164	7.9	40.7	55.7	1.80	
Private household	343	208	0.1	135	0.0	60.6	39.4	2.68	
Service	59,479	24,895	16.9	31,289	6.5	41.9	52.6	1.85	
Farm labor	9,442	2,546	1.7	6,408	1.3	27.0	67.9	1.19	
Laborers	34,141	14,275	9.7	18,238	3.8	41.8	53.4	1.85	
Not reported	0	0	0.0	0	0.0	0.0	0.0	0.00	
Total	652,454	147,340	100.0	483,223	100.0	22.6	74.1	1.00	33.24
Women									
Professional and technical	119,388	27,333	16.3	89,789	22.2	22.9	75.2	0.80	
Managers, officials, proprietors	89,113	18,568	11.0	68,976	17.0	20.8	77.4	0.73	
Clerical	178,110	52,979	31.5	122,643	30.3	29.7	68.9	1.04	
Sales	78,592	18,455	11.0	58,220	14.4	23.5	74.1	0.82	
Craftsmen, foremen	11,759	3,833	2.3	7,168	1.8	32.6	61.0	1.14	
Operatives	23,458	10,930	6.5	11,100	2.7	46.6	47.3	1.62	
Private household	4,648	3,048	1.8	1,471	0.4	65.6	31.6	2.28	
Service	72,330	29,234	17.4	40,543	10.0	40.4	56.1	1.41	
Farm labor	1,637	229	0.1	1,317	0.3	14.0	80.5	0.49	
Laborers	7,445	3,497	2.1	3,467	0.9	47.0	46.6	1.64	
Not reported	0	0	0.0	0	0.0	0.0	0.0	0.00	
Total	586,480	168,106	100.0	404,694	100.0	28.7	69.0	1.00	15.52
Total population	1,238,934	315,446		887,917		25.5	71.7		

Source: U.S. Department of Commerce 1992.

For African American men, no similar large opening of formerly segregated jobs occurred, although over- and underrepresentation did decline. Still, in 1990, 33 percent of men would have had to change jobs to bring about racial representativeness in occupations. Women, who tend to have jobs characterized by lesser earnings and authority, have come relatively close to parity, requiring a shift of only 15.5 percent to achieve representativeness.

Occupations, Job Racial Composition, and Earnings

An analysis of jobs held by African Americans, as reported in the GANS, shows that occupations with the greatest disproportion of majority-black jobs are service, sales, and laborers (see figure 9.3). These are also occupations with low levels of unionization and low wages. Most professional and technical jobs are also majority black, although the imbalance is not as pronounced. Predominantly majority-white occupations are manager, official, and administrator, clerical craft, and operative.

When the average earnings of blacks in majority-black and majority-white jobs are considered by occupation, it is found that the largest gaps in earnings exist in laborer, service, and sales jobs, which average 25 to 50 percent (see figure 9.4). The earnings differential also exists with managerial, clerical, craft, and operative jobs, but the gap is smaller, particularly with the latter three pink- and blue-collar jobs. The higher earnings in majority-white manager, official, and administrator positions, plus the preponderance of majority-white positions of this type, helps drive the earnings gap between majority-black and majority-white jobs in a manner consistent with Weberian analyses of earnings differentials due to differential authority held by the worker.

Professional and technical jobs present an anomaly, however, as majority-black jobs pay more than majority-white jobs. Greater earnings to employment in majority-black jobs in the central business district and Fulton County, for women in particular, are unexpected. Despite the overall low returns to employment in majority-black jobs, why do professional and technical jobs and those located in Fulton County, particularly those held by women and in the central business district, yield higher earnings? This is the question to which we now turn.

Higher Earnings in Majority-Black Jobs: Authority and Enclaves
Authority Relations Within Firms

Higher earnings in majority-black jobs may reflect placement in firms with well-developed authority hierarchies. It is in the dimension of au-

FIGURE 9.3   *Black Workers by Occupational Group and Racial*
Majority of Job

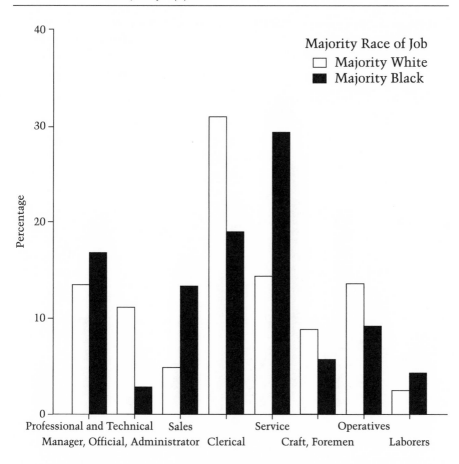

Occupational Group

Source: Greater Atlanta Neighborhood Study 1994.

thority that the greatest discrimination, and the greatest labor returns, are seen. Most managerial hierarchies have traditionally relied on strong mentoring and assimilation to yield bonds of trust among a homogeneous leadership (Domhoff 1983). Economic theories of organization have stressed the economies obtained through low transaction costs (Williamson 1991), one source of which is the reproduction of authority hierarchies (Kanter 1977). This is supported by the work of James R. Kluegel (1978), who found that on average, across occupations, the ex-

FIGURE 9.4   *Average Yearly Earnings by Occupational Group and Racial Majority of Job*

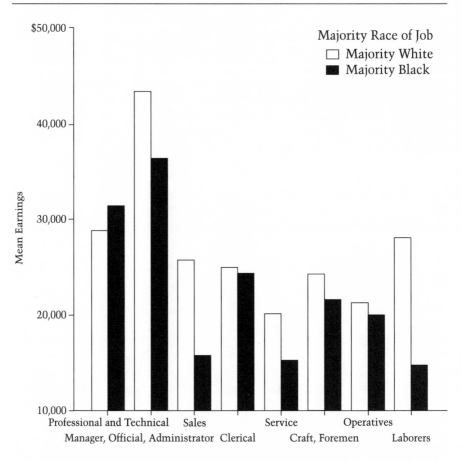

Occupational Group

Source: Greater Atlanta Neighborhood Study 1994.

clusion of African American men from positions of authority accounted for approximately one-third of the total black-white income gap.

Ethnic Enterprise and the African American Experience: Politicized Markets

Employment with higher levels of authority may occur in ethnic enterprises (Jiobu 1988). Study of ethnic enterprise in the U.S. was renewed in the 1970s, after the pioneering work of W. E. B. Du Bois (1898), Joseph Pierce (1947), and Abram L. Harris (1936). Ethnic enterprise theory has come to focus on the ability of a cohesive ethnic group to develop ownership of enterprises and to organize market relationships such that the outcome for the group is greater than without cooperation. (Light 1972; Bonacich and Modell 1982; Wilson and Martin 1982). However, unlike earlier theorists, recent theorists have tended not to consider African Americans as involved in ethnic enterprise because they are viewed as lacking a unifying ethnic-based solidarity. They show the importance of the creation of downward and upward linkages in an ethnic enclave to increased ethnic group control over market segments and the creation of multiplier effects by buying from co-ethnics.[5]

Robert M. Jiobu (1988) shifted the study of ethnic enterprises from a focus on location, ethnic customers, segmented markets, and immigration. He theorized a more general market process, which he terms the ethnic hegemonization of industrial arena(s). The concept of ethnic hegemony refers to an ethnic group obtaining an influential share of an industrial niche in the larger economy, such that the group achieves sufficient power in those markets to attain average or better economic returns.

Butler (1991) theorizes that, historically, African Americans have taken the route of ethnic enterprise like other minorities, however, they were blocked from most levels of participation in the greater U.S. economy. At the time of Booker T. Washington's famous Atlanta Compromise speech in 1898, it was felt that if African Americans abstained from politics and social equality, they would be able to cooperate and freely participate economically. Instead, in most areas of the south, they were driven out of particularly lucrative industries, such as oilfields in Arkansas, not allowed to practice skilled crafts, such as brickmasonry and mechanics, driven out of downtown business districts, refused banking and insurance services, and not allowed to open their places of entertainment to interracial clientele. They were "detoured" from the larger market route to prosperity, and thus developed businesses serving the black community. Unlike other minorities, blacks were forced to remain within the confines of their community.

Two important conclusions can be drawn from the theory of economic detour. First, true social and economic liberty to pursue a livelihood is dependent on full access to the larger market, not just to ethnically segmented markets. Second, political power is inextricably linked with economic power in the regulation of, and interference in, the market. It is this latter point that has heretofore been so often neglected.[6] A combined political and economic analysis takes into account how groups organize within racial and national solidarities to create political power, shape market outcomes that result in control over capital (ethnic hegemony), or resist others' use of capital to dominate their group (ethnic hegemonic contestation).

The Government Sector and Enterprise

Along with the denial that African Americans exhibit ethnic solidarity, it is popular to deny that the government sector can serve as a valid economic asset for creating business linkages (Waldinger 1986; Wilson 1978; Wilson and Martin 1982; Jiobu 1988). The public sector is seen as siphoning off black talent that could have gone toward business development or achieved influence in private-sector labor markets. However, first, the public sector clearly has been the source of the greatest accumulation of savings among African Americans which could be invested in business development. Oliver and Shapiro (1995) find that African Americans held net financial assets averaging $1,200 for workers in the secondary sector, $3,700 for those in the primary sector, and $4,300 for those in government employment (1995, 85). Further, Bates (1993) found that African American presence as mayors and significant city administrators was a major factor in increased ability of African American–owned businesses to become large enough no longer to be classified as primarily self-employment. The importance of the use of municipal political power to engender large-scale stable employment among other American ethnic groups is well documented (Lieberson 1980; Clark 1975, 1994).

African American Ethnic Hegemony Contestation

I argue here that African Americans in Atlanta have come to exercise a degree of ethnic solidarity that is sufficient for them to contest white market dominance in several industries. This argument is consistent, for the most part, with the theory of Jiobu (1988), who suggests the primary determinants for "ethnic hegemony" (he provides six aspects, which I have combined into four).

First, ethnic hegemony is predicated on the creation of a sheltered market for ethnic labor, a sort of internal labor market characterized by protection from "adverse effects of economic cycles, political attacks, insecure tenure, and competition from other workers" (Jiobu 1988, 355). The civil service of a government is given as an example, and is the primary arena employed by Atlanta's African Americans.

Second, the sheltered "internal market-like" situation is characterized by ethnic saturation. "Saturation increases the likelihood that minority individuals will find employment" (Jiobu 1988, 356). I focus here on majority-black jobs, which are those most likely to reflect saturation.

Third, this saturation will reflect minority group members crowding into low-wage jobs unless it is combined with ethnic economic control. This means that "ethnics are in positions to make important economic decisions, such as hiring, firing and business strategy" (Jiobu 1988, 356). In Atlanta, spreading from the government sector, African Americans waged a determined battle to force the opening of white-dominated labor markets and business markets.

Wayne Santoro (1995) studied the determinants of the translation of black political power into economic power, defined as the existence of viable affirmative-action employment and affirmative-action contracting programs. He tested the importance of black political incorporation—defined by Rufus P. Browning, Dale Rogers Marshall, and David H. Tabb (1984) as the presence of blacks in the local dominant political coalition, as opposed to simple representation within government. Based on his index, which incorporates whether a city has a black mayor, a black city council president or vice president, and the total number of remaining black council members, Atlanta has had an incorporated black political regime since 1974. He found that political incorporation was a significant factor for both employment and contract affirmative-action policies. This suggests that the organization of the ruling regime has a significant effect on market structuring decisions and outcomes related to the development of ethnic economic power.

In Atlanta, African Americans have achieved a considerable measure of influence over hiring, firing, and joint-enterprise and subcontracting decisions in industries within the government sector, or in industries in which the city government is heavily involved. Industries largely within the government sector include government employment, education and social services, and transportation and utilities.

Fourth, Jiobu states that "to be upwardly mobile the minority must hegemonize products or services that are in high demand by the majority, forcing the majority to deal with them. An *economic interface* between the majority and minority must exist" (1988, 356). Government involvement in the construction and real estate and finance industries creates the economic interface. A consistent set of industries has been influenced by the advent of local political power by particular minority ethnic groups—the Irish in New York and the Italians in Providence, Rhode Island, for example. Stanley Lieberson (1980) identifies construction, law, and related professions as particular provinces of political patronage that lead to amassing of capital, growing enterprise, and eventual differentiation and effective economic betterment for the ethnic group. Wilson and Martin (1982) show the initial importance of the construction industry to local business enterprise development, and the unique degree to which Cubans bought from and sold to other Cuban-owned enterprises, creating both upward linkages to professional services and real estate and important downward linkages to construction and manufacturing. Construction projects must pass code and zoning inspection, major projects often require tax abatements or public bond issues, and the value of real estate is integrally connected to city infrastructure, services, and urban planning decisions.

Therefore, it is hypothesized that five industries—construction, FIRE (finance, insurance, and real estate), transportation and utilities, social services and education, and government—would be the locus of ethnic hegemonic contestation precisely because of African American political incorporation in Atlanta.

Specific benefits within an ethnically hegemonized economic area are said to include the following:

(1) Discrimination against the minority is largely absent;

(2) The minority group achieves at least partial command over its own economic destiny, as it is not dependent solely on the goodwill of the majority nor forced into marginal secondary-sector jobs;

(3) A sheltered labor market is open to the minority members with more steady employment and upward mobility;

(4) Spillover effects such as described by Jiobu: "For example, unions wishing to organize that labor market are more likely to accept minority members; majority customers are more likely to deal with minority retailers and wholesalers; majority financial institutions are more likely to advance capital to minority businesses" (1988, 356).

Findings

Analysis of the GANS data provides support for employing a theory of contested hegemony to help explain the earnings outcomes of African Americans by racial composition of jobs. First, majority-black jobs may be divided into those that are theorized to belong to the sector contested by black political incorporation and those that do not. The latter are considered primarily a legacy from the historically segregated occupations. The contested sector jobs are in government, transportation and utilities, social services, construction and finance, insurance, and real estate. Industries with hiring patterns not directly affected by municipal linkages, and therefore most likely reflective of historic hiring patterns

TABLE 9.11   *Descriptives for Analysis of African American Earnings by Job Type and Other Variables*

Measure	Majority-White Jobs N = 165	Saturated Jobs (Majority Black)		Standard Deviation
		Contested Jobs N = 102	Historically Segregated Jobs N = 125	
Mean earnings	$24,139	$22,396	$14,951[a]	11,846.94
Job distribution	42.1%	26.0%	31.9%	—
Percentage female	58.8	66.7	68.8	—
Mean hours worked	40.7	39.6	38.5	8.95
Mean years education	13.5	13.5	12.5	2.23
Mean years experience	17.5	18.3	16.0[b]	11.08
Mean years tenure	7.1	8.1	4.9	7.62
Days on-the-job training	36[b]	14	8[b]	84
Percentage primary-sector jobs	29.9	24.5	12.1	—
Percentage unionized	12.1	32.4	6.4	—
Percentage large firms	52.7	46.1	33.6	—
Percentage small firms	14.5	16.7	29.6	—
Percentage government jobs	21.2	44.1	0	—
Percentage high-skilled	6.6	8.5	3.0	—
Percentage with authority	7.9	5.9	12.8	—

Source: Greater Atlanta Neighborhood Study 1994.
[a] t-Test significant at .01.
[b] t-Test significant at .05.

of segregation, are manufacturing, wholesale, retail, and services. When so divided, majority-black job outcomes display a bimodal pattern: labor outcomes in the black contested sector more closely resemble those in majority-white jobs than those in historically segregated jobs (see table 9.11). Mean earnings for full-time black workers in majority-white jobs are $24,139; $22,396 for black contested jobs; and $14,951 for historically segregated jobs. Earlier occupational analysis showed that in the professional and technical occupations, African Americans with majority-black co-workers earn more or the same as those with majority-white co-workers, unlike in every other occupational category. Average education attainment is equal among hegemonized job holders and majority-white job holders, which is consistent with greater professional and technical employment.

The high unionzation of contested jobs indicates primary-sector status or conditions such as found there. Consistent is the finding that significantly fewer historically segregated jobs are found in large firms.

TABLE 9.12   *Job Quality Descriptives for African American Workers by Job Type*

Measure	Majority-White Jobs (Percentage)	Saturated Jobs (Majority Black)	
		Contested Jobs (Percentage)	Historically Segregated Jobs (Percentage)
Respondent discriminated against in past year	16.7	11.8	9.8
Other promoted faster due to race	31.5	16.7[b]	25.8
Formal training provided	41.7	31.4	18.4[a]
Retirement plan provided	76.2	70.6	34.4[a]
Paid sick leave	77.4	73.5	44.8[a]
Health insurance for self provided	81.1	77.5	47.2[a]
Health insurance for family provided	75.9	72.2	44.2

Source: Greater Atlanta Neighborhood Study 1994.
[a]Pearson test significant at the .01 level.
[b]Pearson test significant at the .05 level.

There are also more women employed in historically segregated jobs, which may reflect their lower level of power in society, and the continued relegation to historically less-valued work. However, women employed in the central business district and Fulton County did not appear to suffer these conditions to a similar degree.

Average weekly hours and number of weeks worked (not shown) show no significant variation across the three job categories, although a slight hierarchy of more steady employment and more hours are found for white-majority jobs and contested jobs than for historically segregated jobs.

Contested sector jobs are also more similar to majority-white jobs in job quality (see table 9.12). The levels of nonwage benefits, such as training provided on the job, paid sick leave, health care, and retirement plans all show similarity between majority-white and contested jobs, and significantly higher levels than provided by historically segregated jobs.

The levels of supervisory responsibility at first appear to present something of an anomaly, as it is the sole dimension where historically segregated jobs provide more advantage. This is consistent, however, with findings that the majority of African Americans in authority positions are supervising other African Americans (Mueller, Parcel, and Tanaka 1989).

TABLE 9.13   *Mean Earnings of African American Workers by Job Type, Job, and Residential Location*

Work Location						
				Majority-Black Jobs		
	Majority-White Jobs		Contested Jobs		Historically Segregated Jobs	
Works in	$	N	$	N	$	N
Central business district	20,700	5	23,338	7	19,781	6
Fulton[a]	19,100	28	23,177	25	14,410	35
DeKalb	21,621	11	15,892	6	13,097	14
Northern suburbs	17,911	14	17,456	3	17,831	5
Residential Location						
Resides in						
Fulton	21,061	77	18,314	54	13,882	69
DeKalb	27,735	67	27,198	41	16,193	42
Northern suburbs	22,890	13	29,474	5	17,440	8

Source: Greater Atlanta Neighborhood Study 1994.
[a]Fulton County outside of Atlanta has mean earnings of $18,751 (N = 23) for majority-white jobs, $23,155 (N = 18) for contested jobs, and $13,299 (N = 29) for historically segregated jobs.

Spatial analysis also supports the existence of ethnic hegemonic contestation.[7] In the central business district and Fulton County, contested sector jobs have the greatest returns, $23,338 and $23,177, respectively (see table 9.13). For jobs located in DeKalb County, which is predominantly outside the city of Atlanta's political influence, earning patterns by racial majority of co-workers are the same as the overall pattern of largest earnings for majority-white jobs ($21,621), while majority-black jobs show low earnings; $15,892 (contested) and $13,097 (segregated).

Table 9.14 shows that blacks are more often employed in Fulton County, and contested jobs are disproportionately located in the central business district or Fulton County.

The GANS survey also provides some evidence of the strength of African American group solidarity. Table 9.15, which we will return to presently, shows the results of two questions related to notions of outcomes to group identity. The first question, "Do you think what happens generally to Black people in this country will have something to do with what happens in your life?" taps a feeling of group mutual destiny and is supported by 80 percent of respondents.

TABLE 9.14   *Job and Residential Location by Job Type for African American Workers in the Atlanta MSA*

| | | Majority-Black Jobs | |
Location	Majority-White Jobs	Contested Jobs	Historically Segregated Jobs
	Job Location		
Works in (N = 147)			
Central business			
district[a]	9.3	19.4	10.5
Fulton	51.9	69.4	61.4
DeKalb	20.4	20.4	24.6
Clayton	1.9	1.9	5.3
Northern suburbs	26.0	8.3	8.3
Total[b]	100.0	100.0	100.0

Source: Greater Atlanta Neighborhood Study 1994.
[a]Included in figures for Fulton and DeKalb as well.
[b]1 to 3 percent of cases located in other counties (see notes to table 9.4).

The Politics of Solidarity: Implications

Affirmative action is frequently attacked as ineffective; however, affirmative action and minority contracting can be seen as the most evident change in the social regulation of markets. It is in the arena of state power that dispossessed majorities (as for instance blacks in Atlanta) can contest the private control of capital which gives the power to dominate market exchanges, creating patterns of racial concentration and earnings in jobs. The ability of social groups who are supportive of affirmative action to assemble the resolve to continue this political protection is an open question. However, within cities like Atlanta, the continued maintenance of African American population concentration provides a kernel of political *power* that has the possibility, through the linkages of local government to contested industries, to maintain this protection *regardless* of whether it is legitimated as law. It is perhaps this implicit understanding that draws the tremendous African American migration—almost twice the white rate (chapter 2), giving Atlanta its reputation as a black mecca.

In this ensuing struggle, what is important to the future of mankind is an understanding of the workings of *solidarity*. That there is ambivalence to exercising dominance through group solidarity within the African American community is displayed by their disinclination to equate increased African American political power with *monopolization* of political power. For instance, the second question reported in table 9.15

TABLE 9.15   *Indicators of Racial Solidarity for African American Workers in Atlanta*

Do you think what happens generally to black people in this country will have something to do with what happens in your life? N = 386				
Yes = 80 percent		No = 20 percent		
(Do you agree that) the more influence blacks have in local politics, the less influence whites will have in politics? N = 93				
Strongly Agree	Generally Agree	Neither	Generally Disagree	Strongly Disagree
4 percent	16 percent	11 percent	23 percent	46 percent

Source: Greater Atlanta Neighborhood Study 1994.

relates to perceptions of African American political involvement as the enactment of a zero sum game. Only 4 percent of African Americans strongly agree while 73 percent strongly or generally disagree that if blacks gain political power, whites will lose political power. This is one strong reason for viewing the process of their exertion of political power to affect markets as one of *contesting existing white ethnic hegemony.* Further, to the extent that the greatest benefits were seen among African American women, it can be theorized that the proposed process of contesting racial domination in government-related industries involved the creation of openings for *excluded* workers previously disadvantaged by both race and gender. If the process were more correctly characterized as the imposition of a new domination, it would more likely resemble other power consolidations which tend to privilege males.

Conclusion

African Americans with majority-black co-workers earn less on average than those with majority-white co-workers, thus reflecting a situation of job saturation. A review of the history of job segregation and integration provides considerable support for relating this saturation of certain low-wage jobs by African Americans to processes of historic segregation and split-labor market conflict. Support is also found for explaining relatively higher earnings in jobs with majority-white composition as the product of civil rights struggles to open the white-dominated employment sectors of the Atlanta labor market. Further, for a significant proportion of majority-black jobs, higher earnings and other outcomes more similar to, or the same as, majority-white jobs have been found. A respecification of the theory of Jiobu (1988) to include viewing local government and industries affected by linkages with it as an economic sphere capable of *ethnic contestation* led to the finding of significant evidence of the existence of African American labor market contestation in Atlanta.

Analysis suggests that the black community has utilized political influence over the structuring of the market in five key industries (construction; real estate and finance; transportation and utilities; education and social services; and government employment) to create a sheltered labor market, which largely dispels the negative effects of low master status/low capital ownership. On the other hand, majority-black jobs that are the legacy of historic segregation, clustered in the urban center of DeKalb County, continue to provide the lowest returns, both monetarily and in terms of benefits. The contrast can be seen particularly in the central business district and Fulton County, where African American political incorporation exists and employment in majority-black jobs in contested industries provides earnings and conditions on par with those obtained in majority-white jobs.

The importance of processes of market monopolization as described by dual-economy theory are given support in that decreased labor force outcomes of traditional majority-black jobs correlate with their preponderance in the secondary sector. The contested jobs, however, have greater primary-sector composition and characteristics. There was little evidence to test the possibility of increased earnings in suburban jobs, which were more often integrated, but hegemonic processes in the city of Atlanta and Fulton County do appear to trump spatial disadvantages of distance from job growth, and yield robust earnings for African Americans.

These findings give support to the extension of theory of ethnic hegemony to consider political considerations as inextricably intertwined with economic processes. There is evidence that important political and social linkages are available through the government sector that can increase market outcomes for excluded groups. Theories of ethnic enterprise can broaden the perspective and enrich the study of outcomes to integration or ethnic concentration, particularly when they are extended to take into consideration the political economy of the African American experience.

Notes

1. Self-selection of African Americans into situations of majority-black co-workers that pay less due to location in financially circumscribed black neighborhoods is a fourth explanation that cannot be adequately evaluated here.

2. Further, neighborhood conditions within these counties cannot be equated with inner-city underclass conditions, as they range the full

gamut from dense public housing to new housing subdivisions and condominiums.

3. The agrarian middle class are farmers. The traditional middle class was made up primarily of agricultural and business owners, while the new middle class is primarily white-collar workers in clerical, sales, administrative, managerial, technical, and professional occupations. The traditional lower class were manual workers, primarily farm and household. The working class includes craft and operative workers, transport, service, and laborers (Black and Black 1987, 51).

4. Index of dissimilarity $=[.5(\Sigma|((n_1/N_1) - (n_2/N_2)|)]^* \ 100$, where n_1 and n_2 refer to the number of people in the job in status categories 1 and 2, and N_1, and N_2 refer to the total number of people in those status categories in the population, and the index is summed over the whole population.

5. Although the extent to which returns were better for employees versus owners remained debated for groups such as Chinese-Americans (Portes and Jenson 1992; Sanders and Nee 1987).

6. For instance, Robert M. Jiobu (1988) documents (but does not stress) the connections between the rise of Japan as a Pacific rim power, the government support for colonization and overseas land use by its people and the creation of conditions within the United States for their horticultural industry ethnic hegemony. Similarly, Kenneth L. Wilson and W. Allen Martin (1982) point to (but do not stress) the connection between the Cuban American role as pivotal allies in the political struggle against socialism, and their close ties economically and militarily, which were rewarded with unusually generous refugee relocation assistance provided directly by the U.S. government, and the success of Cuban ethnic enclave development.

7. Spatial mismatch theory would predict greater earnings in the northern suburbs, an area of rapid economic and job growth. However, there are too few cases in the northern suburbs to make a valid comparison.

References

Atlanta Regional Commission. 1993. *Economic Trends*. Atlanta, Ga.

Bates, Timothy. 1993. *Banking on Black Enterprise*. Washington, D.C.: Joint Center for Political and Economic Studies.

Bayor, Ronald H. 1996. *Race and the Shaping of Twentieth-Century Atlanta*. Chapel Hill: University of North Carolina Press.

Beggs, John J. 1995. "The Institutional Environment: Implications for Race and Gender Inequality in the U.S. Labor Market." *American Sociological Review* 60(August): 612–33.

Black, Earl, and Merle Black. 1987. *Politics and Society in the South.* Cambridge, Mass.: Harvard University Press.

Bonacich, Edna, and J. Modell. 1982. *The Economic Basis of Ethnic Solidarity.* Berkeley: Univ. of California Press.

Boston, Thomas D. 1988. *Race, Class and Conservativism.* Boston: Unwin Hyman.

Browning, Rufus P., Dale Rogers Marshall, and David H. Tabb. 1984. *Protest Is Not Enough.* Berkeley: University of California Press.

Butler, John Sibley. 1991. *Entrepreneurship and Self-Help Among Black Americans, a Reconsideration of Race and Economics.* Albany, N.Y. State University of New York Press.

Clark, Terry N. 1975. "The Irish Ethic and the Spirit of Patronage." *Ethnicity* 2: 305–59.

——. 1994. *Urban Innovation.* Thousand Oaks, Calif.: Sage Publications.

Cross, Theodore. 1984. *The Black Power Imperative, Racial Inequality and the Politics of Nonviolence.* New York: Faulkner.

Dawson, Michael C. 1994. *Behind the Mule: Race and Class in African American Politics.* Princeton, N.J.: Princeton University Press.

Department of Housing and Consumer Services, Extension Service. 1994. *The Georgia County Guide.* Atlanta: University of Georgia.

Domhoff, G. William. 1983. *Who Rules America Now?* Englewood Cliffs, N.J.: Prentice-Hall.

Du Bois, W. E. B. 1898. *The Negro in Business.* Atlanta: Atlanta University Press.

Farley, Reynolds. 1984. *Blacks and Whites, Narrowing the Gap?* Cambridge, Mass.: Harvard University Press.

Foner, Philip S. 1974. *Organized Labor and the Black Worker 1619–1973.* New York: International Publishers.

Frisbie, W. Parker, and Lisa Neidert. 1977. "Inequality and the Relative Size of Minority Population: A Comparative Analysis." *American Journal of Sociology* 82: 1007–30.

Guinier, Lani. 1994. *The Tyranny of the Majority: Fundamental Fairness in Representative Democracy.* New York: Free Press.

Harmon, David Andrew. 1996. *Beneath the Image of the Civil Rights Movement and Race Relations.* New York: Garland Publishing.

Harris, Abram L. 1936. *The Negro as Capitalist.* College Park, Md.: McGrath.

Hirsch, Barry T., and Edward J. Schumacher. 1992. "Labor Earnings, Discrimination, and the Racial Composition of Jobs." *Journal of Human Resources* 27(4): 602–28.

Hodson, Randy. 1983. *Worker's Earnings and Corporate Economic Structure.* New York: Harcourt Brace Jovanovich.

Hodson, Randy, and Robert L. Kaufman. 1982. "Economic Dualism: A Critical Review." *American Sociological Review* 49: 308–22.

Holmes, Bob. 1993. *The Status of Black Atlanta 1993.* Southern Center for Studies in Public Policy, Clarke Atlanta University.

———. 1994. *The Status of Black Atlanta 1994*. Southern Center for Studies in Public Policy, Clarke Atlanta University.

———. 1995. *The Status of Black Atlanta 1995*. Southern Center for Studies in Public Policy, Clarke Atlanta University.

Holzer, Harry. 1992. "Spatial Mismatch Theory." In *Urban Labor Markets and Job Opportunity*, edited by George E. Peterson and Wayne Vroman. Washington, D.C.: Urban Institute.

Ihlanfeldt, Keith R., and David L. Sjoquist. 1989. "The Impact of Job Decentralization on the Economic Welfare of Central City Blacks." *Journal of Urban Economics* 26: 110–30.

———. 1990. "Job Accessibility and Racial Differences in Youth Employment Rates." *American Economic Review* 80: 267–76.

Jiobu, Robert M. 1988. "Ethnic Hegemony and the Japanese of California." *American Sociological Review* 53(June): 353–67.

Kanter, Rosabeth. 1977. *Men and Women of the Corporation*. New York: Basic Books.

Kasarda, John D. 1983. "Entry Level Jobs, Mobility, and Urban Minority Unemployment." *Urban Affairs Quarterly* 19: 21–40.

———. 1989. "Urban Industrial Transition and the Underclass." *The Annals of the American Academy of Political and Social Science* 501: 34–47.

Kluegel, James R. 1978. "The Causes and Cost of Racial Exclusion from Job Authority." *American Sociological Review* 43: 285–301.

Lieberson, Stanley. 1980. *A Piece of the Pie: Blacks and White Immigrants Since 1880*. Berkeley: University of California Press.

Light, Ivan. 1972. *Ethnic Enterprise in America*. Berkeley: University of California Press.

Light, Ivan, and Carolyn Rosenstein. 1995. *Race, Ethnicity, and Entrepreneurship in Urban America*. New York: Aldine De Gruyter.

Model, Suzanne. 1987. "A Comparative Perspective on the Ethnic Enclave: Blacks, Italians, and Jews in New York City." *International Migration Review* 19(1): 64–81.

Mueller, Charles W., Toby L. Parcel, and Kazuko Tanaka. 1989. "Particularism in Authority Outcomes of Black and White Supervisors." *Social Science Research* 18: 1–20.

Oliver, Melvin L., and Thomas M. Shapiro. 1995. *Black Wealth, White Wealth, a New Perspective on Racial Inequality*. N.Y.: Routledge.

Orfield, Gary, and Carole Askhinaze. 1991. *The Closing Door: Conservative Policy and Black Opportunity*. Chicago: University of Chicago Press.

Pierce, Joseph. 1947. *Negro Business and Business Education*. New York: Harper and Bros.

Pomerantz, Gary M. 1996. *Where Peachtree Meets Sweet Auburn, The Saga of Two Families and the Making of Atlanta*. New York: Scribner.

Portes, Alejandro, and Robert L. Bach. 1985. *Latin Journey, Cuban and*

Mexican Immigrants in the United States. Berkeley: University of California Press.

Portes, Alejandro, and Leif Jensen. 1992. "Disproving the Enclave Hypothesis." *American Sociological Review* 57: 418–20.

Quadagno, Jill. 1994. *The Color of Welfare.* New York: Oxford.

Sanders, Jimy, and Victor Nee. 1987. "Limits of Ethnic Solidarity in the Enclave Economy." *American Sociological Review* 52(December): 745–73.

Santoro, Wayne. 1995. "Black Politics and Employment Policies: The Determinants of Local Government Affirmative Action." *Social Science Quarterly* 76 (December): 794–806.

Stone, Clarence N. 1989. *Regime Politics, Governing Atlanta, 1946–1988.* Lawrence: University of Kansas Press.

Szafran, Robert F. 1982. "What Kinds of Firms Hire and Promote Women and Blacks? A Review of the Literature." *Sociological Quarterly* 23 (Spring): 171–90.

Tomaskovic-Devey, Donald. 1993. *Gender and Racial Inequality at Work: The Sources and Consequences of Job Segregation.* Ithaca, N.Y.: IRL Press.

Turner, Susan C. 1996. "Barriers to a Better Break: Wages, Race and Space in Metropolitan Detroit." Wayne State University. Unpublished paper.

U.S. Department of Commerce, Bureau of the Census. 1962. *Census of Population: 1960, Characteristics of Population*, vol. 1, Part 12, Georgia. Washington: U.S. Government Printing Office.

———. 1992. *1990 Census of Population, Social and Economic Characteristics, Georgia* Washington: U.S. Government Printing Office.

U.S. Department of Labor. 1994. *Employment and Earnings* 41(1).

Waldinger, Roger. 1986. "Changing Ladders Musical Chairs: Ethnicity and Opportunity in Post-industrial New York." *Politics and Society* 15(4): 369–402.

Williamson, Oliver E. 1991. "Comparative Economic Organization: The Analysis of Discrete Structural Alternatives." *Administrative Science Quarterly* 36: 269–96.

Wilson, Kenneth L., and W. Allen Martin. 1982. "Ethnic Enclaves: A Comparison of the Cuban and Black Economies in Miami." *American Journal of Sociology* 88(1): 135–60.

Wilson, William Julius. 1978. *The Declining Significance of Race.* Chicago: University of Chicago Press.

———. 1987. *The Truly Disadvantaged: The Inner City, the Underclass, and Public Policy.* Chicago: University of Chicago Press.

10

FINDING WORK IN ATLANTA: IS THERE AN OPTIMAL STRATEGY FOR DISADVANTAGED JOB SEEKERS?

Nikki McIntyre Finlay

C HAPTER 6 discussed the role of spatial mismatch in explaining the Atlanta paradox, and concluded that access to job opportunities is important. Certainly, one of the important aspects of job policy is to ensure that job seekers who are poor know how to appropriately search the job opportunities that do exist. Unfortunately, job seekers living in poor areas are often at a double disadvantage when looking for work. First, they often live in areas suffering from declining employment, and thus may suffer from spatial mismatch. Second, family and friends of these workers often have little information about good jobs, while much of the empirical literature on job search concludes that the single best method for finding work is talking to family and friends (Corcoran, Datcher, and Duncan 1980; Hilaski 1971; Holzer 1988; Rees 1966).

The objective of this chapter is to explore how search strategy affects the outcome of a search and whether the poor use less effective strategies. Search strategy comprises two dimensions: effort expended and methods used. This chapter focuses on the search methods used, including referrals from family and friends, newspaper ads, direct application, and formal methods (such as employment agencies). (Finlay [1998] provides a more detailed analysis of the choice of the level of effort.) We explore the factors that determine which search method results in a job, and the effect of the search method on the outcome of the search. The outcome of a search has three dimensions: whether an acceptable offer arrives, the amount of time it takes for an acceptable offer to arrive (the duration of the search), and the compensation offered.

To determine both the choice of search strategy and the influence of that strategy on the outcome of a search, we developed a model of search outcome as a function of search strategy, the searcher's human capital, and an extensive set of control variables. This model assumes not only that the search strategy affects the outcome of a search, but also that the expected outcome of a search influences the strategy chosen. Highly skilled workers may be better able to use certain search methods, and therefore are more likely to use these methods than are lower-skilled workers. Highly skilled job seekers may also be more likely to know people with good jobs, and therefore better able to use these connections to find work.

Most models of job search outcome do not account for differences in strategy choice caused by human capital and other individual characteristics; Harry J. Holzer (1988) is the primary exception. As a result, parameter estimates of the impact of strategy on outcome may capture differences in job seekers. Additionally, parameter estimates of the impact of individual differences on outcome may capture some of the influence of strategy. Therefore, separating the influence of the choice of search strategy on the outcome from the influence of the ability of the job seeker himself is important. To overcome these problems, we use a two-stage estimation procedure to determine the impact of a particular strategy on the outcome of a search. Appendix 10A.1 presents additional details of the statistical methodology. (Finlay [1998] contains a detailed presentation of the methodology, which is also described in Maddala [1983, chap. 8.])

The models are estimated using the extensive information on job search characteristics and individual characteristics provided in the Greater Atlanta Neighborhood Study. (See the appendix to chapter 1 for a discussion of the GANS.) The variables of interest in this analysis are the probability that the search method will result in a job offer, the probability that a job seeker will use a particular method, and the effect of the search strategy on the outcome of the search—that is, the duration of a search and the hours and wage in the accepted job. Several results from these estimates demonstrate that strategy does influence the outcome and that disadvantaged workers often make different choices than skilled workers. The goal of this analysis is to determine whether job seekers in poverty areas can effectively overcome the problems of poor geographic location and job information deprivation.

How Jobs are Found

In his seminal article, Albert Rees (1966) explored the importance of information source in the hiring process. Nearly thirty years later, Heidi

L. Golding (1995) notes that information source is still an important gateway for job seekers. Both Rees and Golding use case studies of firm data. Studies of job seekers (Holzer 1988; Corcoran, Datcher, and Duncan 1980; Schiller 1975; Bradshaw 1973; Hilaski 1971) also confirm the importance of information source in determining whether a job offer arrives. Specifically, all of these studies show that the most common way to find work is through referrals by family and friends.

Several explanations support the hypothesis that referral by family and friends is the best method for getting a job. Rees's explanation, which centers on the cost of making a bad hiring decision, suggests that firms will view applicants referred by its current (presumably satisfactory) workforce with more favor than applicants arising from other sources of information. Current employees have a stake in the organization and will, therefore, be unwilling to refer unreliable acquaintances. Employees also know job seekers who are like themselves. As a result, the firm can hire from a pool of applicants whose abilities and attitudes are similar to its current workforce. This minimizes the likelihood of a hiring mistake. Additionally, the current workforce will know what a particular job requires and what kinds of working conditions arise (Montgomery 1991). Therefore, a referred applicant can minimize the risk of taking a job that doesn't meet his requirements.

In addition to the reasons given by Rees, the relationship between risk and the effectiveness of a given search method may be affected by the tasks that a potential worker is expected to perform. Firms may be more concerned about who fills jobs that require employees to have contact with customers, since these employees represent the firm. Therefore, having an employee who has the right attitude is important, and referrals reduce the risk of hiring a worker who does not have the proper attitude. On the other hand, firms may view jobs requiring easily demonstrable skills as less risky. For these jobs, firms may be more willing to accept applicants who use search methods other than referrals. Firms desperate for workers will also be more likely to accept applicants who are not referred by family and friends (Goodwin and Carlson 1981). In general, the other informal methods will be more important if the risk of hiring an inappropriate person is smaller or the labor market is tighter.

To a firm and to the employee, the jobs for which a hiring mistake is the most costly are highly paid, highly visible jobs, for example, professional jobs requiring both a high level of skill and the right attitude (Bartlett and Miller 1985; Ullman 1968). Furthermore, these jobs are rarely advertised (Gieseking and Plawin 1994). Although firms use executive recruiters to fill these positions, they are likely to prefer referrals by acquaintances, who in this case are usually colleagues who work for other companies (Payne 1987). Even if a pool of applicants comes from secondary sources, part of the screening process will involve calling references. For a member of the hiring firm to be able to contact someone he knows is ideal. Thus, highly skilled workers seeking highly paid jobs will be most likely to be hired through referrals by friends. Therefore, workers with higher levels of human capital should find that using referrals by friends is the most effective method of search.

There is one group, however, who may be better off using other methods. These are workers with poor access to information about jobs (Green, Tigges, and Browne 1994). These include workers living in depressed neighborhoods and workers whose acquaintances do not already have good jobs. While these job seekers often attempt to use formal methods to replace these poor connections, this may be unwise. Formal sources are costly to the firm and are therefore reserved for two classes of hiring. The first is a pressing demand for workers of a certain caliber. For example, retail stores often conduct interviews in college placement offices in the fall to get ready for Christmas. The other class is a need for a worker with very specific skills or types of experience. Displaced and disadvantaged workers are unlikely to meet either requirement. For these workers, the other informal methods may provide the best alternative to using family and friends to find work.

Unfortunately, direct application is also unlikely to be helpful. Disadvantaged job seekers may attempt to use walk-ins because it is easy. But living in a depressed area means that vacancy notices will be rare. Responding to newspaper ads may be more effective. Displaced workers may attempt to send resumes because this is what most highly skilled and highly educated workers have been taught to do. The chance of a resume finding someone who has both the authority and the need to hire the worker is slim (Payne 1987; Gieseking and Plawin 1994; Bolles 1994). Sending resumes is unlikely to be useful for another reason. The resume will emphasize experience in the worker's old industry. If the industry is declining, the worker may attempt to change industries, but a firm currently hiring workers in another industry may not see the experience as relevant. In this case, newspaper ads and Internet postings may help the worker pinpoint emerging opportunities.

The analysis of the GANS data provides some support for these previous findings of the relative success of search methods in various types of situations. Tables 10.1 through 10.4 present, by various categories, the search method that the respondent identified as resulting in the respondent's current job. While referrals are more likely to generate a job offer, walk-ins and newspaper ads are important sources of job information. Some interesting patterns emerge from the data. The success of using family and friends declines with education, while the success of

TABLE 10.1   *Successful Search Method, by Education*

| | Search Method | | | |
Education	Family and Friends	Newspaper Ads	Walk-in	Employment Agency
No degree	64.2%	9.9%	12.3%	4.9%
High school degree	57.1	16.2	15.8	8.3
Associate's degree	53.7	22.2	12.0	9.3
Bachelor's degree	43.5	25.0	17.7	11.3
Graduate degree	64.2	15.8	10.5	7.9

Source: Greater Atlanta Neighborhood Study 1994.

all other methods increases (see table 10.1). However, this pattern does not hold for those with graduate degrees, which provides some support for the hypothesis that among highly skilled workers, referrals are more effective. No clear pattern emerged by the type of task performed in the job, although the successfulness of using employment agencies increases with easily demonstrable skills (table 10.2).

Table 10.3 shows that the successful method differs by the industry in which the respondent found employment, with workers using referrals having the most success in the construction industry.[1] Workers in the financial, insurance, and real estate industry have the greatest success finding work through newspaper ads, while in the retail trade it is through direct application.

Table 10.4 shows that those living in thriving communities (as measured by employment growth) are more likely to obtain jobs from refer-

TABLE 10.2   *Successful Search Method, by Job Tasks Performed*

| | Search Method | | | |
Job Task	Family and Friends	Newspaper Ads	Walk-in	Employment Agency
Personal contact	58.5%	16.5%	16.7%	6.4%
Phone contact	55.3	20.2	14.6	8.4
Read instructions or reports	53.9	19.4	15.6	10.6
Write paragraphs	54.9	19.2	14.7	10.9
Computer skills	51.0	21.5	16.2	10.6
Arithmetic skills	56.1	17.2	15.8	9.4

Source: Greater Atlanta Neighborhood Study 1994.

TABLE 10.3   *Successful Search Method, by Industry*

Industry	Percentage Change in Employment[a]	Search Method			
		Family and Friends	Newspaper Ads	Walk-in	Employment Agency
Construction	−9.79%	64.1%	17.9%	7.7%	10.3%
Manufacturing	−3.03	57.1	17.9	10.7	14.3
Retail	1.37	54.5	11.4	28.0	5.3
Finance, insurance, real estate	1.83	54.8	31.0	7.1	7.1
Government	2.97	52.9	20.6	16.2	10.3
Services	11.61	59.1	20.9	10.2	6.5
Other		45.2	16.4	14.4	12.5

Source: Atlanta Regional Commission 1994; Greater Atlanta Neighborhood Study 1994.
[a]Appendix 10A.2 describes the employment data.

rals. (See appendix 10A.2 for a discussion of how employment growth was measured.) Surprisingly, those living in areas experiencing moderate job loss (up to 10 percent) are more likely to have found their jobs from walk-ins and formal search methods. Those living in areas experiencing heavy job loss (over 10 percent) find more success using newspaper ads. This suggests that these job seekers attempt to find work in other areas, where personal knowledge of job opportunities and the knowledge of friends and family may be limited. These results indicate the problem with referrals by family and friends. Informal networks are very useful for those who have good contacts in the labor market. Those lacking

TABLE 10.4   *Successful Method, by Neighborhood Employment Change[a]*

Percentage Change in Employment by Residential Location	Search Methods			
	Family and Friends	Newspaper Ads	Walk-in	Employment Agency
< −10 percent	56.5%	19.4%	11.3%	7.3%
0 percent to −10 percent	54.0	18.0	25.0	12.7
10 percent to 0 percent	53.0	19.7	18.8	8.0
> 10 percent	63.0	16.3	15.2	3.3

Source: Greater Atlanta Neighborhood Study 1994.
[a]Appendix 10A.2 describes the employment data.

such contacts may be shut out of potentially good employment opportunities if they rely on the informal networks they do have.

These data also show that alternatives to referrals can be a viable option for certain workers. Nearly 40 percent of all workers in the GANS found work through methods other than referrals.

To investigate this issue more fully, we estimated, using Probit analysis, structural regressions of the probability that a particular search method led to the respondent's current job. Several types of variables were used to estimate these structural equations, including search methods used, search effort, expected search outcome, human capital variables (education and training), labor supply variables (tenure), labor demand variables, demographic variables, transportation mode choice, search location, and social network variables. We believe that search methods used and search effort are endogenous, and thus use the predicted value of these variables from regressions estimated as part of the first stage regressions. (See appendix 10A.1 for more details on the estimation procedure.)

We focus on the parameters on a subset of variables included in the regression, in particular, access to search location, transportation mode, market demand for labor, and social network variables. (See Finlay [1998] for the complete set of parameters.) The first set of variables measures access to selected search areas. The GANS identified seven geographic areas (see map 10.1; see chapter 1 for a description of these seven areas), and for each area the respondent was asked if he or she had searched there. These variables were interacted with a dummy variable that equaled 1 if the respondent lived near the area being searched.[2] Transportation mode is measured by the means the respondent uses to get to work. As noted, the type of access a job seeker has plays an important role in determining the successfulness of referrals by family and friends. Labor market conditions are expected to contribute to the usefulness of a particular method, so measures of labor demand, as measured by the percent change over the period 1990 to 1993 in the level of employment in the respondent's community and in the respondent's industry of employment, are included. The GANS includes a set of questions concerning the characteristics of the individuals who make up the respondent's social network. Given the importance that the literature places on the role of social networks in the job search process, the set of explanatory variables includes attributes of the primary support person.

The selected parameters are presented in table 10.5. Many of the coefficients are insignificant. The first set of variables measures geographic access to search areas. Proximity to one of the identified search areas is expected to have an effect on how jobs are found. None of the

MAP 10.1   *Metropolitan Atlanta*

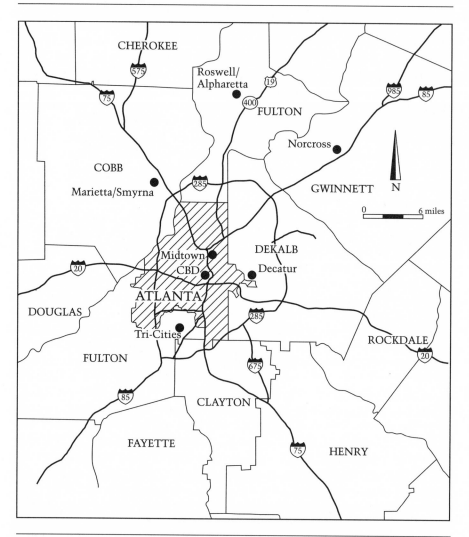

Source: Cartographic Research Laboratory, Department of Geography, Georgia State University, 1999.

coefficients on these variables is significant in affecting the success of formal search methods. In general, searching close to home increases the likelihood of finding a job through direct application (walk-ins) and decreases the likelihood of finding a job through family and friends. The exception to the pattern is for Atlanta residents who search in Midtown.

TABLE 10.5 *Successful Job Search Methods: Selected Parameter Estimates (Standard Error in Parentheses)*

| | Search Method Resulting in a Job | | | |
Variable	Family and Friends	Newspaper Ads	Walk-in	Formal
Search in				
Atlanta X lives in Atlanta	-0.83^a	0.54	2.17^a	-0.15
	(0.41)	(0.60)	(0.94)	(0.70)
Decatur X lives in DeKalb	-0.42	0.30	0.61	-0.46
	(0.37)	(0.68)	(0.85)	(0.59)
Tri-Cities X lives in South Metro	-0.87^a	0.22	0.07	-0.60
	(0.41)	(0.56)	(0.90)	(0.61)
Midtown X lives in Atlanta	-0.41	1.21^a	-2.76^a	-0.66
	(0.38)	(0.57)	(1.03)	(0.72)
Marietta-Smyrna X lives in Cobb	-0.26	0.44	2.14^a	-0.68
	(0.32)	(0.55)	(0.76)	(0.82)
Midtown X lives in DeKalb	-0.12	-0.51	-0.04	0.46
	(0.38)	(0.68)	(0.79)	(0.63)
Alpharetta-Roswell X lives in North Fulton	-0.97^b	1.12^c	-5.71	0.98
	(0.54)	(0.73)	(26.1)	(1.04)
Norcross X lives in Gwinnett	-1.12^a	0.89	1.59^c	0.80
	(0.53)	(0.73)	(1.04)	(0.79)
Public transportation			3.05^a	-2.61^a
			(1.53)	(1.27)
Walk to work			-1.11	-3.06^b
			(1.95)	(1.71)
Car to work			1.66^c	-3.11^a
			(1.18)	(1.21)
Carpool to work			-3.90	-6.63
			(23.2)	(19.4)
Car to search		0.74^c		
		(0.46)		
Percentage change in employment in respondent's community		-0.043^a	-0.018	0.006
		(0.021)	(0.033)	(0.033)
Percentage change in employment in respondent's industry	-0.036^c	0.039^c	0.11^c	-0.09^a
	(0.021)	(0.028)	(0.06)	(0.04)
Characteristics of social network				
Gender (female = 1)	-0.55^a	0.64^b	0.79^b	0.36
	(0.21)	(0.33)	(0.46)	(0.37)
Relationship (co-worker = 1)	-0.16	0.12	0.69^b	0.59^b
	(0.24)	(0.52)	(0.39)	(0.32)
Marital status (married = 1)	-0.05	0.02	-1.43^a	0.58^c
	(0.20)	(0.29)	(0.51)	(0.37)
Lives in same neighborhood	0.36^c	-1.08^a	0.25	-0.30
	(0.21)	(0.37)	(0.44)	(0.39)

TABLE 10.5   *Continued*

| Variable | Search Method Resulting in a Job | | | |
	Family and Friends	Newspaper Ads	Walk-in	Formal
Lives in same neighborhood	−0.34	1.68[b]	−0.58	
and is high poverty	(0.65)	(0.90)	(5.49)	
Respondent helped support	0.49[a]	−1.10[a]	−0.41	0.79[b]
person	(0.21)	(0.36)	(0.42)	(0.42)
Support person will help	−0.33	0.36	0.24	−1.08
in crisis	(0.45)	(0.83)	(1.05)	(0.87)
Support person is employed	−0.44[c]	0.62[c]	−0.01	0.06
	(0.26)	(0.45)	(0.57)	(0.51)
Support person receives	0.51	−0.20	−2.65[a]	−0.47
public assistance	(0.52)	(0.75)	(1.28)	(0.93)
Education	0.04	−0.07	0.21	−0.17
	(0.08)	(0.13)	(0.17)	(0.15)
Race (black = 1)	−0.07	0.73[b]	0.08	−0.23
	(0.23)	(0.41)	(0.54)	(0.48)
N	294	294	294	331
Likelihood ratio	99.2	120.9	144.9	67.2
(d.f.)	(57)	(59)	(62)	(54)

Source: Author's tabulations.
[a]Significant at the 5 percent level.
[b]Significant at the 10 percent level.
[c]Significant at the 20 percent level.

Searching in that area increases the effectiveness of newspaper ads and decreases the effectiveness of walk-ins and direct application. Since Midtown is becoming the secondary financial district, many jobs are advertised. Additionally, the Midtown area has experienced tremendous job growth. In this situation, firms are more likely to post job listings in the classifieds.

Those living in North Fulton County (near Roswell-Alpharetta) have a higher chance of finding a job through newspaper ads if they search close to home. Jobs and residences in this area are spread out. Going through newspaper ads can help narrow the search. For residents of Gwinnett and Cobb, searching close to home increases the chances of finding a job using walk-ins. These are both high growth areas suffering from local labor shortages. Gwinnett has experienced the highest growth in high-tech jobs in the country.

The kind of transportation used also has an impact on the method most likely to result in an acceptable job offer. Using public transportation or a car increases the probability of finding a job through direct application and reduces the chances of finding a job through formal methods. Having a car available to search increases the chances of finding work through newspaper ads, in keeping with the results cited here.

The next two variables measure labor market demand. The higher the percent change in the number of jobs within the respondent's residential area, the lower the probability that newspaper ads will result in a job. This is in keeping with the results in table 10.4. The coefficient on the percent change in employment within the neighborhood for success of walk-ins is not significantly different from zero. This is unexpected. However, overall growth in employment does not necessarily indicate growth in jobs requiring direct application. For example, the downtown area lost jobs during this period. However, job seekers looking for work in the government sector have the second highest probability of finding work through direct applications (table 10.3), and most federal and state government jobs are located in the downtown and midtown areas.

The other variable measuring labor demand is the percent change in employment in the industry in which the respondent is employed. This has a positive influence on the probability that responding to newspaper ads and direct application will result in an offer. This is expected, since expanding industries are more likely to recruit workers through newspaper ads and to accept walk-ins. A higher percent change in employment in the respondent's industry leads to a lower likelihood of finding work through formal methods and through family and friends.

The attributes of the primary support person also influence how jobs are found. Of the demographic indicators, the gender of the support person is most influential. If the support person is female, then the probability of finding a job through family and friends is lower, while the probability of finding a job through direct application or newspaper ads is higher. If the support person is married, then the probability of finding a job through formal methods is higher and the probability of finding a job through direct application is lower. These results may reflect labor market attachment as well as access to people with information about good jobs.

In contradiction to Rees's hypothesis (1966) that referral by a co-worker is the best method for getting a job, if the primary support person is a co-worker, then the chance of finding work through direct application is higher. This may result from using more than one method to find out about a job opening (Golding 1995).

The most interesting results come from the neighborhood variables. Living in the same neighborhood as the primary support person increases the probability of finding a job through family and friends and reduces the probability of finding a job through newspaper ads. However, the reverse is true if the respondent lives in a poverty area. Again, those living in poor neighborhoods do better if they can find other sources of job information and can look farther afield. Supporting these findings, having friends who receive public assistance also decreases the chances of finding work though walk-ins. Those who know people on public assistance may be more likely to live in depressed areas of the Atlanta region.

Knowing people who are working increases the usefulness of newspaper ads and decreases the usefulness of family and friends. These findings contradict Rees's hypothesis. Mark Granovetter's (cited in Green, Tigges, and Browne 1994, 6) hypothesis that weak social ties matter more than strong social ties may explain these odd results. If the respondent has strong social ties, primarily family relationships, to most of the people in the network, then these ties may be less helpful in seeking work. Given that GANS oversampled poverty neighborhoods, this is a reasonable conclusion. Interestingly, having a black primary support person increases the chances of successfully using newspaper ads. If the respondents have social ties to people who are like themselves, then this suggests that black job seekers in Atlanta have a better chance of finding work through newspaper ads. Yet, the results presented here indicate that black workers are more likely to use direct application.

The final network variable is the ability of the respondent to aid the support person. If the respondent is able to give aid, then the usefulness of family and friends and formal methods increases and the usefulness of newspaper ads decreases. Those who have the resources to help their friends are more likely to have friends who know about good job openings. These workers are also more likely to be able to use placement services successfully.

While an offer is an important indicator of the success of a search, the actual attributes of the job offer also need to be considered. Finding a job that has the right hours and an acceptable wage within a reasonable amount of time is the reason most workers undertake a search. The next section analyzes the influence of the choice of strategy and the successfulness of that strategy on hours, wages, and the duration of the search.

How Search Strategy Influences the Outcome of a Job Search

While determining which search method is most helpful in finding work is important, determining how that strategy influences the actual job found is also important. For example, table 10.6 shows that direct application (walk-ins) is the quickest way to find work, but also yields the lowest wages. We consider three outcomes—duration of the search, hours worked, and wages—which are measured as log wages. There are several categories of variables that are expected to affect the three out-

TABLE 10.6   *Impact of Successful Method on Outcome*

	Search Duration in Weeks			Hours at Work			Hourly Wage		
	N	Mean	Standard Deviation	N	Mean	Standard Deviation	N	Mean	Standard Deviation
Found job using family and friends	162	22.9	73.2	304	39.2	11.79	274	9.27	5.79
Found job using newspaper ads	50	25.6	57.0	103	39.8	8.94	82	9.58	4.77
Found job using walk-in	35	17.8	28.6	71	38.1	13.9	54	8.32	5.32
Found job using employment agency	27	33.5	77.1	46	38.8	12.2	38	9.65	4.87
Total	282	23.2	65.6	530	39.3	11.7	452	9.22	5.47

Source: Author's tabulations.

comes and that, therefore, should be included in the regressions. The following discusses these sets of variables.

Indicators of investment in human capital (education and experience) are expected to have a major positive impact on wages and hours. However, the appropriateness of the search strategy should also have a direct impact on wages and hours. The direct impact on hours is the result of the increased tendency for highly skilled workers to choose full-time work. Referrals by family and friends should generate better job matches for those seeking high-paying and high-skilled positions. Responding to newspaper advertising and direct application (walk-ins) should be most useful for lower-paying jobs. Again, those who are more able should be more likely to choose the most appropriate strategy. Additionally, firms may reward certain kinds of search behavior, particularly if that behavior reliably signals reduced risk of an inappropriate hire. It may seem that only the actual method that generates an offer, rather than the methods used, is of importance. This is what the firm sees and rewards. However, since search effort and methods used may influence the number and kinds of opportunities a job seeker actually encounters, these variables also belong in the outcome equation (Schwab, Rynes, and Aldag 1990). Different search methods may give a job seeker access to different employment opportunities.

Prior work on the influence of search strategy on the wage rate has been inconclusive (Allen and Keaveny 1980; Reid 1972). As noted, the choice of search strategy is likely to be influenced by the expected outcome. In addition, the ability of the worker influences both the outcome of a search and the choice of search method. Workers with more education and experience should receive higher wages and work longer hours. They should also spend more time looking for a job when they do search. In addition to measures of human capital, duration and compensation depend on how the market rewards the individual characteristics of workers, such as perceived labor market attachment.

The spatial mismatch hypothesis suggests that duration and compensation in geographically dispersed areas like Atlanta will also depend on where the job seeker looks for work. Therefore, measures of geographic access are included in the regressions. The regressions also included labor supply variables (such as whether the respondent quit his or her previous job), measures of liquidity, and measures of labor demand as explanatory variables.

The estimation approach mirrors that used above—that is, the search variables are estimates from the (unreported) first-stage regression. Table 10.7 contains selected coefficients from the regressions; see Finlay (1998) for the full set of parameters. The results are for job seekers who had found work.

As with the regressions reported in table 10.5, many of the coefficients are not significant. The first set of regression coefficients of interest includes measures of the impact of the search method that actually results in an offer; the values of these variables come from the first-stage regressions. Two significant results emerge: finding work through direct application (walk-in) results in a lower wage, and formal search methods lead to an increase in hours worked. The first result is in keeping with the previously published results. Direct application is the easiest method to use, but does not always generate the best outcome.

The second set of regression coefficients shows the impact of search method used, regardless of whether it was successful. Using family and friends increases the duration of a search, as does using newspaper ads. The positive effects on duration from using family and friends and from using newspaper ads are as expected and are consistent with previously stated results.

The search method does affect the hours worked. Using family and friends and formal search results in fewer hours, while use of walk-ins results in a job with more hours.

Using newspaper ads results in lower wages. This result is not completely surprising, for two reasons. First, the use of newspaper ads is helpful for poverty-area respondents. These job seekers may have less education and experience than workers in nonpoverty areas, or they may be less likely to have the demonstrable skills that newspaper ads cater to. Second, using newspaper ads is, from the firm's perspective, a

TABLE 10.7   *Selected Parameter Estimates for the Outcome of a Search (Standard Errors in Parentheses)*

	Duration	Hours	Log Wage
Prob (job found using family and friends)	0.30	1.63	−0.09
	(0.47)	(2.02)	(0.11)
Prob (job found using newspaper)	−0.13	0.54	0.01
	(0.11)	(0.52)	(0.03)
Prob (job found using walk-in)	−0.23	0.41	−0.15[a]
	(0.31)	(1.29)	(0.07)
Prob (job found using employment agency)	−0.01	0.33[b]	−0.005
	(0.05)	(0.20)	(0.010)
Prob (used family and friends)	0.53[a]	−2.37[a]	−0.03
	(0.25)	(1.13)	(0.06)
Prob (used newspaper)	0.42[c]	1.58	−0.11[c]
	(0.28)	(1.34)	(0.07)
Prob (used walk-ins)	−0.08	3.64[a]	0.03
	(0.22)	(0.97)	(0.05)
Prob (used formal)	−0.03	−3.16[a]	0.004
	(0.32)	(1.32)	(0.07)
Race (Black = 1)	0.24	3.55[a]	−0.06
	(0.36)	(1.78)	(0.08)
Race (Hispanic = 1)	−0.41	−3.24	0.003
	(0.84)	(4.86)	(0.21)
Married × Female	0.46	0.16	−0.09
	(0.41)	(2.93)	(0.10)
Gender (Female = 1)	−0.01	−3.69[a]	−0.01
	(0.33)	(1.82)	(0.08)
Searched in central business district	−0.21		−0.05
	(0.40)		(0.08)
Search in Decatur	0.20		−0.04
	(0.38)		(0.08)
Search in Midtown	0.38		−0.004
	(0.36)		(0.08)
Search in Marietta-Smyrna	0.03		−0.03
	(0.30)		(0.07)
Search in Alpharetta-Roswell	−0.15		−0.07
	(0.36)		(0.08)
Search in Norcross	0.17		0.25[a]
	(0.39)		(0.09)
Search in Tri-Cities	−1.21[a]		0.06
	(0.39)		(0.09)
Car to work			0.33[b]
			(0.19)
Lives in Atlanta	0.90[a]		
	(0.36)		
N	290	470	475
Scale	1.30		

TABLE 10.7   *Continued*

	Duration	Hours	Log Wage
(Standard error)	(0.09)		
F-statistic		3.19	5.11
R-squared		.34	.61
Density		−12.42	−1.19
(Standard error)		(7.01)	(0.58)

Source: Author's tabulations.
[a]Significant at the 5 percent level.
[b]Significant at the 10 percent level.
[c]Significant at the 20 percent level.

more risky method of recruitment. Therefore, the firm will pay lower wages to compensate for the increased risk. None of the other search usage variables in table 10.7 is significant for the wage equation.

These disappointing results may indicate that search strategy variables do not explain much of the variation in the outcome of a search. There are two reasons to remain hopeful. First, this estimation uses observations for job searches conducted from five years prior to the survey up to the time of the survey. Even if the chosen job search strategy conveys information to both the job seeker and the firm, it is likely that the effects will dissipate over time (Allen and Keaveny 1980). Also, including these variables does alter the behavior of other variables in the outcome regressions, as compared to a straightforward simultaneous equations system that only models the outcome. These results are noted below.

The third set of variables is the demographic variables, and contains perhaps the most interesting findings. For job hunters who had completed their search, neither race nor gender is significantly different from zero in the duration and wage equations. Contrary to the usual finding, blacks and women who have recently completed job searches do not receive wages that differ significantly from white men. The only demographic variables that are significant are race and gender in the hours equation.

These results suggest that previously cited (Holzer 1987a, 1987b) race and gender differentials may be capturing differing returns to search or different strategy choices. In a preliminary study using GANS, Edwards (1994) found that blacks do not choose to search differently than whites, although blacks are heavier users of all methods than whites. However, when differences in human capital, the expected gains from search, and other individual attributes are accounted for in the choice of strategy, blacks do, in fact, search differently than whites. Blacks are much more likely to use direct application, which is associated with lower wages, as noted in table 10.6.

Two alternative explanations are worth noting. First, GANS oversampled in poor neighborhoods. Inside the Perimeter (that is, Interstate 285), poor neighborhoods are usually black. Poor white neighborhoods tend to be located in the suburban and exurban areas of the metropolitan Atlanta area. Poor black neighborhoods are therefore more likely to be sampled than poor white neighborhoods. It may be that different choices attributed to racial differences should be ascribed to income differences. It is interesting to note, however, that Hispanics are more likely to choose newspaper ads, and that there is no wage differential.

The fourth set of variables of interest in this analysis includes the areas searched. Searching in Norcross (one of the fastest-growing employment centers in the metro Atlanta area) has a positive impact on wages. Searching around the airport (Tri-Cities) decreases the duration of a search. Many of the job offers in this area may require direct application, leading to shorter search spells. Union activity is also higher in this area.

Finally, transportation mode influences the wage outcome of a search; using a car for commutes leads to higher wages. Those with cars have access to a wider variety of jobs, since many areas of rapid employment growth cannot be reached by public transportation. As a result, these job seekers can find a higher-paying job more quickly than job seekers with restricted transportation access. Living in the city of Atlanta results in longer search spells, a finding that may reflect the absence of a car. This is an important issue for disadvantaged workers in the Atlanta area. Since jobs are dispersed over a large geographic area, not having a car may interfere with the job search process. Nevertheless, there are areas of the city that are accessible by public transportation and that are experiencing job growth in industries that often rely on newspaper ads to recruit workers. The question remains, Do disadvantaged workers use search methods that will allow them to find out about these jobs?

Job Search Strategies for Disadvantaged Workers

This section focuses on the respondent's choice of search methods. In contrast to much prior empirical work, direct application was the most heavily used search method (see tables 10.8 through 10.11). This is true even for workers who would not be considered disadvantaged. From the tables we see that only five groups used referrals (family and friends) more often than direct application (walk-ins)—namely, respondents without a high school degree, respondents with a graduate degree, respondents working in the construction and manufacturing industries, and respondents living in areas experiencing moderate job loss. While

TABLE 10.8   *Search Methods Used, by Education[a]*

Education	Family and Friends	Newspaper Ads	Walk-in	Employment Agency
No degree	80.3%	52.5%	73.8%	33.8%
High school degree	78.0	66.8	78.0	43.1
Associate's degree	69.7	73.2	83.5	52.8
Bachelor's degree	78.7	75.6	88.5	56.2
Graduate degree	92.3	65.8	81.6	63.2

Source: Greater Atlanta Neighborhood Study 1994.
[a]Respondents listed all methods used.

direct application is associated with shorter search duration, it is also associated with lower wages.

Four explanations for these patterns are worth noting. First, the average level of education is a high school diploma. The use of referrals may be positively related to the level of education. Workers with higher levels of education should be more capable of using the more complicated methods of job search. The easiest method to use is direct application.

Responding to newspaper ads requires a certain level of reading comprehension, as well as access to newspapers. Using placement services or other formal methods requires the ability to follow directions and the tenacity to maintain contact with the placement specialist. Further, certain placement services are accessible only to certain workers. Union halls accept only members, college placement offices work only with alumni, and executive recruiters call only experienced, senior-level workers. For noneducational classifications, the average education level may be influencing the usage proportions.

TABLE 10.9   *Search Methods Used, by Job Tasks Performed[a]*

Job Task	Family and Friends	Newspaper Ads	Walk-in	Employment Agency
Personal contact	77.4%	67.0%	83.5%	47.5%
Phone contact	77.2	70.4	85.0	49.9
Read instructions or reports	77.9	69.6	84.1	51.8
Write paragraphs	77.1	71.2	85.3	55.5
Computer skills	75.8	71.0	86.6	56.4
Arithmetic skills	76.5	68.7	84.3	49.0

Source: Greater Atlanta Neighborhood Study 1994.
[a]Respondents listed all methods used.

TABLE 10.10   Search Methods Used, by Industry Demand[a]

Industry	Percentage Change in Employment	Search Methods			
		Family and Friends	Newspaper Ads	Walk-in	Employment Agency
Construction	9.79%	87.2%	59.0%	81.6%	49.5%
Manufacturing	−3.03	78.6	78.2	71.8	41.0
Retail	1.37	75.2	57.7	85.7	54.6
Finance, Insurance, Real Estate	1.83	78.1	71.4	82.4	34.4
Government	2.97	76.4	71.0	85.4	51.2
Services	11.61	79.4	61.8	80.9	51.5
Other		79.4	73.5	81.6	49.5

Source: Greater Atlanta Neighborhood Study 1994.
Respondents listed all methods used. Appendix 10A.2 describes the additional data used to construct these tables.

Another possibility is that some job seekers used more than one method for the same job. A friend or relative could give the respondent information about a job that leads to a direct application. Since direct application includes sending resumes, this is very plausible. A third possibility is that patterns of job seeking have changed over time.

The final possibility is related to informational constraints. The GANS data oversampled households from poverty areas. If network quality is an important determinant of method choice, then respondents from poorer households are likely to exhibit a different pattern of behavior. For using family and friends to be successful, the worker must know people with better jobs. Ideally, these contacts should have "weak" so-

TABLE 10.11   Usage of Methods, by Neighborhood Demand[a]

Percentage Change in Employment by Residential Location	Search Methods			
	Family and Friends	Newspaper Ads	Walk-in	Employment Agency
< −10 percent	76.8%	72.0%	83.2%	47.2%
0 percent to −10 percent	81.4	69.5	78.7	49.2
10 percent to 0 percent	75.6	67.6	79.7	47.6
> 10 percent	78.3	58.2	83.7	42.2

Source: Greater Atlanta Neighborhood Study 1994.
[a]Respondents listed all methods used.

cial ties to the job seeker (Green, Tigges, and Browne 1994; see also chapter 11). That is, these contacts should not be relatives or neighbors, but acquaintances whom the job seeker knows from work, school, or other organizations. People with higher levels of human capital are more likely to live in different neighborhoods from their co-workers, to maintain ties to former classmates, and to join other formal organizations. Having a broad range of acquaintances, particularly in a city as large and as spread out as Atlanta, increases the chances of hearing about new job opportunities. As noted by Hal Gieseking and Paul Plawin (1994), finding out about job opportunities before they are officially posted can be the most effective means of getting a new job.

The results from the regressions on the probability that a job seeker will use a particular search method provide some support for the above hypotheses. Although space precludes a discussion of these more formal analyses of the choice of search methods, several results merit attention. Table 10.12 presents selected parameters from these regressions; see Nikki McIntyre Finlay (1998) for a discussion of all the parameters.

The first result of interest is that respondents who live in the same neighborhood as the members of their informal support network are less likely to use referrals and direct application. However, this result becomes significantly positive (in one-tailed tests) if the respondent lives in a nonpoor census tract. (A nonpoor census tract has few residents with incomes under the poverty threshold.) These results indicate the importance of both geographic access and information access. Another indicator of information access—the number of years the respondent has lived in the Atlanta area—is also positively associated with the use of family and friends.

Transportation access is an important component of geographic access and an important determinant of the probability that a job seeker will use a given method. Having a car available to look for work increases the use of newspaper ads and walk-ins, as expected. However, those who looked for work in the Midtown area, which is highly accessible by public transportation, also chose to use newspaper ads. This result shows the importance of the recruiting methods preferred by an industry. This also shows that it is possible to use newspaper ads successfully in the Atlanta area when a car is not available.

Disturbingly, for all respondents in the Atlanta survey who searched for work, the pattern of search methods used (table 10.8) differs greatly from the pattern of search methods that resulted in a job. Referrals account for more than 50 percent of all offers, while other informal methods account for less than 30 percent of all offers. Tables 10.8 through 10.11 show that job seekers overuse newspaper ads and direct applications, considering the relative ineffectiveness of these methods.

TABLE 10.12   *Selected Parameter Estimates for the Choice of Methods (Standard Errors in Parentheses)*

| | Search Methods Used | | | |
	Family and Friends	Newspaper Ads	Walk-in	Formal
Same neighborhood as primary support person	−0.81[b]	−0.49	−0.48	−0.39
	(0.47)	(0.36)	(0.40)	(0.40)
Same neighborhood as primary support person X nonpoor	1.01[a]	0.38	0.53	0.28
	(0.48)	(0.37)	(0.43)	(0.36)
Years lived in Atlanta	0.020[a]	0.002	0.006	−0.010[c]
	(0.008)	(0.007)	(0.008)	(0.007)
Car to search	−0.36[c]	0.78[a]	0.57[a]	−0.29
	(0.26)	(0.26)	(0.29)	(0.23)
Search Midtown	−0.06	0.59[a]	0.54[b]	−0.31[c]
	(0.24)	(0.26)	(0.29)	(0.21)
Race (black = 1)	−0.36	0.34	1.29[a]	0.22
	(0.40)	(0.37)	(0.38)	(0.37)
N	407	412	427	423
Likelihood ratio	105.2	148.3	125.8	147.0
(d.f.)	(66)	(72)	(70)	(71)

Source: Author's tabulations.
[a]Significant at the 5 percent level.
[b]Significant at the 10 percent level.
[c]Significant at the 20 percent level.

This is particularly true for black job seekers. Blacks are much more likely to use direct applications than are whites. This may be because contacting firms through family and friends is very inexpensive in terms of time and money outlays, which allows more time to allocate to less effective methods. Or, this may be because direct application is easy to use.

Conclusion

The results from the estimation do indicate that while the actual strategy may have little influence on the outcome, there is an optimal search strategy for disadvantaged workers. The important step is choosing to search. Changing jobs generally leads to higher salaries and more contacts. Using newspaper ads results in lower wages, as does successful use of direct application. However, using newspaper ads is helpful for two kinds of job seekers. Workers with poor information access and workers living in depressed areas of the metro area benefit from the information provided in the classified, particularly when a car is available. It would appear that different search strategies do convey different information. No other study has found these positive effects for using classified ads.

These findings also suggest how public employment assistance programs might improve placement services for disadvantaged workers. Helping those job seekers who have difficulty accessing and comprehending newspaper postings may prove a more worthwhile form of assistance than sending these workers directly to potential employers. Although Internet postings are usually aimed at highly skilled workers, providing job seekers with access to these services may also improve placement service.

These results also support the hypothesis that access to jobs is very important. This analysis used two kinds of variables to control for access: information about the quality of the respondent's social network and indicators of transportation access. The results generated by this analysis confirm many of the problems that other researchers have found. Those with poor access to job information will have trouble finding good jobs simply because they lack ties to people who are working.

One of the aspects of information access explored in this research is locational. Those who have ties outside their families and neighborhoods are more likely to find good jobs using referrals. The more geographically widespread a job hunter's informal network, the better the jobs obtained using informal search methods will be. Those who know people in other areas of the city are at an advantage. This is often inherent. Those with greater ability are more likely to have larger personal communities and to be able to exploit that knowledge base. However, certain kinds of workers can successfully use other informal methods until they have established ties to the labor market that go beyond neighborhood boundaries.

This chapter is drawn from my dissertation. I would like to thank the chair of my committee, Keith Ihlanfeldt, and the other members, Chris Bollinger, Julie Hotchkiss, Lynn Shore, and Paula Stephan, for their assistance.

Appendix 10A.1
Empirical Methodology

This research uses an adaptation of the search theoretic model of Holzer (1988). Job search inputs (a certain amount of time devoted to search and a choice of methods used to search) are combined with the latent ability of the worker to produce job offers. Wage, hours, and the duration of the search spell characterize offers. To analyze the impact of strategy choice and productivity on outcome, this research estimates a simultaneous equations model. This model comprises three subsystems. The search strategy variables compose the first subsystem, indicators of search productivity compose the second subsystem, and search outcome variables compose the third subsystem.

Were this system linear, the procedure would entail use of two-stage least squares or three-stage least squares. Unfortunately, eleven of the endogenous variables are dichotomous and three are censored. We use a limited-information estimation approach. G. S. Maddala (1983) and D. F. Nelson and L. Olsen (1978) outline two-stage procedures similar to two-stage least squares for these kinds of variables. Although more efficient estimation procedures exist, the emphasis in this analysis is on consistent estimation. The rest of this appendix provides a general overview of the estimation procedure and the selection problems encountered.

Two-Stage Estimation

This analysis uses the two-stage procedure to keep the estimation of a fifteen-equation system with mixed variables manageable. The two-stage procedure estimates the reduced form for each equation using the union of the set of exogenous variables that are available for all those in the sample. The procedure estimates reduced forms for effort, number of contacts, the number of interviews, wages and hours equations using ordinary least squares (OLS), reduced forms for the employment status (whether employed or unemployed at the time of search), method and jobfind equations using probit, and the reduced form for duration using censored regression. The procedure then generates structural estimates for each endogenous variable using the reduced form estimates of the included endogenous variables as instruments. This is similar to the ordinary two-stage least squares estimation used for most simultaneous equations models. According to Donald Cox and George Jakubson (1995), this procedure provides consistent estimates.

To identify parameters, each equation includes at least one unique exogenous variable. An additional problem with the instrumental variables approach occurs when the instruments do not adequately represent the endogenous right-hand side variables. John Bound, Dana A. Jaeger, and Regina Baker (1995) suggest testing the significance of the excluded instruments to determine whether the instruments themselves are causing an additional source of bias in the parameter estimates. F-tests on the excluded instruments were also run. Each of these statistics indicates that the instruments are probably not an additional source of bias in the structural estimates.

Selection

There are two potential sources of selection bias. The first is the standard wage-hours selection problem. Generally wages and hours are unknown for individuals not currently working. This is not a major problem in the GANS data, since the data set reports wages for all those who have worked within the previous five years.[3] (This analysis does exclude recent entrants. However, of the 660 job seekers in the GANS data, only 11 were new entrants. The GANS data differs significantly from other data sets used to study job search in that all respondents are over twenty-one.) Therefore, some measure of wage is available for all those in the sample. Most of those excluded are permanently out of the labor force.

The second source of selection is that outcomes are unknown for those who still had not completed their searches at the time of the survey. Fortunately, job search theory provides a method for dealing with this difficulty. For those who have searched and found new jobs, the accepted wage exceeds the reservation wage. For those who had quit their previous job or who were searching while employed, and had not yet found work, the current wage is less than the reservation wage.[4] (Generally, those who had not found work at the time of the survey had not searched as long as those who had found work.) A variation of the method used by Nicholas M. Kiefer and G. R. Neumann (1979) fits the theoretical model and results in a good fit.

Appendix 10A.2
Employment Data

Additional data come from *Employment 1994* published by the Atlanta Regional Commission (ARC). This analysis uses two measures of labor demand constructed from these data. The first is the percent change in employment by superdistrict from 1990 to 1993. A superdistrict is an area within a county encompassing several contiguous census tracts and sharing a common geographical or economic designation (see chapter 2). These years correspond approximately to the time frame of the GANS survey. Since the ARC experienced some data collection problems with the 1991 data, data were not reported for 1991 and 1992.[5] The GANS data identify the residential census tract of each respondent and this analysis codes the residential county, the closest business district, and the superdistrict. Using the superdistrict rather than the census tract allows the analysis to avoid cumbersome gravity measures of proximate employment, while still giving a reasonable picture of the employment prospects close to the respondent.

   The second measure of labor demand is the percent change in employment by industry from 1990 to 1993. A handful of GANS respondents did not report an industry. The analysis uses the overall level of employment growth in Atlanta for these respondents. Additionally, since the ARC changed the industry assignment for approximately 6,000 hospital jobs, the analysis uses the weighted average of the two industries (services and government) for medical services (SIC codes 810-819). Finally, in some of the equations the analysis uses dummy variables representing the occupation and industry of the job seeker.

Notes

1. This may differ from findings in other cities for two reasons. First, Georgia is a right-to-work state, so union activity has always been limited. Also, in the Atlanta area, many construction workers are recent immigrants from Central and South America, relying on word-of-mouth from other immigrants.

2. The residential areas are larger than the defined search areas.

3. Wage inflation was minimal during this time frame.

4. This analysis also excludes the twenty-five job seekers who were fired and had not found work. Again, the GANS data gives a different perspective. In this case, most job seekers are employed.

5. Approximately 1,500 jobs were allocated to DeKalb County when these jobs should have been allocated to Gwinnett County. Using the longer time frame gives a truer picture of employment growth for these two areas.

References

Allen, Robert E., and Timothy J. Keaveny. 1980. "The Relative Effectiveness of Alternative Job Sources." *Journal of Vocational Behavior* 16: 18–32.

Atlanta Regional Commission. 1995. *Employment, 1994.* Atlanta: Atlanta Regional Commission.

Bartlett, Robin L., and Timothy I. Miller. 1985. "Executive Compensation: Female Executives and Networking." *American Economic Review Papers and Proceedings* 75: 266–70.

Bolles, Richard Nelson. 1994. *What Color Is Your Parachute.* 1997 ed. Berkeley, Calif.: Ten Speed Press.

Bound, John, David A. Jaeger, and Regina Baker. 1995. "Problems with Instrumental Variables Estimation When the Correlation Between the Instruments and the Endogenous Variable is Weak." *Journal of the American Statistical Association* 90: 443–50.

Bradshaw, Thomas F. 1973. "Job-Seeking Methods Used by Unemployed Workers." *Monthly Labor Review* 96 (February): 35–40.

Corcoran, Mary, Linda Datcher, and Greg J. Duncan. 1980. "Information and Influence Networks in Labor Markets." In *Five Thousand American Families—Patterns of Economic Progress*, vol. 8. Ann Arbor, Mich.: Institute for Social Research.

Cox, Donald, and George Jakubson. 1995. "The Connection Between Public Transfers and Private Interfamily Transfers." *Journal of Public Economics* 57: 129–67.

Edwards, Barbara. 1994. "Job Search Methods: Does the Neighborhood Affect the Outcome?" Policy Research Center, Georgia State University, Atlanta. Unpublished paper.

Finlay, Nikki McIntyre. 1998. "The Relationship Between Job Search Strategy and Job Search Outcome." Ph.D. diss., Georgia State University.

Gieseking, Hal, and Paul Plawin. 1994. *30 Days to a Good Job*. New York: Fireside.

Golding, Heidi L. W. 1995. "The Effects of Job Matching Methods on Employment Outcomes: An Analysis of Two Firms' Employment Records." Paper presented at SEA meetings, Department of Economics, University of Maryland, Baltimore.

Goodwin, William B., and John A. Carlson. 1981. "Job-Advertising and Wage Control Spillovers." *Journal of Human Resources* 16: 80–93.

Green, Gary P., Leann M. Tigges, and Irene Browne. 1994. "Social Resources, Job Search, and Poverty in Atlanta." Working paper. Emory University.

Hilaski, Harvey J. 1971. "How Poverty Area Residents Look for Work." *Monthly Labor Review* 94 (March): 41–45.

Holzer, Harry J. 1987a. "Informal Job Search and Black Youth Unemployment." *American Economic Review* 77: 446–52.

———. 1987b. "Job Search by Employed and Unemployed Youth." *Industrial and Labor Relations Review* 40: 601–11.

———. 1988. "Search Methods Used by Unemployed Youth." *Journal of Labor Economics* 6: 1–20.

Kiefer, Nicholas M., and G. R. Neumann. 1979. "Estimation of Wage Offer Distributions and Reservation Wages." In *Studies of the Economics of Search*, edited by S. A. Lippman and J. J. McCall. New York: North Holland.

Maddala, G. S. 1983. *Limited-Dependent and Qualitative Variables in Econometrics*. Cambridge: Cambridge University Press.

Montgomery, James D. 1991. "Social Networks and Labor-Market Outcomes: Toward an Economic Analysis." *American Economic Review* 81: 1,408–18.

Nelson, F. D., and L. Olsen. 1978. "Specification and Estimation of a Simultaneous Equation Model with Limited Dependent Variables." *International Economic Review* 19: 695–710.

Payne, Richard A. 1987. *How to Get a Better Job Quicker*. New York: New American Library.

Rees, Albert. 1966. "Information Networks in Labor Markets." *American Economic Review Papers and Proceedings* 56: 559–66.

Reid, Graham L. 1972. "Job Search and the Effectiveness of Job-Finding Methods." *Industrial and Labor Relations Review* 2: 479–95.

Schiller, Bradley R. 1975. "Job Search Media: Utilization and effectiveness." *Quarterly Review of Economics and Business* 15: 55–63.

Schwab, Donald P., Sara L. Rynes, and Ramon J. Aldag. 1990. "Theories and Research on Job Search and Choice. In *Organizational Entry*, edited by G. R. Ferris and K. M. Rowland. Greenwich, Conn.: JAI Press.

Ullman, Joseph C. 1968. "Interfirm Differences in the Cost of Clerical Workers." *Journal of Business* 41: 153–65.

11

"SOMEONE TO COUNT ON": INFORMAL SUPPORT

Gary Paul Green, Roger B. Hammer, and Leann M. Tigges

A GROWING debate in the urban poverty literature focuses on whether African American poverty is accompanied by social isolation (Fernandez and Harris 1992; Wilson 1987, 1996). *Social isolation* refers to poor individuals' lack of social ties with others, especially those with jobs, higher levels of education, and resources that could provide them with support, especially informal employment information. Social isolation, it is alleged, is primarily the result of the declining number of jobs for unskilled African Americans in the inner city, coupled with residential segregation by race and income (Wilson 1996).[1] The loss of middle-income jobs, and employed people, in the inner city restricts the mobility of the poor and the number of role models for youth. Residential concentration of the impoverished, many of whom are not employed, decreases the potential of associating with individuals who have information about jobs, and creates a so-called underclass, whose behaviors in some ways deviate from mainstream society. Members of the underclass are doubly disadvantaged because they have fewer personal ties, and their social contacts do not provide them with resources leading to employment or support (Huckfeldt 1983).

Why is social isolation important for understanding urban poverty? Social relationships often provide informal support for individuals. Support can assume a variety of forms, including emotional support, material aid and services, information, and new social contacts. The types of interpersonal contacts that provide the bulk of informal support are with kin, friends, and neighbors and through social organizations such as the church (Fernandez and Harris 1992). In this chapter, we examine the influences on instrumental support provided to and received from those outside the household among Atlanta residents. By "instrumental support" we mean assistance with a variety of activities and needs, such as taking care of children, getting a ride somewhere, and lending money.

The Atlanta paradox—strong economic growth accompanied by the persistence of poverty among a large percentage of the black population—presents an interesting context for the study of informal support and social isolation. Although the recent economic growth may not have affected the overall material well-being of the poor in Atlanta, there are two possible scenarios for its effect on their social resources.

First, the poor may be socially isolated and may not have been in a position to benefit either directly or indirectly from the economic growth in the region. If the poor have few social contacts with others outside their neighborhood or with those who are not poor, economic growth should have little effect on the availability of social resources, and class and racial differences in the availability of social resources should persist. This scenario does not preclude social networks among poor individuals and households with strong reciprocal commitments but limited material resources.

An alternative scenario emphasizes social support rather than isolation. Although the rapid economic growth that has occurred in the Atlanta metropolitan area may not have directly benefited those left in poverty, it may have affected those who are linked to the poor in a variety of ways, such as through kinship and friendship. Thus, as a result of economic growth there may be more social resources available to the poor. The large black middle class in the city may provide greater opportunities for the urban poor to establish social ties across class lines. Kin ties across class lines may be especially effective in reducing the social isolation that is so endemic in poor neighborhoods.

Social networks resulting from historical migration patterns from rural areas into Atlanta also may provide greater access to social support. Annie Barnes (1985) found that many families in Atlanta belonged to clubs established by migrants from specific rural localities. These clubs provided stronger ties than did neighborhood organizations. Barnes's study suggests that recent arrivals whose kin were already established in the city have larger, more effective interpersonal networks and potentially greater access to informal support than those without these established ties. This argument would suggest that there should be few racial or class differences in the availability of social resources.

Much of the existing literature on informal support focuses on the role of social networks in influencing the income and mobility of individuals (Bridges and Villemez 1986; Granovetter 1974; Lin, Ensel, and Vaughn 1981; Marsden and Hurlbert 1988). Here we focus on access to instrumental support, especially child care, transportation, and money.

Access to child care is critical to mothers' labor force participation (Stolzenberg and Waite 1984), and it is influenced by employment opportunities and interpersonal networks. Transportation is also an important determinant of labor force participation. In many urban areas in the United States, there is evidence of a growing spatial mismatch between where the poor live and where jobs are being created (Holzer 1991, chap. 6). Access to monetary resources for housing and other basic needs is essential for many younger individuals and families who are less financially established, as well as others experiencing financial instability. There is a continuing question of whether informal access to monetary resources through social networks is influenced more by race or class (Eggebeen 1992).

In this chapter, using the Greater Atlanta Neighborhood Study (GANS), we explore the factors that contribute to the use of informal support among Atlanta residents. (See the appendix to chapter 1 for a discussion of the GANS.) We examine individual characteristics, family structure, and neighborhood influences on instrumental support. We begin by examining the race, gender, and class differences in the use and provision of informal support. The purpose of this analysis is to examine whether race, gender, and class effects persist even while controlling for family/household and neighborhood structure. Recent research has emphasized the need to study the context of informal support (Beggs, Haines, and Hurlbert 1996; House, Umberson, and Landis 1988). Our research focuses especially on the effects of living in single-headed households and poor neighborhoods on access to and availability of informal sources of support.

Class, Race, and Gender Differences in Informal Support

The literature on informal support has tended to focus on class, race, and gender differences. We briefly review some of the basic findings from this literature and identify specific research questions for Atlanta.

Social Class

A central premise in the literature is that informal support is based on both economic need and capacity. Individuals with few economic resources may need to rely more heavily on social ties to compensate for their lack of resources in the marketplace. The poor, therefore, have to rely on informal arrangements for child care and other forms of support rather than purchasing these services.

Among African Americans, for example, H. P. McAdoo (1978) finds stronger obligations of reciprocity among persons from lower socio-economic backgrounds. Carol Stack's (1974) study of ties among poor urban blacks indicates strong and large networks of mutual obligation among the poor. Karen E. Campbell and Barrett Lee (1992) report that neighborhood income and status are positively associated with the size of neighborhood networks, but low-income individuals have more frequent contact with neighbors than do those with higher incomes.

Although lower-income individuals may have stronger ties within their networks, their lack of resources may actually limit the size of their networks and make these social ties less effective in providing or accessing informal support. Members of their social network may have fewer resources to provide, and conversely, individuals may not be able to provide much assistance to others in their network. Controlling for family structure will probably reduce some of the effects of class on informal support, because family economic circumstances are related to the number of working adults in the family. Many single mothers are likely to live in poverty. Yet, single mothers may have stronger ties with individuals outside the household. Thus, based on the literature, we expect poverty status to be strongly related to use of informal support. Although the poor may have more limited social networks, it is expected that they will have a greater dependence on their networks for material support.

Race

Racial differences frequently exist in the size of social networks and frequency of social interaction (Taylor 1986). Data from the 1985 General Social Survey show that whites have the largest networks, followed by Hispanics, and then blacks. Networks of blacks have a lower proportion of kin than do those of whites, while the proportion of women is highest in the networks of whites, even when kin/nonkin composition is controlled (Marsden 1987, 129). Similarly, Melvin Oliver (1988) reports that whites rely more heavily on kin in their social networks, while blacks rely on kin and church associations. African Americans' social networks are likely to consist of close friends of the family as well as blood relations and to go beyond the nuclear family (Stack 1974). Blacks are tied to more neighbors, have more frequent contact with their neighbors, and rely more heavily on neighbors for instrumental assistance (such as child care, transportation, and money) than do whites (Lee, Campbell, and Miller 1991).

Studies generally find, however, that blacks receive less informal support from their social networks than do whites. James M. Gaudin and Kathryn B. Davis (1985), for example, indicate that rural Georgia

247

low-income black families receive less informal support than do white families. Eggebeen (1992) also reports that blacks are much less likely to receive any sort of assistance from kin than are whites. He argues that this difference may be the result of the different financial situations of the kin of blacks and whites; class may be influencing the level of support informal social networks are able to provide.

Research examining the relationship between race and informal support frequently does not control for the influence of family structure, social class, and especially neighborhood composition. A few studies suggest that racial differences in social ties are due to differences in family structure and social class (see Hofferth 1984). We expect blacks to be disadvantaged in the receipt of informal support, but we also expect the disadvantage to disappear after class and social context are controlled.

Gender

Research indicates that although women generally have smaller social networks, they place greater emphasis on close relationships than do men (House, Umberson, and Landis 1988). Women tend to play different roles than men in social relationships and to have different network structures than men. Women generally are more likely to seek or accept informal support, even when controlling for need (Logan and Spitze 1994b; Spitze and Logan 1989). Overall, the close ties and smaller networks of women should influence informal support; compared to men, women should have greater access to, and be more likely to provide, informal support to others. These relationships between gender and the composition of networks, however, may be influenced by family structure. Women are more likely to be single parents, and single parents generally have fewer social ties than do two-parent families (Hurlbert and Acock 1990). Having fewer ties may in turn reduce access to social support.

Unfortunately, few studies have been able to disaggregate the effects of class, race, and gender on the receipt and provision of informal support. Are racial differences in instrumental support a product of class position, or are they due to cultural differences between blacks and whites? Researchers have seldom considered the impact of family structure and neighborhood organization on the availability of informal support. As we suggested, family structure may be the underlying factor in the relationship between class, race, and gender and the use and provision of instrumental support. Wilson's work also suggests that neighborhood structure should have an effect over and above the influences of individual characteristics on the availability of informal support. Poor neighborhoods simply provide fewer opportunities to access this form of support. In the following analysis, we attempt to untangle some of these interrelated factors influencing the provision and receipt of informal support in Atlanta.

The Data
Variables

To examine the size and nature of social networks among Atlanta residents, GANS respondents under the age of sixty-five were asked with whom they discussed important matters. The questions were modeled after those used in the 1985 General Social Survey. Respondents were asked: "From time to time, most people discuss important matters with other people. Looking back over the last six months, who are the people, other than people living in your household, with whom you discussed matters important to you?" Respondents were allowed to name up to three persons; they were prompted for other discussion partners if they named fewer than three. Although it would have been desirable to have information on all people who were discussion partners for the respondents, other studies show that most people name three or fewer people even when given the opportunity to name more.[2] In Atlanta, the average respondent named two.

Respondents were then asked whether they had given help to each of their discussion partners—specifically, whether during the past month, they helped that person "do everyday things like giving them a ride somewhere, lending them a little money, or running errands." Finally, respondents were asked whether the discussion partner was someone they could count on for help in a major crisis, such as a serious illness or needing a place to stay.

Respondents also were asked how frequently (very often, fairly often, not too often, or never) they received help from family (including children, grandparents, aunts, uncles, in-laws, and so on) and from people they knew through their church. These questions pertained to all church and family contacts and were not limited to their discussion partners.

Respondents were asked a set of questions about the type of assistance they received most often from family members and the type of assistance from family that is most important to them—the choices included child care, household items (furnishings, clothing, and so on), household chores, help with bills or food, advice-support, transportation, or something else.

Finally, respondents were asked whether in the past year they received or gave various types of assistance from or to anyone outside the household. The types of assistance included child care while a parent is working, transportation, money, or anything else. Our multivariate analysis focuses on modeling the factors affecting whether respondents have received help from or given help to others outside the household with respect to child care, transportation, or money. Logistic regression analysis is used to conduct these analyses.

The central independent variables in the analysis are gender, race, and class. All of these variables are coded as dichotomous variables (women = 1; black = 1; and poor = 1). Because there are few respondents in our sample who were neither (non-Hispanic) white nor black, we limit our analysis to blacks and non-Hispanic whites. Our measure of social class is poverty status. We use the federal government's official definition of poverty, which considers total family annual earnings and family size. Because earnings may fluctuate from year to year, we considered families to be poor if their household income was not 25 percent above the poverty level during the previous year (1992).

Many of the relationships that we are examining may be a function of influences other than race, class, and gender. To consider this possibility, we use multivariate models to control for other factors. In addition to race, class, and gender, our models include the age and educational level of the respondent. Older and more educated individuals may have more resources and less need for assistance from others. On the other hand, older and more educated individuals may have developed more social ties, which may be essential to developing social networks necessary for receiving instrumental aid.

Because the length of time an individual has resided in a community may influence the likelihood of developing social support, we control for the number of years respondents lived in the Atlanta metropolitan area. Labor force participation also is used as a control variable because it may increase the opportunities to develop social relationships. Conversely, those individuals who are not full-time labor force participants may have more need to receive help from others. A dichotomous variable was created for full-time labor force participation; part-time workers and those not in the labor force are the omitted category. Full-time employment is defined as working an average of thirty-five hours or more per week.

Family structure is measured by two variables: whether there is a child in the household; and whether there is another adult in the household. Both variables are dichotomous (1 = yes; 0 = no). Having a child should increase social contacts and possibly increase the likelihood of receiving assistance. Having another adult in the household may reduce

TABLE 11.1   *Percentage of Respondents Reporting Zero to Three Discussion Partners (Distribution for Total Sample, Sex, Race, and Class Groups)*

Number of Partners	Total	Female	Male	Black	White	Poor	Not Poor
0	11.9	11.7	12.0	17.0	10.0	12.8	8.5
1	17.5	13.0	22.7	27.7	13.8	28.7	16.3
2	21.2	19.2	23.5	23.1	20.5	25.5	20.8
3	49.4	56.1	41.8	32.2	55.8	33.1	54.3
Mean	2.081	2.197[a]	1.951	1.705[a]	2.221	1.789[a]	2.210
SD	(1.067)	(1.059)	(1.061)	(1.093)	(1.023)	(1.050)	(1.002)
N	1263	670	593	342	921	58	970

Source: Greater Atlanta Neighborhood Study 1994.
[a]Difference of means statistically significant at $p \leq 0.01$.

the need for assistance, but it also increases the social contacts the household may have with those who can provide or need assistance.

Our measure of neighborhood structure is percent poverty in the census tract. These data are drawn from the 1990 Census of Housing and Population (Summary Tape Files [STF3]). (Data from the census tract in which the respondent lived were matched with his or her address.) We include this variable because Wilson (1996) argues that neighborhood structure plays an independent role in affecting individual behavior and labor market outcomes. Individuals living in poor neighborhoods may be less likely to receive help or assistance, but they may be more likely to provide assistance.

Analysis

In table 11.1, we provide information on the number of discussion partners by race, gender, and class. Twelve percent of all respondents reported that they had no one outside their household with whom they discussed matters important to them. About 18 percent had one discussion partner, 21 percent had two, and almost half (49.4 percent) reported three discussion partners. Contrary to previous research, women were shown to have more discussion partners than men had. Whites had more discussion partners than blacks did. More than half (55.8 percent) of white respondents had three discussion partners, while only one-third (32.2 percent) of black respondents had that many. Consistent with our expectations, the poor tended to have fewer discussion partners than did

TABLE 11.2   *Percentage of Respondents Reporting Zero to Three Discussion Partners Who Have Been Helped by Them to Do Everyday Things (Distribution for Total Sample, Sex, Race, and Class Groups)*

Number of Partners	Total	Female	Male	Black	White	Poor	Not Poor
0	44.8	43.0	46.9	59.6	39.3	50.5	38.6
1	26.2	24.0	28.8	22.0	27.8	27.0	27.5
2	17.4	19.1	15.4	12.7	19.1	14.1	20.2
3	11.6	13.9	9.0	5.7	13.8	8.4	13.7
Mean	0.958	1.040^b	0.865	0.646^b	1.073	0.805^a	1.090
SD	(1.042)	(1.085)	(0.983)	(0.911)	(1.064)	(0.981)	(1.063)
N	1263	670	593	342	921	58	970

Source: Greater Atlanta Neighborhood Study 1994.
[a]Difference of means statistically significant at $p \leq 0.05$.
[b]Difference of means statistically significant at $p \leq 0.01$.

the nonpoor. Almost half (54.3 percent) of the nonpoor had three discussion partners, while only one-third (33.1 percent) of the poor did.

Next, we examined the number of discussion partners the respondent had helped do everyday things like giving them a ride somewhere, lending them a little money, or running errands for them (see table 11.2). About half (45 percent) of the respondents had not helped their discussion partners in these ways. Only 12 percent had provided help to three discussion partners. Women, whites, and the nonpoor were more likely than men, blacks, or the poor to help their discussion partners with everyday things. Probably the most striking finding was that almost 60 percent of blacks said they had no discussion partners whom they had helped in the previous month.

It could be argued that receiving help with everyday things is not as important as having someone on whom one can rely in a major crisis. To assess if there are differences in the level of crucial resources, respondents were asked if each of their discussion partners was someone on whom they could rely for help in a major crisis, such as a serious illness or needing a place to stay (see table 11.3). While very few respondents had provided help to three of their discussion partners, approximately 40 percent said that they could count on three discussion partners for help in a major crisis. Only about 14 percent said they had no discussion partners on whom they could count in a crisis. This is just 2 percentage points higher than the number reporting zero discussion partners; it appears that most respondents regarded their discussion partners as people they could count on in a crisis.

TABLE 11.3   *Percentage of Respondents Reporting Zero to Three Discussion Partners on Whom They Can Rely for Help in a Major Crisis (Distribution for Total Sample, Sex, Race, and Class Groups Number of Discussion Partners)*

Number of Partners	Total	Female	Male	Black	White	Poor	Not Poor
0	13.8	13.4	14.2	20.0	11.4	13.7	10.6
1	22.1	17.4	27.5	28.6	19.8	37.7	21.5
2	24.1	23.8	24.5	23.3	24.4	17.0	24.4
3	40.0	45.4	33.8	28.1	44.4	31.7	43.4
Mean	1.903	2.012[b]	1.779	1.595[b]	2.017	1.666[a]	2.007
SD	(1.078)	(1.080)	(1.064)	(1.099)	(1.049)	(1.072)	(1.037)
N	1263	670	593	342	921	58	970

Source: Greater Atlanta Neighborhood Study 1994.
[a]Difference of means statistically significant at $p \leq 0.05$.
[b]Difference of means statistically significant at $p \leq 0.01$.

Gender, race, and class differences also existed in the number of discussion partners respondents could count on in a crisis. Again, women, whites, and the nonpoor had more of this kind of social resource. For both cases—providing help to and counting on discussion partners—the race effects were especially strong. These relationships may be a function of the smaller number of discussion partners named by African Americans, males, and the poor. We will examine this possibility in the multivariate analyses.

Providing and Receiving Help

Access to informal support may not be limited to people in one's immediate social network. These resources may be available from other family members or organizations such as the church. The GANS asked Atlantans how often, if ever, they received assistance from other family members and from people they know through their church. Surprisingly few had received help from people they knew through church (see table 11.4). Almost half of the churchgoers said they never received help from someone in their church. About one-tenth received assistance very often from someone in their church. When they did receive help, it tended to be for the same things given by families: advice or support, help with bills or food, and household chores and meals. There were no significant differences by sex, race, or class in the receipt of assistance from this source.

Most people obtained some help from family—including children,

TABLE 11.4   *Percentage of Respondents Who Received Assistance from People Known Through Church (Churchgoers Only) (Distribution for Total Sample, Sex, Race, and Class Groups)*

Frequency	Total	Female	Male	Black	White	Poor	Not Poor
Very often	10.6	12.1	8.7	11.2	9.8	16.1	10.0
Fairly often	11.0	11.2	11.0	13.0	10.2	16.1	11.4
Not too often	30.1	29.6	30.6	27.9	31.9	27.4	29.9
Never	48.3	47.1	49.7	47.9	48.2	40.3	48.7
N	1156	626	529	330	778	62	892

Source: Greater Atlanta Neighborhood Study 1994.

grandparents, aunts, uncles, in-laws, and others. Only about one-fourth said they never received assistance from family (see table 11.5). And about one-fourth reported receiving help from their family very often. Women and whites were more likely to obtain assistance from family members than were men and blacks.

Among types of help, Atlantans were most likely to receive advice or support, followed by help with household chores (see table 11.6). Women were more likely to receive assistance in the form of child care and were much more likely to receive household items than were men. Women were also more likely than men to view help with child care, household items, and household chores as being the most important types of assistance they received from family members. Blacks were more likely than whites to stress the importance of child care and help with bills or food. Finally, the poor were both more likely to receive and

TABLE 11.5   *Percentage of Respondents Who Received Assistance from Family (Distribution for Total Sample, Sex, Race, and Class Groups)*

Frequency	Total	Female[a]	Male	Black[a]	White	Poor	Not Poor
Very often	26.4	31.3	20.9	20.7	28.0	35.1	26.3
Fairly often	20.1	21.0	19.1	21.3	19.1	15.6	23.5
Not too often	28.6	27.1	30.2	25.5	29.7	28.6	26.7
Never	25.0	20.6	29.8	32.4	23.1	20.8	23.4
N	1500	786	712	376	1067	77	1118

Source: Greater Atlanta Neighborhood Study 1994.
[a]Statistically significant at $p \leq 0.01$.

TABLE 11.6　　*Type of Assistance Received Most Often and Considered Most Important by Respondents (Distribution for Total Sample, Sex, Race, and Class Groups)*

	Total	Female	Male	Black	White	Poor	Not Poor
Assistance received most often							
Child care	11.1	13.0	8.8	14.8	10.0	8.1	11.6
Household items	13.9	14.5	13.3	10.2	15.0	11.3	13.4
Household chores	21.3	22.8	19.3	20.1	22.3	30.6	21.1
Help with bills or food	19.0	16.4	22.3	25.8	16.6	35.5	17.5
Advice-support	26.3	23.9	29.3	20.1	28.4	6.5	28.3
Transportation	2.0	3.1	0.6	2.9	1.7	4.8	1.8
N	1116	498[a]	614	244[a]	821	62[a]	852
Assistance received most important							
Child care	11.0	12.3	9.4	16.7	9.4	11.3	11.7
Household items	7.6	12.3	5.7	7.5	7.8	8.1	7.0
Household chores	22.2	22.9	21.4	17.9	24.3	35.5	20.8
Help with bills or food	17.5	16.7	18.5	25.8	14.4	25.8	15.4
Advice-support	35.7	33.4	38.7	26.3	38.4	14.5	38.9
Transportation	1.8	2.6	0.6	2.9	1.3	4.8	1.7
N	1109	616[a]	491	240[a]	818	62[a]	843

Source: Greater Atlanta Neighborhood Study 1994.
[a]Statistically significant at $p \leq 0.01$.

more likely to emphasize the importance of help with household chores and with bills or food, compared to the nonpoor. The poor are also less than one-fourth as likely to list advice as the most frequent type of support received, and less than one-half as likely to list it as most important. This probably demonstrates their greater need for more material types of support. Although the percentages who reported transportation as either the most frequently received or most important form of support were very small, females, blacks, and the poor were substantially more likely to emphasize it as being important.

We also consider whether there were gender, race, and class differences in the type of assistance given to and received from anyone outside the household (see table 11.7). There were few gender differences in

TABLE 11.7   *Type of Assistance Given to and Received from Others Outside the Households (Distribution for Total Sample, Sex, Race, and Class Groups)*

	Total	Female	Male	Black	White	Poor	Not Poor
Type of assistance given							
Child care	24.6	29.3	19.6[b]	29.2[a]	23.0	31.3	26.6
N	1506	777	729	377	1073	80	1119
Transportation	44.2	41.4	47.0[a]	43.2	44.7	30.4[b]	49.0
N	1509	725	783	377	1074	79	1122
Money	41.6	38.6	44.8[a]	49.2[b]	38.6	31.2[a]	42.5
N	1504	724	779	378	1071	77	1119
Type of assistance received							
Child care	14.2	14.3	14.0	14.8	13.6	19.0	16.0
N	1503	777	726	372	1074	79	1119
Transportation	33.8	34.8	32.6	36.3	32.9	48.8[b]	34.2
N	1503	778	724	375	1071	80	1118
Money	23.4	25.2	21.5	32.7[b]	19.6	45.5[b]	24.1
N	1506	722	782	376	1074	77	1122

Source: Greater Atlanta Neighborhood Study 1994.
[a]Statistically significant at $p \leq 0.05$.
[b]Statistically significant at $p \leq 0.01$.

the type of assistance received, but some differences in the type of assistance given. Women were much more likely to provide child-care assistance than were men. Men were somewhat more likely to provide help with transportation or money. Racial differences existed in the probability of helping others financially and with child care. Blacks were more likely than whites to provide child care and financial assistance; they were also more likely to receive money from others. The poor were both much more likely to receive money and less likely to help others by giving them money. The strongest differences between the poor and the nonpoor were in transportation: the poor were much more likely to receive transportation assistance and much less likely to provide it.

The racial effects on the type of assistance given and received were especially striking because of the earlier finding that blacks have smaller social networks and fewer people in their network on whom they can count in a crisis. These findings suggest that blacks may have more intensive networks and be much more likely to rely on these resources. It could also be that there are more expectations for mutual assistance

TABLE 11.8   Logistic Regression Analysis of Providing Money to
and Receiving Money from Someone Outside the
Household

	Provided Money		Received Money	
	B	SE	B	SE
Black	−0.474[b]	0.121	−0.305[a]	0.129
Female	−0.039	0.094	0.255[a]	0.104
Poor	−0.186	0.251	0.022	0.266
Age	−0.011	0.010	−0.047[b]	0.012
High school or GED	−0.025	0.226	0.265	0.246
Full-time worker	−0.344[a]	0.154	−0.632[b]	0.191
Years in Atlanta	0.015	0.011	0.000	0.012
Child in household	0.267[b]	0.101	−0.020	0.111
Other adult in household	−0.078	0.104	0.268[a]	0.112
Network size	0.164	0.096	0.217[a]	0.110
Percent poverty tract	−0.999	1.336	0.568	1.404
Constant	−0.379	0.567	0.177	0.619
−2 log likelihood	708.859		601.318	
Goodness of fit	546.285		562.813	
Model chi-square	32.174		60.115	

Source: Greater Atlanta Neighborhood Study 1994.
[a]Statistically significant at $p \leq 0.05$.
[b]Statistically significant at $p \leq 0.01$.

among blacks compared to whites—so that discussion partner networks
may not be adequate indicators of informal support networks for blacks.

Multivariate Analysis

We conducted multivariate analyses to assess whether these bivariate
relationships between individual characteristics and use and provision
of instrumental informal support (money, transportation, or child care)
persisted while controlling for other factors (see table 11.8). Because network size may influence the extent of assistance (Logan and Spitze
1994a), we used the number of discussion partners as a control variable
in these analyses.

The two strongest influences on the likelihood of the respondent
providing money to someone outside the household were race and having a child in the household. Blacks were less likely to provide money to
someone outside the household, and those with children in the household were more likely. Blacks were also less likely to receive money
from others. The direction of the relationship between race and instru-

TABLE 11.9   *Logistic Regression Analysis of Providing Transportation to and Receiving Transportation from Someone Outside the Household*

	Provided Transportation		Received Transportation	
	B	SE	B	SE
Black	0.155	0.121	0.132	0.123
Female	0.140	0.092	0.052	0.096
Poor	−0.484	0.277	0.136	0.267
Age	0.041[a]	0.010	0.053[a]	0.011
High school or GED	0.081	0.228	−0.429	0.233
Full-time worker	−0.076	0.140	−0.108	0.145
Years in Atlanta	−0.036[a]	0.011	−0.010	0.011
Child in household	0.116	0.098	0.063	0.103
Other adult in household	0.047	0.103	−0.180	0.107
Network size	−0.133	0.095	−0.081	0.099
Percent poverty tract	1.341	1.359	1.075	1.373
Constant	−0.485	0.574	−2.003[a]	0.595
−2 log likelihood	728.25		681.586	
Goodness of fit	549.729		540.518	
Model chi-square	31.873		44.51	

Source: Greater Atlanta Neighborhood Study 1994.
[a]Statistically significant at $p \leq 0.01$.

mental support reversed once we controlled for other factors. There may be several reasons for this finding. Blacks have smaller networks and are less likely to have another adult in the household—two factors that tend to increase the likelihood of receiving assistance.

Younger respondents and those individuals who are not employed full-time were more likely to receive money from others. Network size increases the likelihood of receiving money, as does having another adult in the household. Overall, race continues to have a strong effect even when controlling for other factors, and assistance is not influenced as much by poverty as it is by social contacts.

The models for providing and receiving transportation assistance offer somewhat different results than the models for providing and receiving money (see table 11.9). Transportation assistance was not affected by the gender, race, or class of the respondent. Age had the strongest influence, with older individuals being more likely both to provide and to receive help with transportation. Surprisingly, length of time in the community was negatively related to providing transportation to someone outside the household.

TABLE 11.10   *Logistic Regression Analysis of Providing Child Care to and Receiving Child Care from Someone Outside the Household*

	Provided Child Care		Received Child Care	
	B	SE	B	SE
Black	0.410[b]	0.135	0.342	0.214
Female	−0.085	0.107	0.126	0.151
Poor	0.321	0.278	0.599	0.428
Age	0.007	0.33		
High school or GED	0.090	0.251	−0.395	0.370
Full-time worker	−0.573[b]	0.146	−0.248	0.203
Years in Atlanta	−0.025[a]	0.012	−0.027	0.017
Child in household	0.125	0.111		
Other adult in household	0.394[b]	0.128	0.620[a]	0.249
Network size	−0.076	0.112	−0.353	0.184
Percent poverty tract	0.049	1.468	1.804	2.285
Constant	0.581	0.654	0.582	0.785
−2 log likelihood	575.68		277.063	
Goodness of fit	539.914		215.346	
Model chi-square	49.679		18.345	

Source: Greater Atlanta Neighborhood Study 1994.
[a]Statistically significant at $p \le 0.05$.
[b]Statistically significant at $p \le 0.01$.

Finally, we examined the influence of the independent variables on providing and receiving child care (see table 11.10). In our model for receiving child care, we considered only those individuals with a child in the household. We also did not consider the influence of age here, because most householders with children present are relatively young. Overall, receiving child care from others did not appear to be influenced by race, class, or gender. Surprisingly, respondents with another adult in the household were more likely to receive assistance in child care than were single parents. Blacks were more likely than whites to provide child care, as were those individuals with another adult in the house-hold and those who worked less than full-time.

Conclusion

Overall, we find some evidence that the poor in Atlanta are more so-cially isolated than those who are not poor. They have smaller discussion networks, which means they have fewer people on whom they can rely for assistance. But there is evidence that many of the poor continue to receive and provide help. They especially value and accept help with household chores. Almost one-half of the poor receive assistance with transportation and money as well. These findings suggest that informal support continues to be important for the poor in Atlanta. Remarkably, about one-third of the poor provide monetary support to others. The multivariate regression analyses suggest that class does not have an independent effect on providing or receiving money, transportation, or child care. The social networks of the poor do not provide less help than the social networks of the nonpoor.

A central argument in the urban poverty literature is that family structure and neighborhood structure may help explain away the effects of race, gender, and class on the types of social relationships maintained by individuals. Yet, there has been very little empirical research that controls for all of the relevant factors. We find little evidence that level of neighborhood poverty influences the likelihood of households providing or receiving money, transportation, or child care. Having a child in the household does increase the likelihood of providing money, and having another adult in the household increases the likelihood of providing child care and of receiving child care and financial assistance. Interestingly, the evidence suggests that providing and receiving help are influenced more by factors associated with developing strong social ties to others.

Although bivariate relationships show blacks more likely to provide and receive money from others outside the household, when we control for class, family structure, and neighborhood structure, this relationship reverses. This finding suggests that race differences in financial assistance are primarily the result of other individual and household characteristics. Thus, there is not much support for the argument that cultural differences explain the different patterns of social support. They tend to be due to other structural factors.

Another interesting result from the multivariate analysis is that network size has a minimal effect on receiving or providing help with money, transportation, or child care. This finding tends to support previous work suggesting that network size may not be related to the level of interaction in the network. Informal support appears to be more a result of mutual expectations than just the development of numerous close or confidential social relationships.

What do these findings mean for our understanding of poverty and inequality in Atlanta? We do find evidence that the poor are more socially isolated than the nonpoor, and that this frequently means they have fewer people they can count on in a crisis. Yet, the poor continue to rely on family support to compensate for their lack of resources in the marketplace. Although the social web that links individuals to neighbors, friends, and others may not be as strong in poor neighborhoods as it once was, there remain some important bonds of social support. This finding suggests that although the economic growth Atlanta has experienced may not have directly benefited many of the poor, it may have helped increase the potential for obtaining social resources.

These results suggest several different avenues for future research. First, we need a better understanding of the consequences of these relationships. If an individual's discussion partners are limited to relatives or neighbors, does this limit job information and access to other resources? Do co-workers provide individuals with access to important resources that other discussion partners may not, especially because they are employed, while relatives or neighbors may not be?

Finally, there always is the question of whether Atlanta is somehow different from other cities. Earlier chapters described some characteristics of Atlanta that make it different, especially the large black middle class and the rural-to-urban migration pattern that may provide greater opportunities for informal support across neighborhoods and class lines. More research on informal support in other settings is needed.

Support for this research was provided by the University of Wisconsin Graduate School. We appreciate the comments and suggestions of Brenda Sullivan.

Notes

1. For recent evidence that disputes the spatial mismatch thesis, see Samuel Cohn and Mark Fossett (1996).

2. To a similarly worded question, Peter V. Marsden (1987) reports that 60 percent of respondents named three or fewer discussion partners and 75 percent named four or fewer in their close personal network.

References

Barnes, Annie. 1985. *The Black Middle Class Family*. Bristol, Ind.: Wyndham Hall Press.

Beggs, John J., Valerie A. Haines, and Jeanne S. Hurlbert. 1996. "Situational Contingencies Surrounding the Receipt of Informal Support." *Social Forces* 75(1): 201–22.

Bridges, William P., and Wayne J. Villemez. 1986. "Informal Hiring and Income in the Labor Market." *American Sociological Review* 51(4): 574–82.

Campbell, Karen, and Barrett Lee. 1992. "Sources of Personal Neighbor Networks: Social Integration, Need, or Time?" *Social Forces* 70(4): 1,077–1,100.

Campbell, Karen E., Peter V. Marsden, and Jeanne S. Hurlbert. 1986. "Social Resources and Socioeconomic Status." *Social Networks* 8(2): 97–117.

Cohn, Samuel, and Mark Fossett. 1996. "What Spatial Mismatch? The Proximity of Blacks to Employment in Boston and Houston." *Social Forces* 75(2): 557–72.

Eggebeen, David J. 1992. "From Generation unto Generation: Parent-Child Support in Aging American Families." *Generations* 17(3): 45–49.

Fernandez, Roberto, and David Harris. 1992. "Social Isolation and the Underclass." In *Drugs, Crime, and Social Isolation*, edited by Adele Harrell and George Peterson. Washington, D.C.: Urban Institute.

Gaudin, James M., Jr., and Kathryn B. Davis. 1985. "Social Networks of Black and White Rural Families: A Research Report." *Journal of Marriage and the Family* 47(4): 1,015–21.

Granovetter, Mark. 1974. *Getting a Job: A Study of Contacts and Careers*. Cambridge, Mass.: Harvard University Press.

Hofferth, Sandra. 1984. "Kin Networks, Race, and Family Structure." *Journal of Marriage and the Family* 46(4): 791–806.

Holzer, Harry. 1991. "Spatial Mismatch Hypothesis: What Has the Evidence Shown?" *Urban Studies* 28(3): 105–22.

House, J. S. 1981. *Work, Stress and Social Support*. Reading, Mass.: Addison-Wesley.

House, J. S., D. Umberson, and K. R. Landis. 1988. "Structures and Processes of Social Support." *Annual Review of Sociology* 14: 293–318.

Huckfeldt, R. Robert. 1983. "Social Contexts, Social Networks, and Urban Neighborhoods: Environmental Constraints on Friendship Choice." *American Journal of Sociology* 89(3): 651–69.

Hurlbert, Jeanne, and Alan Acock. 1990. "The Effects of Marital Status on the Form and Composition of Social Networks." *Social Science Quarterly* 71(2): 163–74.

Lee, Barrett, Karen Campbell, and Oscar Miller. 1991. "Racial Differences in Urban Neighboring." *Sociological Forum* 6(3): 525–50.

Lin, Nan, Walter M. Ensel, and John C. Vaughn. 1981. "Social Resources and the Strength of Ties: Structural Factors in Occupational Status Attainment." *American Sociological Review* 46(4): 393–405.

Logan, John R., and Glenna Spitze. 1994a. "Family Neighbors." *American Journal of Sociology*. 100(2): 453–76.

———. 1994b. "Informal Support and Use of Formal Services by Older Americans." *Journal of Gerontology* 49(1): 25–34.

Marsden, Peter V. 1987. "Core Discussion Networks of Americans." *American Sociological Review* 52(1): 122–31.

Marsden, Peter V., and Jeanne S. Hurlbert. 1988. "Social Resources and Mobility Outcomes: A Replication and Extension." *Social Forces* 66(4): 1,038–59.

McAdoo, H. P. 1978. "Black Mothers and the Extended Family Support

Network." In *The Black Woman*, edited by L. Rodgers-Rose. Beverly Hills, Calif.: Sage Publications.

Massey, Douglas, and Nancy Denton. 1993. *American Apartheid*. Cambridge, Mass.: Harvard University Press.

Oliver, Melvin. 1988. "The Urban Black Community as Networks: Toward a Social Network Perspective." *Sociological Quarterly* 29(4): 623–45.

Spitze, Glenna, and John R. Logan. 1989. "Gender Differences in Family Support: Is There a Payoff?" *Gerontologist* 29(3): 108–13.

Stack, Carol. 1974. *All Our Kin: Strategies for Survival in a Black Community*. New York: Harper & Row.

Stolzenberg, Ross, and Linda Waite. 1984. "Local Labor Markets, Children, and Labor Force Participation of Wives." *Demography* 21(2): 157–70.

Taylor, Robert Joseph. 1986. "Receipt of Support from Family Among Black Americans." *Journal of Marriage and the Family* 48(1): 67–77.

Verbrugge, Lois M. 1979. "Multiplexity in Adult Friendships." *Social Forces* 57(4): 1,286–1,309.

Wilson, William Julius. 1987. *The Truly Disadvantaged: The Inner City, the Underclass, and Public Policy*. Chicago: University of Chicago Press.

———. 1996. *When Work Disappears: The World of the New Urban Poor*. New York: Knopf.

12

URBAN INEQUALITY IN ATLANTA: POLICY OPTIONS

David L. Sjoquist

T HE CHAPTERS in this volume have explored many of the possible causes of what we have called the Atlanta paradox—the existence and persistence of substantial racial inequality in Atlanta in the face of an extremely dynamic economy. These causes can be grouped into four categories.[1]

- *Discrimination* Several chapters provided at least indirect evidence that racial and gender discrimination exists in Atlanta's labor market, and that racial discrimination exists in its housing market.

- *Access to employment* Substantial evidence was presented showing that racial differences in access to jobs exist. In particular, chapter 6 presents strong evidence concerning the existence of a spatial mismatch between residential locations in the inner city and job locations in the suburbs. Chapter 10 found that job-search strategies that are employed by minorities limit their access to jobs.

- *Human capital* In several chapters, the racial differences in the level of human capital were noted and the implications explored. The results of these differences are that minorities earn less and are less able to find employment in higher-skilled, better-paying occupations.

- *Segregation and segmentation* Chapter 3 discussed the century of racial segregation in Atlanta, which led to an isolated minority population detached from the formal economy and labor market. Several of the other chapters that focused on housing and employment patterns provided evidence that the legacy of the policies and programs adopted by whites to segregate blacks has not been overcome. Furthermore, evidence was presented that, while racial attitudes have improved, many whites are still reluctant to live in a neighborhood that contains a substantial number of blacks. The implication is that beyond the other three causes listed here, minorities are still burdened by a legacy in which, for example, certain jobs and certain neighborhoods are considered black. While the segregation and segmentation of blacks are in part the results of discrimination, they also appear to be due, in part, to underlying patterns or expectations built up since the Civil War that continue to be perpetuated out of inertia, lack of understanding, or fear.

In this chapter, we explore possible policy options implied by this list of causes and address race as an issue that affects all of them.

Discrimination

Substantial evidence has been presented in this book, although some of it is indirect, that housing and employment patterns in Atlanta are in part due to discriminatory behavior.[2] We first consider discrimination in the housing market and then turn to the labor market.

Housing Market

The issue of housing discrimination and segregation has been widely addressed by many writers, and policy prescriptions for reducing discrimination in the housing market are well known. They include greater enforcement of fair-housing and fair-lending laws and the creation of public information campaigns focused on the principals involved in the housing market and lending agencies.

One of the most extensive and recent analyses of housing market discrimination is by John Yinger (1995), who presents an extensive program to combat housing discrimination. The following discussion of actions to improve fair housing enforcement is based on Yinger's program.

The first step is to ensure that complaints filed under the Fair Housing Act are effectively handled. In Atlanta, Metro Fair Housing Services, Inc., has a twenty-year history of enforcing fair housing. It is funded mainly by the city of Atlanta and Fulton and DeKalb counties. It has not received substantial funding, however, and hence has had to survive on a bare-bones budget (Ihlanfeldt 1998). Thus, in addition to the federal government's (the Department of Housing and Urban Development) support for complaint conciliation, increased funding for Metro Fair Housing Services, Inc.—including funding from other local governments as well as local businesses—would be desirable. A stronger Metro Fair Housing Services would also mean that the victims of housing discrimination would not have to bear the responsibility for enforcing the law.

Yinger recommends applying two fair-lending programs—the Home Mortgage Disclosure Act and the Community Reinvestment Act—to the housing market.[3] This would yield information regarding the housing market outcomes of minorities, and would give real estate intermediaries the formal responsibility of providing equal access to available housing in all neighborhoods.

In Atlanta, additional fair-housing audits should be conducted in order to reduce housing discrimination. (In a fair-housing audit, a black and a white person or couple, who are trained and with the exception of race are otherwise identical, search for housing at the same site.) Such audits frequently reveal that rental units are available when the white couple applies but not when the black couple applies. The results could be used to sue violators of the fair-housing law, or otherwise obtain compliance. With limited resources, the audits should be targeted to where discrimination is suspected. Periodic broader-based audits, while more expensive, would provide the community at large with direct evidence of the extent of housing market discrimination. Metro Fair Housing Services, Inc., has conducted housing audits, but would need increased funding to expand this activity.

Local public information campaigns that inform the relevant parties regarding prohibited contacts, appropriate conduct, and the availability of recourse measures would also be of great help. In addition, state licensing requirement for real estate brokers could include more extensive training in fair housing.

In addition to possible discriminatory behavior by real estate agents and landlords, housing discrimination is also sometimes the result of discrimination by mortgage lenders. Yinger has argued that nationally, the fair lending–enforcement system has improved considerably in recent years. But given the nature of the lending process, it is much harder to document discriminatory lending practices, despite the fact that there is much more information about the treatment of minorities in mortgage lending than there is about the renting and buying of homes. The evaluation of creditworthiness is very subjective. Thus, attempts at determining whether blacks are denied loans because of race must face the possibility that the mortgage denial is for some credit-related factor not observed by the researcher. This is one reason some authors have suggested that credit scoring may be a way to reduce lending discrimination.[4] With credit scoring, the lending institution must specify its criteria for making loans, as well as the relative importance of each factor, thereby eliminating or reducing the subjective opinion of the lender.

Labor Market

This book has also provided indirect evidence of racial and gender discrimination in the labor market in Atlanta. Employment discrimination takes multiple forms, including hiring, promotion, and wage discrimination.

Harry J. Holzer (1996), who employs the Multi-City Study of Urban Inequality Employer Surveys in his study, finds that employer discrimination is more pervasive in smaller establishments and in the suburbs. He further suggests that some of these firms have moved to suburban areas in order to avoid hiring minority employees. Joleen Kirschenman, Philip Moss, and Christopher Tilly (1996), using their employer survey, find that most businesses have a negative assessment of the workforce in concentrated minority and/or low-income areas. To the extent that this is true, it helps explain at least part of the spatial mismatch. Furthermore, Harry J. Holzer and Keith R. Ihlanfeldt (1998), using the four Multi-City Survey of Urban Inequality surveys, find that the higher the percentage of white customers, the lower the probability that a black will get hired and the lower the wage blacks will receive. In other words, customer discrimination, at least in part, drives employer discrimination. Thus, part of the strategy needs to address employment discrimination in the suburbs and the other largely white communities.

Enforcement of equal employment opportunity (EEO) laws is one obvious policy prescription, and is suggested by Holzer.[5] However, research on the effects of EEO laws come to differing conclusions.[6] EEO enforcement is a federal government policy; nothing like it exists at the local level. And, while the state of Georgia could pass its own EEO law, that's not likely to occur.

Similar to the fair-housing audits, fair-employment audits of employers could be conducted in the Atlanta area.[7] They have been conducted as part of a national study and in various communities. An organization similar to Metro Fair Housing Services, Inc., could be formed to conduct such audits in Atlanta on an ongoing basis.

The legal and political attacks on affirmative action, including the substantial decline in enforcement, suggest that alternatives to continued reliance on government or legal remedies need to be found. Relying on the voluntary actions of employers will obviously not be enough.

Spatial Mismatch

Chapter 6 concludes that the lack of access to employment is an important factor in explaining inequality in Atlanta. When evidence accumulated in the late 1980s and early 1990s in favor of the spatial mismatch hypothesis, the policy recommendation that was advanced was to improve the ability of low-skilled workers to commute from the inner city to suburban job sites. This was perhaps naive. There are less subtle implications of the literature that should be considered before such single-focus programs are adopted.

The early spatial mismatch studies revealed only that access matters; they did not determine the cause of that effect. As discussed in chapter 6 in the section on the perpetuation of spatial mismatch, the effect of access may be driven by commuting difficulties, lack of information about job availability at distant sites, job discrimination by suburban firms, or a feeling of a lack of acceptance by minorities at suburban job sites. The limited research on these aspects of spatial mismatch and the evidence presented in chapter 6 suggest that all of these factors play a role, although their relative importance has not been determined. The implication is that commuting programs may not be sufficient, or even necessary, to overcome the problem of access.

There is no shortage of policy prescriptions for addressing spatial mismatch (see, for example, Evelyn Blumenberg and Paul Ong [1998]). The policies are grouped into three broad categories: moving jobs closer to the workers (inner-city development strategy), making it easier for workers to get to existing jobs (mobility strategy), and moving people closer to jobs (desegregation strategy). We consider the first two in this section.

Inner-City Development

Inner-city development programs, such as Enterprise Zones, have been politically popular but subject to much criticism. One of the strongest opponents is John Kain (see Kain and Persky 1969 and Kain 1992). John Kain and Joseph J. Persky describe such programs as "ghetto gilding," and claim that they are an inefficient way of increasing employment and earnings. Instead, such programs encourage inner-city residents to remain in the ghetto. Mark Alan Hughes (1993) also voices his opposition to such programs.

Several studies have concluded that programs such as Enterprise Zones are not cost-effective (Papke 1993; Ladd 1994; Boarnet and Bogart 1996; see also Fisher and Peters 1998). Other results are more encouraging. A study of the New Jersey Enterprise Zone program estimated that participating firms provided more than 9,000 new jobs and $242 million in additional wages. However, the cost per job was estimated to be approximately $13,070, and because of the growth in the New Jersey economy during this time, it is not clear whether these jobs truly resulted from the Enterprise Zone (Rubin 1991).

The city of Atlanta has several Enterprise Zones, although most are focused on housing. It also has one of the Federal Empowerment Zones.[8] While businesses have located in Atlanta's industrial Enterprise Zones, a substantial percentage of the workers do not live nearby, and the lost property tax per job is high. There has been no formal evaluation of the Atlanta Empowerment Zone, but the belief seems to be that it has not had much effect to date.

Mobility

Hughes (1993, 1995) has been one of the most vocal advocates for a mobility strategy, but not everyone agrees. Some writers have expressed concern that if inner-city residents are provided improved access to suburban jobs, then employers will have even less reason to locate in the inner city. And Yinger (1995) argues that there is "no evidence to support the claim that we could design a cost-effective national policy that links inner-city residential locations to typically dispersed employment sites" (371).

A mobility strategy should address all four reasons why access matters: commuting, job information, job discrimination, and social distance. Much of the attention for mobility strategies has focused on commuting. Attempts at using public transit system for reverse commuting have been relatively unsuccessful, however, especially those that have not taken into account the particular problems of low-skilled workers and former welfare recipients—single parents with child-care issues.

In Atlanta, only three of the twenty counties in the metropolitan region are served by mass transit: Fulton and DeKalb are served by MARTA, while Cobb is served by Cobb County Transit (CCT). MARTA has an extensive bus system in addition to its rail system, but the dispersed nature of suburban jobs makes reverse commuting by public transit difficult.

One approach is to establish employment centers at the end of MARTA's rail lines. A system of targeted van pools could be organized that would transport individuals from the station to job sites. There is some evidence that more community-based, small-scale projects such as these have worked better than mass transit (Hughes 1995; American Public Transit Association 1994).

Since there is empirical evidence that getting information about jobs is a problem (Ihlanfeldt 1997), these unemployment centers could serve as job information centers as well. There is evidence that many suburban employers do not widely advertise job openings, relying instead on window signs and word of mouth. Thus, such centers should make a major effort to encourage suburban businesses to list job openings and to conduct job interviews there on a periodic basis. The center could be set up to take completed application forms and forward them to the employers, who could then arrange interviews. It could also provide child-care services, even for workers who do not work 9-to-5 hours.

Finally, there is limited evidence that inner-city minority workers may avoid suburban job settings out of concern for how they might be treated (Sjoquist 1996). Solving such a problem seems complex. Efforts would have to be put into making the inner-city worker feel comfortable in the suburban setting and making the firm understand the issues facing the perspective minority employee. One approach is for the employment center to operate a temporary job service (Wilson 1996). Such an operation would allow employers to screen potential employees "on the job" and would allow employees to gain a view of the job setting.

Lack of Human Capital

Nearly every study of poverty and inequality recommends improved education and training as policy prescriptions. As measured by standardized test scores, completion rates, attendance, and the like, the performance of the Atlanta public school system is very poor. In fact, Georgia generally ranks low relative to other states in terms of educational performance. There is no lack of calls for improving the performance of public schools, but little agreement on how to accomplish this goal. We simply echo others here by noting the importance of improving the performance of inner-city schools, increasing retention rates, and developing effective school-to-work programs.

Recent studies have identified barriers to adopting reforms in Atlanta-area school systems (O'Neill 1995). While parents and educators support the concept of reform, they often oppose implementation of change in their own schools. This resistance is in part due to the lack of communication between reformers and parents and teachers. But the lack of support at the school level also reflects a lack of leadership, both inside and outside the schools, with the vision and will to carry out reform. There is also widespread concern among school officials regarding the repercussions of advocating change. Reforms that are generally advocated by educators and the business community are frequently opposed by groups such as political and religious conservatives, with the resulting controversy often inflamed by the media. Consequently, individuals are loath to take on the task of initiating change. Finally, many of the attempted reforms do not have the funding to be carried out.

Attention must be given to overcoming these barriers. The business community, as expressed through the efforts of the Atlanta and Georgia Chambers of Commerce, has a strong interest in improving education. The organizations that have been established to promote educational reform need to move beyond determining what needs to be done, and consider how to overcome the barriers to implementing the desired changes.

Improving general education is a long-term solution, since it focuses on future generations of workers; it does nothing for the current workforce. Although improving primary and secondary education in the city of Atlanta is important to the students who attend Atlanta public schools, a large percentage of future residents of the city of Atlanta will have been educated elsewhere (about 20 percent of those who lived in the city of Atlanta in 1990 did not live there in 1985). Thus, improving the city's schools will not necessarily lead to significant improvements in the future population of the city.

A six-month training program, though certainly not a substitute for a high school degree and two years of postsecondary vocational education, has been found to be cost-effective. Rebecca M. Blank (1994, 190), based on a review of employment training programs, concludes that they "can provide small and positive effects" for disadvantaged workers in terms of employment and earnings (see also Moffitt [1992]). Blank also concludes, however, that there is a great deal that is unknown about running effective job-training programs for disadvantaged workers, especially men and youth.

There are many training programs in Atlanta, including those funded through the Private Industry Councils and the Georgia Department of Technical and Adult Education, and programs offered by various nonprofit organizations, such as the Atlanta Urban League. However, there is little coordination among these providers and no master list of training programs.

As chapter 8 points out, very few minorities or white females hold supervisory positions. In addition to confronting this through legal action where appropriate, training programs that provide insight into supervisory roles and a nongovernmental program promoting affirmative action within businesses might be beneficial. A consortium of human resource managers (perhaps organized through the Society for Human Resource Management), the Metropolitan Atlanta Chamber of Commerce, and others could develop a program that encourages firms to promote and hire minorities into supervisory positions. The consortium could provide technical assistance, particularly to smaller firms, on how to manage the diversity issues such promotion or hiring might raise. At the same time, a management-training program could be offered to minorities who have an interest in becoming supervisors. In addition to addressing how to be a supervisor, such a program should include a discussion of issues such as how to make it known to the firm that one is interested in becoming a supervisor and how to reduce racially based concerns that the decision-maker might have about promoting a minority worker. Such a program could be a way of providing a certification, and hence help overcome a decision-maker's reluctance to promote a minority into a supervisory position.

The concentration of female-headed households in the central city (see chapter 2), particularly those on welfare, poses a particular challenge. The new welfare program limits the time these women can remain on welfare, making the task of obtaining employment critical.[9] In addition to the obvious act of providing job-training programs (including job-readiness training), other programs might increase the likelihood of their obtaining employment. Many of these individuals lack basic skills in math and reading, and thus, for certain types of training to be successful, it may be necessary to incorporate a component of basic education.

There are other possible barriers to employment of current welfare recipients. Since many of these women have not had previous employment, they are unable to provide any independent verification of their ability to perform in a work setting. Thus, firms consider it risky to hire these women. This has implications for search strategies (see chapter 10); sending in a resume without referral from a current employer has a low probability of resulting in a job. One way of gaining employment credentials is through a series of temporary positions, which would eliminate at least part of the risk that a firm would otherwise face. One programmatic option aimed at adults with little or no experience is for local social service agencies to operate a temporary employment business, which would allow these workers to gain on-the-job experience and build a resume. A job placement center should be operated as part of such an employment office. In addition, welfare-to-work programs should encourage firms to modify their employment selection criteria to accommodate welfare recipients who lack identifiable experience.

Another potential barrier to hiring former welfare recipients (or anyone without verifiable experience) is unemployment insurance. Given that firing a worker may affect a firm's unemployment insurance rating, particularly a smaller firm's, it will be reluctant to hire workers who are seen as running a high risk of being dismissed. Thus, the state should consider modifying its unemployment insurance–rating system in order to reduce or eliminate this incentive.

Segmentation and Segregation

The effects of a century of racial segregation practiced by whites in Atlanta can still be seen. Certainly substantial improvement has been made over the past thirty to forty years, but, as shown in this volume, there is still a large isolated minority population with weak links to the formal economy and labor market. Beyond the causes discussed here, the observed segmentation of minorities in terms of housing and employment appears to be the result of underlying patterns built up over the post–Civil War period and that continue to be perpetuated out of inertia, a lack of understanding, or fear. In this section, we address ways to overcome these forces, first with respect to housing and then with respect to employment, focusing on actions other than enforcement of antidiscrimination laws.

Housing

There are two related objectives regarding housing: reducing the concentration of the poor and racially integrating housing. Overcoming the social isolation of the poor means either deconcentrating them by dispersing subsidized housing or increasing the supply of low-income housing in other parts of the Atlanta region, or bringing more of the middle class back into the city. We consider each in turn.

Deconcentrating the Poor   Keith R. Ihlanfeldt (1998) discusses the concentration of the poor in Atlanta and policy options, and the following is based on his work. The Atlanta Housing Authority (AHA) has taken steps to deconcentrate public housing within the city. Under the Olympic Legacy Program, five large public housing projects are being converted into privately managed mixed-income apartment complexes. The goal is to have public housing, low-income (tax-credit) housing, and market-rent housing each representing a third of the units within each complex.

These efforts, while laudable, do not address the possibility of dispersing subsidized-housing recipients into suburban areas. Currently, there are a number of impediments that tend to keep those households receiving certificates and vouchers from the AHA from leaving the city of Atlanta:

- Many of these households do not consider the suburbs when searching for housing. They have poor information about the suburban housing market, and find it difficult to search there because public transit is rarely available (Goering, Stebbins, and Siewert 1995).

- Holders of certificates cannot pay more than the Fair Market Rent (FMR), defined by HUD as a reasonable rent for a standard low-income dwelling unit. The lion's share of the apartments in nonimpacted suburban neighborhoods (those with few households that receive housing subsidies) have rents exceeding the FMR.

- Landlords in nonimpacted suburban neighborhoods are reluctant to participate in the Section 8 program because they are concerned that their nonsubsidized tenants will move out (Finkel and Kennedy 1994).[10]

- Although certificate and voucher recipients are allowed to use their rental assistance anywhere within the metro area, accommodating tenant moves from one housing authority jurisdiction to another is administratively complex. The biggest problem is that programs are not uniform; payment standards, occupancy standards, and utility allowances generally differ among housing authorities.

- When households that have been issued certificates and vouchers by the AHA find apartments in another jurisdiction, the AHA retains only 20 percent of HUD's serving fee. This creates a disincentive to help certificate and voucher recipients move to the suburbs.

While the elimination of these impediments would require significant federal involvement (in the form of regulatory changes and additional funding), steps can be taken locally to improve the mobility of Section 8 recipients:

- The single most important determinant of whether certificate and voucher recipients extend their housing search into suburban areas is whether they receive counseling (Polikoff 1995; Urban Policy Brief 1994). Effective counseling should both inform recipients of suburban housing opportunities and canvass suburban landlords seeing their participation in Section 8 programs. Counseling can be provided by the AHA or by an independent fair-housing or community organization.
- Cooperation among local housing authorities could also result in greater uniformity in Section 8 regulations throughout the region. This would enhance the portability of certificates and vouchers, and thereby the mobility of their holders.
- Two approaches could be taken to increase landlord participation in nonimpacted suburban neighborhoods. First, a number of local housing authorities have targeted up-front bonuses to such landlords (Polikoff 1995), which appear to have been successful in increasing the supply of units in nontraditional areas. Second, marketing efforts could be focused on these landlords.

Increasing the Supply of Low-Income Rental Housing   The two major obstacles to increasing the supply of low-income rental housing in low poverty areas are the opposition of local residents and the low rates of return on such investment. Policies that might overcome each of these obstacles will be considered in turn.

While opposition is typically registered through public forums, in the suburbs it has been institutionalized in the form of restrictive zoning (for example, general limitations on multifamily housing construction, as well as moratoria on multifamily rezonings). There are three approaches to overcoming this opposition:

- Challenge the legality of the restrictive zoning. There have been numerous legal challenges to local restrictions on the development of lower-income housing, and in some cases the litigation has resulted in court orders requiring suburban communities to provide it. In general, however, both federal and state courts have upheld local communities' restrictive zoning ordinances (Schill 1992).

- State intervention. Several states (including California, Florida, Washington, and Vermont) require each local community to have a plan for providing affordable housing. Georgia requires each jurisdiction to examine issues related to the provision of adequate and affordable housing; however, communities are not required to implement their plans. Serious consideration should be given to passing an "Anti-Snob Zoning Act," giving public and nonprofit developers access to a special permit procedure at the local level, as well as redress if a proposal to build affordable units is rejected in a community where less than 10 percent of the housing is classified as affordable (Burchell, Listakin, and Pashman 1994).

- Educate the public about the benefits of having low-income rental housing within their community. Communities' opposition of low-income housing is based, in part, on the belief that low-income households will increase public service costs by more than they increase tax revenue—a belief supported by empirical evidence. In addition, there is the perception that low-income housing reduces the value of nearby properties—which is not supported by empirical evidence. On the plus side, in many suburban areas throughout the Atlanta region, employers are having difficulty filling lower-end jobs; increases in the supply of low-income rental housing within these areas will alleviate these worker shortages.

The other obstacle to the provision of low-income rental housing in low poverty areas is that it seldom passes the private sector's profitability test. A number of strategies can successfully mitigate this problem:

- Regulations could be changed that would allow owners of existing single-family units to rent accessory apartments. This would bring about a quick and low-cost increase in the supply of low-income rental housing in low poverty areas.

- Private not-for-profit corporations could provide the necessary financial assistance to make low-income housing projects economically feasible.

- Inclusionary zoning could be established that would be voluntary but would include incentives for developers. To maintain private-market profitability, developers would trade inclusion of affordable units for increased density allowances. This has proven to be a popular approach to increasing the supply of low-income housing in low poverty areas; there are 50 to 100 jurisdictions nationally that have such an inclusionary ordinance (Burchell, Listakin, and Pashman 1994).

Bringing the Middle Class Back to the City   The alternative to dispersing the poor are policies aimed at attracting and retaining middle-income households in the city, particularly in lower-income neighborhoods. Other than Mary Beth Walker's (1997), little consideration has been given to the design of such programs. This section is based on Walker's recommendations.

To attract middle-class residents a community must successfully address public school quality, crime, housing availability, fiscal conditions, and city services. It must also aim programs specifically at attracting and retaining the middle class.

One impediment to increasing the number of middle-class households is a lack of middle-class housing. The city could make a very large tract of land available at reduced prices to developers for middle-class housing, as Newark did. Alternatively, the city could follow Baltimore and acquire houses through the Land Bank Authority in designated neighborhoods and sell them at low prices to middle-income households willing to rehabilitate them and live there for a specified number of years.

The city could make each designated neighborhood a housing Enterprise Zone, and through it reduce the property taxes on middle-income housing built or rehabilitated in the zone. (While there has been new housing built in the city's housing Enterprise Zones, no research has determined whether the zones are responsible for the housing construction.) The city could also agree to buy back houses that were purchased in the designated neighborhoods if specific goals for things like crime rates and school test scores are not met.

Several local organizations have been promoting "smart growth"—development projects that are environmentally friendly. A similar effort could be made to encourage mixed-income development. Developers need to be made aware of the opportunities to develop middle-income housing in what are currently low-income communities and taught how to design such projects. Such projects need to be designed so that displacement of low-income households is minimized and the middle class is made part of the community rather than isolated from it by gates and fences.

There are several ways the city could improve neighborhood amenities and services and thereby make the neighborhood more desirable. For example:

- Use Community Development Block Grant funds to improve the appearance of designated neighborhoods and to make significant improvements to parks and other amenities;
- Add extra police foot and car patrols;
- Initiate an aggressive housing code–enforcement program;
- Designate the targeted neighborhoods as special service districts and provide additional public services;
- Allow the designated neighborhoods to arrange privately for public services such as trash collection and park maintenance, with a commensurate reduction in property taxes.

Allowing greater community control over local schools, perhaps by establishing charter schools in the designated neighborhoods, may make the middle class more comfortable with the public schools. A voucher program for residents of the designated neighborhoods might be established, leaving students free to attend any public or private school they wish.

Special economic development benefits could be granted to small businesses that located in or near the designated neighborhoods if the owner lived in one of the designated neighborhoods.

The city could adopt a marketing campaign in cooperation with real estate agents and developers focused on attracting middle-income households into the designated neighborhoods.

The development of a set of programs to attract and retain middle-class residents raises a number of conceptual issues. First, focusing some programs specifically on middle-income households poses a dilemma in that resources allocated to middle-income households leave fewer resources for low-income households. Second, consideration needs to be given to what types of middle-income households might be attracted, for that will drive the selection of programs. For example, should the focus be on families with children, young married couples, singles, empty-nesters? Third, there has to be general agreement on the policies that are adopted. For example, the problem of attracting white middle-class students to the public schools may be related to the racial composition of the schools. Setting up schools in which white students are a substantial majority, or providing vouchers that can be used at private schools, may work to attract middle-class white households. Such a policy would not be likely to be acceptable, however, since it perpetuates the basic problem of racial segregation.

Maintaining Integrated Neighborhoods   As discussed in chapters 4 and 7, maintaining integrated neighborhoods is difficult, given the modest willingness of whites to live in a moderately integrated neighborhood. Thus, steps will need to be taken in order to increase the number of integrated neighborhoods and the racial stability of neighborhoods that are integrated. Integrating neighborhoods by fiat—for example, the housing authority forcing low-income households into a middle-income neighborhood—will not achieve the desired social and attitudinal changes (Merry 1980; Chandler 1992). Furthermore, research suggests that social contact is likely to reduce prejudice only when the contact is between people of equal status. However, there is at least one example in the Atlanta area of an ethnically diverse apartment complex in which the residents have, through the efforts of the landlord, learned to celebrate the diversity.

Several programs have been suggested for supporting integrated housing. Yinger (1995), for example, recommends a three-part program. The first part calls for support in opening the suburbs to low-income housing, an issue just addressed. The second part is a grant program to support efforts to promote integration, a program Yinger calls the Stable Neighborhood Initiatives Program. The grants would be used to fund neighborhood-based programs such as housing information centers, housing maintenance, additional public services, and programs that promote intergroup understanding.

The third part is a suggestion to reinstate the Emergency School Aid Act, a special program to "offset the forces that cause racial and ethnic transition and intergroup conflict" (233). The original version was found to have a positive effect, in terms of both better human relations and improved academic performance.

In 1998, *Cityscape* devoted an entire issue to a set of case studies of fourteen racially and ethnically diverse urban neighborhoods. In the concluding article, Philip Nyden et al. point out some of the similarities across these neighborhoods and the characteristics that set them apart from more homogeneous neighborhoods. All the communities had distinctive physical characteristics or environmental assets that made them more attractive than the average city neighborhood, particularly to younger populations. Nyden et al. also found that in some of the communities, local organizations had emerged to promote diversity. Through efforts to address a communitywide issue, these organizations brought together diverse groups. All the communities needed to address common issues: blight in or near their boundaries, community safety, the perception that the presence of minorities is associated with crime, and the quality of the public schools.

In order to encourage and maintain integrated neighborhoods, a local organization, perhaps called the "Diverse Community Initiative" (DCI), should be established, perhaps as part of the United Way of Metropolitan Atlanta or one of the local universities. The DCI could undertake several activities (these suggestions come largely from Nyden et al. [1998]):

- Not a lot is known about what works to encourage and maintain integrated neighborhoods. Thus, one activity of the DCI would be to serve as a local clearinghouse of information concerning strategies that assist communities and community organizations in stabilizing integrated communities.

- Related to that, the DCI could provide technical assistance to communities and community organizations.

- The DCI could develop a network of community organizations interested in promoting and stabilizing communities with diverse populations. The network would provide an opportunity for these organizations to share information, act as a mutual support group, and serve as a way of publicizing successful neighborhood integration.

- The DCI could provide leadership training for residents interested in encouraging and maintaining diverse communities. In communities that are becoming integrated, fears and emotions run high. Having residents who understand how to deal with the situation and defuse the fears would be beneficial. In integrated communities, knowing how to work with diverse residents, whether it is racial or class diversity, would produce more effective leaders.

Employment

It is now difficult to prevent minorities from buying or renting housing in a specific neighborhood. They may face barriers resulting from discriminatory behavior, but with effort these can largely be overcome, at least for middle- and upper-income minorities. (Restrictions on the placement of low-income housing can keep low-income minorities from moving into certain communities.) With employment, however, there is a sort of gatekeeper in each firm. Overcoming employment segmentation has to be approached differently from overcoming housing segregation, but the policy options appear to be quite limited.

One approach is to resort to imposing various forms of pressure on employers, such as EEO, political power, economic power, and appeals to fairness.

The black population in the Atlanta region has substantial economic power. Efforts to harness that power have traditionally focused on efforts to shop at minority-owned businesses. While that may assist the development of black businesses, it does not accomplish the objective of deconcentrating the employment of blacks. An alternative is to use economic power to force businesses to hire blacks into nontraditional black occupations. But that would seem to require a herculean organizing effort.

A final option is to encourage firms, through moral suasion, to open up positions to minorities. Organizations such as the Atlanta Urban League could take the lead in forming a consortium that would promote voluntary equal employment opportunity. The campaign should include the publication of information showing the degree of occupational segmentation, making the case for individual firms to take appropriate steps, and listing sources that would help firms alter their hiring environment. The consortium could provide meetings, conferences, and training sessions to help firms desiring to hire more minorities into nontraditional positions. It could also sponsor awards for firms that made significant changes in their employment culture.

Richard Jenkins (1989) outlines the obstacles that must be confronted by a firm as it establishes and implements a voluntary affirmative-action program. He concludes that "it is probably true today that voluntarism has, at best, severe limitations as a strategy for combating ethnic or gender discrimination" (123). Thus, expectations for major changes due to the promotion of voluntary actions should not be set high.

Improving Race Relations

It is clear from the research presented in this book that the racial attitudes of whites, particularly toward low-income blacks, continue to play a strong role in maintaining urban inequality in Atlanta. Underlying most of the causes of urban inequality discussed herein is the inability or unwillingness of whites to treat blacks as equals. Furthermore, the success of the policies discussed in this chapter is dependent on changes in racial attitudes. Certainly, improved race relations would make it much easier to integrate both neighborhoods and businesses. Even if all the policies discussed here were implemented, not much would probably change without a significant improvement in white racial attitudes.

In this regard, I share the pessimistic view of George Galster (1992), who presents a cumulative causation model of the black underclass and outlines three categories of policies to address the problem of the underclass: break the linkages, reverse the cycle, and establish a parallel system.

The policies for the "break the linkage" approach include: "anti-'snob-zoning' legislation, affirmative action, job training programs, federal funding of central-city public service employment, assistance for public transit access to suburban work sites, and anti-discrimination laws for jobs and housing" (202–3). But Galster suggests that these pro-grams may not be sufficient to sever the linkages causing the growth of the underclass.

"Reverse the cycle" policies include: Enterprise Zones, dispersed subsidized housing, and retraining programs. Galster is concerned that the jobs created in the Enterprise Zones would be secondary jobs, and he points out, citing Hogan and Lengyel (1985), that dispersal programs have had only mixed results—at least in part since attitudinal and dis-criminatory barriers remain. He suggests that the underclass would be greeted with hostility and would be unwilling to abandon the social net-works of their own neighborhoods.

The third strategy is to create parallel institutions located in and controlled by the underclass community. But Galster doesn't hold out much hope for this approach, either. The strategy is built on an assump-tion "that indigenous institutions can be structured and operated in such a way that they avoid the shortcomings of mainstream institutions yet do not create equally severe handicapped shortcomings of their own" (206). This is consistent with Robert Halpern's (1995) view that "the historic experience with neighborhood initiative suggests that it is at best an ameliorative, not a transforming, problem solving strategy" (221).

I agree with Galster in his conclusion that since racial attitudes are unchanged by these policies, they do not address the fundamental issue: race relations. And I agree with Glenn C. Loury (1998), who argues that the problem of the underclass is "a race problem" (40). Chapter 4 con-cludes that race relations have improved in Atlanta and are expected to continue to do so. But race remains a powerful and significant force and plays a central role in the ability to address the issues associated with urban inequality. In order for fundamental improvements in urban in-equality to come about, the issues to white racial attitudes and race relations must be addressed.

Consideration needs to be given to programs that break down racial barriers. However, the literature on race and race relations is largely concerned with describing and explaining racial attitudes. There is no identifiable research on how to structure community interventions to change racial attitudes among the public at large. What exists are sug-gestions such as those made by Whitney M. Young (1969) for what indi-viduals can do, or discussions of programs such as diversity training. The problem is illustrated by President Clinton's recent effort to hold a public conversation on race. While well intentioned, it was derided by some, ignored by most, and led to no observable changes.

Finding individuals who can lead a public effort is hard. Civil rights leaders can provide leadership in the black community, but are typically disregarded in the white community. The propensity of political candidates in Atlanta to "play the race card" and the disdain that many citizens exhibit toward political officials of the opposite race suggest that the needed leadership is not likely to be found in local governments. Although religious organizations are some of the most segregated bodies in the community, religious leaders are seen as moral exemplars in the community and should be a source of leadership. There are a few biracial groups in Atlanta—for example, Leadership Atlanta and the Atlanta Urban League—that could also provide leadership on this issue.

Even if leaders emerged, however, it is not clear what specific types of programs should be promoted. While it is possible to list programs and activities that seem like good ideas—for example, arranged interracial social gatherings and public forums—not enough is known about what might work to form specific recommendations. It is also easier to suggest programs that involve individuals who are already inclined toward improved race relations. The difficulty lies in finding ways to engage individuals whose propensity is to resist changing their racial attitudes.

Conclusion

Urban inequality of minorities in Atlanta grew out of the mistreatment of blacks by the white community. The continuation of urban inequality can be linked to the continuation of structural arrangements and urban decisions whose historical roots are based on race. On the surface, these structures and processes appear racially neutral, but their operations prevent minorities from reaching equal status in employment and housing.

Confronting the immediate causes, such as access to jobs and lack of human capital, is not easy; nor is it always clear what will work. An ambitious set of policies was laid out in this chapter to address the explanations identified in the preceding chapters. If implemented, these policies will result in some improvement in urban inequality. But until there are changes in white racial attitudes, it is unlikely that significant changes in urban inequality can be realized.

Racial attitudes have improved and are expected to continue to do so, and the economic position of minorities has also improved. In the face of these changes, the large population of poor minorities that reside in the inner city is very troubling and presents a challenge that needs to be addressed by the entire community.

Special thanks to Paula Dressel, Chris Geller, and Keith Ihlanfeldt for helpful comments on an earlier version of this chapter.

Notes

1. Michael B. Teitz and Karen Chapple (1998) present a list of eight possible causes of inner-city poverty.

2. For a general discussion of the existence of racial discrimination, see the symposia in the Spring 1998 issue of the *Journal of Economic Perspectives*.

3. The Home Mortgage Disclosure Act, passed in 1975, requires lenders to provide detailed information regarding the location of loan applications. The Community Reinvestment Act, passed in 1977, is aimed at eliminating redlining and disinvestment in low-income and minority neighborhoods.

4. The pros and cons of advocating increased use of credit scoring as a way of reducing mortgage lending discrimination are discussed by Helen Ladd (1998).

5. Herman Belz (1991) provides a history of the development of U.S. employment discrimination laws and regulations.

6. Jonathan S. Leonard (1998) finds no effect on measured wage discrimination from EEO enforcement during the 1980s, "such as they were" (289). He did find that federal affirmative-action requirements (Executive Order 11246, which required federal contractors to adopt affirmative action programs) increased the number of blacks, both skilled and unskilled, employed by federal contractors during the 1980s (Leonard 1990). He also finds that Title VII of the Civil Rights Act of 1964 "played a significant role over and above that of affirmative action." These findings are similar to what he reports in a review of affirmative action and antidiscrimination law (1986). John J. Donohue III and James Heckman (1991), however, find that the effect of Title VII of the Civil Rights Act was felt only in the South. They suggest that southern employers used the act as cover to defy community norms regarding employing blacks. And James P. Smith and Finis Welch (1987) find that affirmative action has had no impact on racial wage differentials for males. Farrell Bloch (1994) takes a pessimistic view of the effects of federal antidiscrimination efforts.

7. For a discussion of hiring audits and the results of a national test using them, see Margery Austin Turner, Michael Fix, and Raymond J. Struyk (1991).

8. Empowerment Zone is the federal government's term for enterprise zone, that is, an impoverished area to which development incentives such as tax breaks and low-interest loans and other special resources are provided.

9. For a discussion of welfare-to-work programs, see Judith M. Gueron and Edward Pauly (1991).

10. Section 8 is a rent subsidy program that allows low-income individuals to choose where to rent. However, landlords are not required to participate, that is, accept subsidized renters.

References

American Public Transit Association. 1994. *Access to Opportunity: Linking Inner-City Workers to Suburban Jobs*. New York: American Public Transit Association.

Belz, Herman. 1991. *Equality Transformed: A Quarter-Century of Affirmative Action*. New Brunswick, N.J.: Transaction Publishers.

Blank, Rebecca M. 1994. "The Employment Strategy: Public Policies to Increase Work and Earnings." In *Confronting Poverty: Prescriptions for Change*, edited by Sheldon H. Danziger, Gary D. Sandefur, and Daniel H. Weinberg. Cambridge, Mass.: Harvard University Press.

Bloch, Farrell. 1994. *Antidiscrimination Law and Minority Employment*. Chicago: University of Chicago Press.

Boarnet, Marlon G., and William T. Bogart. 1996. "Enterprise Zones and Employment: Evidence from New Jersey." *Journal of Urban Economics* 40(2): 198–215.

Blumenberg, Evelyn, and Paul Ong. 1998. "Job Accessibility and Welfare Usage: Evidence from Los Angeles." *Journal of Policy Analysis and Management* 17(4): 639–57.

Burchell, Robert W., David Listakin, and Arlene Pashman. 1994. *Regional Housing Opportunities for Lower Income Households*. Washington: U.S. Department of Housing and Urban Development.

Chandler, Mittie Olion. 1992. "Obstacles to Integration Program Efforts." In *The Metropolis in Black and White: Place, Power and Polarization*, edited by George C. Galster and Edward W. Hill. New Brunswick, N.J.: Center for Urban Policy Research, Rutgers University.

Donohue, John J., III, and James Heckman. 1991. "Continuous versus Episodic Change: The Impact of Civil Rights Policy on the Economic Status of Blacks." *Journal of Economic Literature* 29(4): 1,603–43.

Finkel, Meryl, and Stephen Kennedy. 1994. *Section 8 Rental Voucher and Rental Certificate Utilization Study: Final Report*. Cambridge Mass.: ABT Associates.

Fisher, Peter S., and Alan H. Peters. 1998. *Industrial Incentives: Competition Among American States and Cities*. Kalamazoo, Mich.: W. E. Upjohn Institute for Employment Research.

Galster, George. 1992. "A Cumulative Causation Model of the Black Underclass." In *The Metropolis in Black and White: Place, Power and Polarization*, edited by George C. Galster and Edward W. Hill. New Brunswick, N.J.: Center for Urban Policy Research, Rutgers University.

Goering, John, Helene Stebbins, and Michael Siewert. 1995. *Promoting Housing Choice in HUD's Rental Assistance Programs*. Washington: U.S. Department of Housing and Urban Development.

Gueron, Judith M., and Edward Pauly. 1991. *From Welfare to Work*. New York: Russell Sage Foundation.

Halpern, Robert. 1995. *Rebuilding the Inner City: A History of Neighborhood Initiatives to Address Poverty in the United States*. New York: Columbia University Press.

Hogan, J., and D. Lengyel. 1985. "Experiences with Scattered-site Housing." *Urban Resources* 2(2): 9–14.

Holzer, Harry J. 1996. *What Employers Want: Job Prospects for Less-Educated Workers*. New York: Russell Sage Foundation.

Holzer, Harry J., and Keith R. Ihlanfeldt. 1998. "Customer Discrimination and Employment Outcomes for Minority Workers." *Quarterly Journal of Economics* 113(3): 835–67.

Hughes, Mark Alan. 1993. "Antipoverty Strategy Where the Rubber Meets the Road: Transporting Workers to Jobs." In *Housing Markets and Residential Mobility*, edited by G. Thomas Kingsley and Margery Austin Turner. Washington, D.C.: Urban Institute Press.

———. 1995. "A Mobility Strategy for Improving Opportunity." *Housing Policy Debate* 6(1): 271–97.

Ihlanfeldt, Keith R. 1997. "Information on the Spatial Distribution of Job Opportunities Within Metropolitan Areas." *Journal of Urban Economics* 41(2): 218–42.

———. 1998. *Breaking the Concentration of Poverty*. Atlanta, Ga.: Research Atlanta.

Jenkins, Richard. 1989. "Equal Opportunity in the Private Sector: The Limits of Voluntarism." In *Racism and Equal Opportunity Policies in the 1980s*. 2nd ed., edited by Richard Jenkins and John Solomos. New York: Cambridge University Press.

Kain, John F. 1992. "The Spatial Mismatch Hypothesis: Three Decades Later." *Housing Policy Debate* 3(2): 371–460.

Kain, John F., and Joseph J. Persky. 1969. "Alternatives to the Gilded Ghetto." *The Public Interest* (Winter): 77–91.

Kirschenman, Joleen, Philip Moss, and Chris Tilly. 1996. "Space as a Signal, Space as a Barrier: How Employers Map and Use Space in Four Metropolitan Labor Markets." Paper presented at the Multi-City Study of Urban Inequality Conference, Russell Sage Foundation, February 8–9.

Ladd, Helen. 1994. "Spatially Targeted Economic Development Strategies: Do They Work?" *Cityscape* 1(1): 193–218.

———. 1998. "Evidence on Discrimination in Mortgage Lending." *Journal of Economic Perspectives* 12(2):41–62.

Leonard, Jonathan S. 1986. "The Effectiveness of Equal Employment Law and Affirmative Action Regulation." In *Research in Labor Economics*, vol. 8 (pt. B), edited by Ronald G. Ehrenberg. Greenwich, Conn.: JAI Press.

———. 1990. "The Impact of Affirmative Action Regulation and Equal Employment Law on Black Employment." *Journal of Economic Perspectives* 4(4): 47–63.

———. 1998. "Wage Disparities and Affirmative Action in the 1980's." *American Economic Review* 86(2): 285–89.

Loury, Glenn C. 1998. "An American Tragedy." *Brookings Review* 16(2): 39–42.

Merry, Sally Engle. 1980. "Racial Integration in an Urban Neighborhood: The Social Organization of Strangers." *Human Organization* 39(1): 59–69.

Moffitt, Robert. 1992. "Incentive Effects of the U.S. Welfare System: A Review." *Journal of Economic Literature* 30(1): 1–61.

Nyden, Philip, John Lukehart, Michael T. Maly, and William Peterman. 1998. "Chapter 13: Conclusion." *Cityscape* 4(2):261–69.

O'Neill, N. Kathleen. 1995. *Overcoming the Barriers to Educational Change.* Atlanta, Ga.: Research Atlanta.

Papke, Leslie E. 1993. "What Do We Know About Enterprise Zones?" In *Tax Policy and the Economy,* vol 7, edited by J. M. Poterba. Cambridge, Mass.: MIT Press.

Polikoff, Alexander. 1995. *Housing Utility: Promise or Illusion?* Washington, D.C.: Urban Institute Press.

Rubin, Marilyn Marks. 1991. "Urban Enterprise Zones in New Jersey: Have They Made a Difference?" In *Enterprise Zones: New Directions in Economic Development,* edited by Roy Green. Newbury Park, Calif.: Sage.

Schill, Michael. 1992. "Deconcentrating the Inner-City Poor." *Chicago-Kent Law Review* 67(3): 795–853.

Sjoquist, David L. 1996. "Spatial Mismatch and Social Acceptability." Working paper. Atlanta: Policy Research Center, Georgia State University.

Smith, James P., and Finis Welch. 1987. "Race and Poverty: A Forty-Year Record." *American Economic Review* 77(2): 152–58.

Teitz, Michael B., and Karen Chapple. 1998. "The Causes of Inner-City Poverty: Eight Hypotheses in Search of Reality." *Cityscape* 3(3): 33–70.

Turner, Margery Austin, Michael Fix, and Raymond J. Struyk. 1991. *Opportunities Denied, Opportunities Diminished: Racial Discrimination in Hiring.* Washington, D.C.: Urban Institute Press.

Urban Policy Brief. 1994. *Residential Mobility Programs.* Washington: U.S. Department of Housing and Urban Development.

Walker, Mary Beth. 1997. *A Population Profile of the City of Atlanta: Trends, Causes and Options.* Atlanta: Research Atlanta.

Wilson, William J. 1996. *When Work Disappears: The World of the New Urban Poor.* New York: Knopf.

Yinger, John. 1995. *Closed Doors, Opportunities Lost: The Continuing Costs of Housing Discrimination.* New York: Russell Sage Foundation.

Young, Jr., Whitney M. 1969. *Beyond Racism: Building an Open Society.* New York: McGraw-Hill.

Index

Numbers in **boldface** refer to full-page figures or tables.